Dancing in the Sun
Hollywood Choreographers, 1915–1937

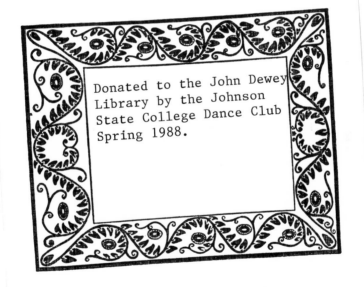

Theater and Dramatic Studies, No. 44

Oscar G. Brockett, Series Editor

Leslie Waggener Professor of Fine Arts
and Professor of Drama
The University of Texas at Austin

Other Titles in This Series

Dancing in the Sun
Hollywood Choreographers, 1915–1937

by
Naima Prevots

UMI Research Press
Ann Arbor / London

Copyright © 1987
Naima Prevots
All rights reserved

Produced and distributed by
UMI Research Press
an imprint of
University Microfilms, Inc.
Ann Arbor, Michigan 48106

Library of Congress Cataloging in Publication Data

Prevots, Naima, 1935-
   Dancing in the sun.

   (Theater and dramatic studies ; no. 44)
   Bibliography: p.
   Includes index.
   1. Choreographers—California—Hollywood (Los
Angeles)—Biography.   2. Dancing—California—
Hollywood (Los Angeles)—History.   I. Title.
II. Series.
   GV1785.A1P74   1987   792.8'2'0922 [B]   87-13859
   ISBN 0-8357-1825-5 (alk. paper)

British Library CIP data is available

Contents

Acknowledgments

I am grateful for the continuous encouragement and thoughtful criticism provided by Judy Alter as friend and colleague at a time when I almost gave up completing this book. Oscar Brochett's incisive comments and support nurtured this project from beginning to end. Others were also important in its early stages: Moshe Lazar, Nancy Ruyter, Nancy Mason Hauser, Allegra Fuller Snyder, Lew Thomas, Meade Andrews, Suzanne Levy, Shelley Berg, Dawn Horwitz, Margaret Bucky, Kayla Zalk.

The work on Norma Gould and Lester Horton would not have been possible without Karoun Toutikian who gave me her time and all her treasures. The Belcher chapter owes a great deal to George Dorris who asked penetrating questions, made me probe more, and published the material in *Dance Chronicle,* 1987. Marge Champion was generous with both her time and her father's precious memorabilia, and Lina Basquette had valuable insights about her stepfather. Helen Caldwell shared intimate knowledge of Michio Ito's work. Amielle Zemach gave me important material on her father; Margot Zemach generously shared her home for an extensive interview with Benjamin. Frieda Maddow and Myriam Rochlin's experiences with Benjamin provided further insights into his work. My thanks also to Giora Manor for translating the Zemach material into Hebrew and publishing both Hebrew and English versions in *Israel Dance,* 1986.

Frank Eng shared everything he had with me and gave me a deeper understanding of Lester Horton. Horton's choreography/teaching were illuminated through conversations with Elizabeth Talbot-Martin, Bella Lewitzsky, and William Bowne. Dorathi Bock-Pierre had a valuable overview of dance history in Los Angeles. Lane Bowling was generous with precious historic material. Debbie Albeyta and Kay Neves were invaluable assistants in proofreading, typing and asking questions.

To Becky, Aaron, Ruth, Jeffrey, Rae, and Albert, a special thanks for just being our family. To Martin Wallen, my husband, for providing love and support and always asking important questions—my love and thanks.

Author's Note

Spelling of dancers names and ballet titles has presented a problem in this study. Many of the choreographers and performers changed name spellings as careers developed. Newspaper reporters and publicists were often careless about spelling, or frequently employed Americanized versions of foreign titles. Programs for the same season at the Hollywood Bowl would often have different spellings of the same works or dancers. In the text, I try to establish a uniformity by identifying performers or works by the most currently accepted form.

Hollywood Map, 1887
Harvey Wilcox filed a map of his ranch with the county recorder for subdivision purposes.
(*Courtesy Hollywood Bowl Museum Archives*)

Prologue

Hollywood and Los Angeles as Dance Meccas

Hollywood never particularly interested me. There was a short period of time, at age eleven, when I collected mass-produced signed movie star pictures. For the most part, my heroes and heroines were the great and glamorous dancers, actors, and actresses that I was privileged to see from a very early age on the various New York stages. Los Angeles was probably even more remote and less interesting to me, and it always seemed a distant and garish country that had little to do with American culture.

Nonetheless, I found myself living in Los Angeles in 1979, and as a Visiting Scholar at UCLA I became involved in a grant proposal to celebrate the Los Angeles centennial in 1981 with a dance history exhibit. UCLA had a large collection of Ruth St. Denis costumes and memorabilia, and much of the exhibit was to center on the contributions of St. Denis and Ted Shawn and the founding of Denishawn in 1915. This institution was widely acknowledged as the cradle of American modern dance, as it had been the training ground for Martha Graham, Charles Weidman, and Doris Humphrey. Lester Horton, who founded his first company in Los Angeles in 1932, and who trained Alvin Ailey, Carmen de Lavallade, and others, was also going to figure in the exhibit. It was unclear what additional artists could be considered important both in the history of dance in the city and also as individuals who shaped American dance.

I began reading about Los Angeles and Hollywood—history, development, changes, etc. I wanted to know why St. Denis, Shawn, and Horton had come to Los Angeles and what else happened in dance. It became clear that Hollywood and the movies had exerted a powerful pull on the imagination of numerous writers, musicians, actors, and visual artists. Film work promised both economic rewards and creative fulfillment. In 1910 Hollywood was a tiny village of just over 3,000 residents when it was incorporated into the small city of Los Angeles

Hollywood, 1903
Picking peas on the Hammel and Decker ranch.
(*Courtesy Hollywood Bowl Museum Archives*)

Hollywood, 1905
(Courtesy California Historical Society)

(population 319,198). In 1911 the first movie studio was created in Hollywood by the Horsley Brothers at the corner of Sunset Boulevard and Gower Street. In those early days it cost almost nothing to acquire a piece of land and build a house. All through the 1930s land and housing were cheap and plentiful. The climate was good, and the image of the western frontier captured the imagination. Large open spaces, with striking views of ocean and majestic mountains, fueled the dream of endless possibilities.

What happened to dancers and choreographers who came to Hollywood and Los Angeles? Who were they, and what did they do in the city? Were the Denishawn School and the Horton studio the only significant institutions for studying serious dance? Ted Shawn came to Los Angeles in 1912 and worked with Norma Gould. After they went to New York and he met Ruth St. Denis, was Gould active again in Los Angeles? Agnes de Mille and George Balanchine had worked in Hollywood briefly, and the accounts indicate their displeasure with the environment and movie work. Were there choreographers who came for the movies and stayed to do other things?

A chance event and a conversation during my first summer in Los Angeles lit a spark that set the course for several years of research and eventually this book. During an evening's concert at the Hollywood Bowl my husband remarked that one of the most striking memories of his childhood was seeing Max Reinhardt's 1934 production of *A Midsummer Night's Dream* on that stage. Looking for more information on Reinhardt and the 1934 production, I found a book by Gottfried Reinhardt, *The Genius: A Memoir of Max Reinhardt*, which had just been published. In writing about his father's arrival and work in Los Angeles, Gottfried Reinhardt wrote that "half of the European and four-fifths of the German speaking civilization moved into this Californian coastal strip. . . . First the German waves swept in, then its Austrian counterpart. They were followed by the French . . . and finally the English. It was the mass migration of a thrown-together elite unprecedented in history, the volume and force of which is hard to grasp even now."

In looking through Reinhardt's book, the list of great artists and intellectuals was very long, among them Igor Stravinsky, Arnold Schoenberg, Herbert Marcuse, Max Reinhardt, Artur Rubinstein, Alexander Archipenko, Thomas Mann, Bertolt Brecht. I remembered reading about the pull Hollywood exerted on famous American artists— George Gershwin, Nathaniel West, F. Scott Fitzgerald, John Dos Passos, William Faulkner, and many others. For some the stay in Los Angeles was fruitful, and they produced work that was important in the totality of their careers. For others the environment proved unsympathetic, and they either left or stayed unhappily.

Where were the dancers and choreographers? There were none listed in Reinhardt's book. There were none listed in other histories of the city. Even if it led nowhere, I wanted to find a way of identifying the concert dance activity in Los Angeles, particularly from the time of the Denishawn School in 1915 through the 1930s—formative years in the development of American dance.

A second visit to the Hollywood Bowl convinced me that a thorough examination of programs for that facility would yield some information. The Bowl seemed to be an old and important institution in the cultural life of Los Angeles and had been operating continuously since the first concert series began there in 1922. Dominating a 65-acre site eight miles from downtown Los Angeles, the stage today has an 83-foot proscenium opening, and the amphitheater currently seats 17,880 people.

The program search proved astounding. Numerous individual choreographers and dancers of diverse backgrounds performed at the Hollywood Bowl in a large variety of concert presentations through the late 1930s. A random list of names would include Ruth St. Denis, Ted Shawn, Norma Gould, Agnes de Mille, Adolph Bolm, Serge Oukrainsky, Andreas Pavley, Albertina Rasch, Muriel Stuart, Fanchon and Marco, Benjamin Zemach, Michio Ito, Lester Horton, Maria Bekefi, Jose Fernandez, Eleanora Flaig, Bronislava Nijinska, Ernest Belcher, Michel Fokine, Vera Fokina, Waldeen Falkenstein, Bella Lewitzky, Thelma Babitz, Frieda Flier, Pearl Wheeler, Francesca Braggiotti, Aida Broadbent, Maria and Marjorie Tallchief, Maud Allan, Maria Gambarelli, Paul Godkin, Martha Deane, Betty Pease, Gwen Verdon, Louis Hightower, Marge Champion, Gower Champion, Robert Bell, Janet Collins, Elise Reiman, James Starbuck, Dimitri Romanoff, Elizabeth Talbot-Martin, Karoun Toutikian, Carmelita Maracci, and Vera Fredowa.

The first question I had to ask was as follows: Hollywood attracted these artists, and they all performed at the Hollywood Bowl. Does that mean that they were also involved in dance in Los Angeles, and what was the relationship between those two places? I began to realize that Hollywood was a state of mind, an image, a symbol. Hollywood is also a specific geographic location, with boundaries that have changed somewhat over the years. Most of the artists who came to "Hollywood" in fact lived and worked in the larger geographic environment known as Los Angeles. The Hollywood Bowl never was a performance facility limited to Hollywood audiences and performers. Today it is owned by the County of Los Angeles. Although Hollywood was the image I was working with, I was looking for artists whose careers had taken place in Los Angeles as a whole.

There were other important questions to ask regarding the long list of dancers listed in the Hollywood Bowl programs: Which of these individuals had lived and worked in Los Angeles for significant periods of time? Which ones concentrated on concert choreography and live performances as opposed to movie work? Which ones had been important influences in Los Angeles in several capacities—as teachers, choreographers, performers? Which ones had a distinct philosophy and made an original contribution to dance in the city? Were there artists not listed on the Bowl programs who should also be investigated further and how would I find them? Then I asked the most important question: Which of the artists seemed to have an importance beyond their work in Los Angeles, thus contributing to the complex development of American dance?

I discovered, at the Hollywood Bowl and at the main branch of the Los Angeles Public Library, scrapbooks organized by year. They contained extensive material: reviews of performances from many newspapers and magazines; interviews with various artists; articles about the Bowl and other performance spaces; complete listings of daily and weekly theater, dance, and music events taking place in Los Angeles—at the Bowl and at other places. I went through scrapbooks from 1910 through 1945.

Eight names that had been prominent on the Hollywood Bowl programs appeared with great frequency in the scrapbooks. Judging from the scrapbooks and the programs (which often provided biographies and publicity information), these eight individuals were considered important figures in the cultural life of the community. They performed, taught, and choreographed extensively in Los Angeles and had made the city their home. They were: Norma Gould, Ernest Belcher, Theodore Kosloff, Serge Oukrainsky, Adolph Bolm, Michio Ito, Benjamin Zemach, and Lester Horton. Several had international reputations; all had performed outside California. It was these eight whose work I decided to study in greater depth. Their careers were minimally documented, their impact went well beyond dance in Los Angeles, and information on their activities in the city would provide insight and leads to their other work. Each one intrigued me. Perhaps other choreographer/teachers would seem more important to someone else. That would be another book.

At this point I had to determine if a split focus was developing: 1) Los Angeles as a major dance center, or 2) eight major choreographer/teachers and a study of their work. I wanted to understand why there was so much dance activity in Los Angeles during the period 1915 through 1937, what impact the city had on choreographers and teachers, why Los Angeles had never developed a major ballet company. On the other hand, I was not interested in documenting every dance event in Los Angeles nor in writing a history of dance in the city. Los Angeles as context was intriguing and important, but had to be integrated with an understanding of work in Los Angeles that had been neglected and was not just regional in impact. Los Angeles as a major focus for dance had brought to light for me a neglected portion of dance history and a significant period of time in the lives of several major figures in the development of American dance.

Los Angeles as a major dance center was background and a jumping off point. Does a city have an impact on an artist's work? Would a study of dance in Chicago, San Francisco, Boston, or Philadelphia bring to light important developments in American dance, and would these various environments all have a particular and different effect on what any choreographer/teacher would do? Los Angeles was unique because of Hollywood and the mythic sense of a last frontier. For all the artists who came, it offered the image of a land of opportunity and freedom. Los Angeles was a city dominated by the movie industry, a strong materialistic, hedonistic culture, and a lack of traditions in the arts. Los Angeles was a major dance center offering dancers space, offering eager but sometimes undisciplined and uneducated bodies, but it was also a place where support for serious artistic endeavors was not a habit and was always difficult to obtain.

In the end, a full study of each artist with an emphasis on their Los Angeles career became the methodology for this book. Theodore Kosloff, Serge Oukrainsky, and Adolph Bolm are mentioned in histories of American ballet, often as significant figures. There are a few scattered articles on their choreography, teaching, and general influence. There is nothing published more recently than 1963 for Adolph Bolm and 1977 for some material on Theodore Kosloff. No books have been written about these three, but their impact on American dance was considerable. Their careers in Los Angeles were extensive, but documentation is almost nonexistent. Much of the information in their respective chapters came from unpublished manuscripts, personal memorabilia, clipping files, newspaper reviews, and articles.

Norma Gould and Ernest Belcher were well-known figures in the dance world during the 1920s and 1930s. They themselves published articles, taught at national dance conventions, and were the subject of several articles written by others. The major sources of information about them came from personal memorabilia, scrapbooks, and special library collections. In 1935, Elizabeth Selden's book *The Dancer's Quest* had several pages devoted to Benjamin Zemach, and she placed him alongside important young artists in New York. However, his career has gone largely undocumented. As with many of the others, the work

Cecil B. de Mille with Cast of *The Squaw Man*, 1914
Together with Jesse L. Lasky, de Mille created this movie, which was the first full-length feature film made in Hollywood.
(*Courtesy Hollywood Bowl Museum Archives*)

in Los Angeles provided clues to his career elsewhere, and material was gathered from interviews, personal collections, and newspapers.

Helen Caldwell wrote a fine book called *Michio Ito, The Dancer and His Dances*. But no other published material exists on this artist, and the Ito chapter in this book provides an overview of his work and in-depth choreographic analysis. Larry Warren's book, *Lester Horton: Modern Dance Pioneer*, is the only one on Horton. The Horton chapter in this book provides an analysis of his work created in Los Angeles—the city in which Horton fully developed as choreographer and teacher.

I determined that 1915 would be the beginning time frame. The Denishawn School, which began then, has been amply documented. Ernest Belcher came to Los Angeles in 1915 and opened his first school. Norma Gould established her first large performing group and began to lecture. In 1915 D. W. Griffith directed his landmark film, *The Birth of a Nation*. The *Lusitania* sank in 1915, and the impact of World War I on the European film industry began to put Hollywood on the international map. Kevin Brownlow and John Kobal quote Anita Loos in *Hollywood: The Pioneers* when they talk about the European film studios: "At the time the war broke out, movies had gained a very substantial place in Europe. . . . But the war broke out and changed the whole scene. It was impossible to work with the economics of war. . . . So I really credit Hollywood on World War One." Serge Oukrainsky left Pavlova's company, on tour in Chicago, in 1915; a year later Ruth Page performed with him, and Doris Humphrey became his student. Michio Ito began working with Ezra Pound and William Butler Yeats in London on translation and production of Noh plays. That year Adolph Bolm in Switzerland was responsible for rehearsing and readying a reconstituted Diaghilev company for the 1916 American tour.

I end the study in 1937. This was the year Lester Horton created a major piece, *Le Sacre du Printemps*, for a large mass public at the Hollywood Bowl. The performance marked his full emergence as a choreographer and integration of the diverse influences he had been exposed to in Los Angeles. Events elsewhere in 1936 and 1937 illuminate the general development of American dance. In 1936 Lincoln Kirstein organized Ballet Caravan to provide opportunities for American dancers, choreographers, composers, and designers. That year Paul Magriel published *A Bibliography of Dancing* in New York, and Doris Humphrey premiered *Theatre Piece* and *With My Red Fires*. Martha Graham premiered *Horizons* and *Chronicle* in 1936, and in 1937 she premiered *Deep Song*. Balanchine presented a Stravinsky festival in 1937 at the Metropolitan Opera House, and Lew Christenson took over the leadership of the San Francisco Ballet Company and School.

By the 1930s there were thousands of dancers in Los Angeles, and for some time the press had been heralding the city as the dance capital of America. In 1929 a *Los Angeles Times* headline read: "L.A. Takes Lead as Dance Center." In that same year the *Los Angeles Times* announced that Michel Fokine and Anna Pavlova were to open schools in the city, although that never happened. In 1931 Ernest Belcher declared there were more dancers being trained in Los Angeles than in any other city in the United States. The first talking movie in 1927, *The Jazz Singer*, generated a large number of movie musicals that required dancers and choreographers. The 1929 depression did not affect the movie industry to any large degree. Nowhere else could dancers be employed during those years with such large and steady salaries.

In 1927 *The American Dancer* magazine was founded in Los Angeles. It was published in the city through 1932 and then moved its headquarters to New York. In 1933 the editor, Ruth Eleanor Howard, wrote as follows (in *Who's Who in Music and Dance in Southern California*): "Artistically, Southern California will prove of inestimable importance in the development of dance in future years." In 1937 the city's dancers organized a Dancers' Federation so that they could provide a strong unified voice in the community. They also attempted to organize a year-round professional ballet company, and as late as 1939 this seemed a possibility.

Information on performances in Los Angeles relies heavily on events that took place at the Hollywood Bowl, which during the 1920s and 1930s was the most prestigious performance space in the city. For choreographers the movies provided money, the Bowl stage artistic recognition. Anything that happened at the Bowl was considered of international importance, and critics from all over the country and the world reviewed performances. The Hollywood Bowl scrapbooks contained articles and reviews from almost all 48 states as well as many in French, German, Yiddish, and Spanish. Events at the Bowl were covered in depth, with preperformance interviews and articles as well as some lengthy critical evaluations. There were not that many performance spaces in Los Angeles in those days, and often a production at the Bowl was repeated during the year elsewhere.

The Hollywood Bowl was created as a community institution. The founders felt a need for presenting great art to the numerous immigrants and new settlers and wanted to provide a spiritual antidote to the burgeoning movie industry. Signs on rooming houses in the period about 1911 through 1920 read: "No dogs, cats or actors allowed." The civic leaders in Hollywood who purchased the Bowl site in 1919 organized the Theatre Arts Alliance to govern the property. The Theatre Arts Alliance, with Ted Shawn as one of its charter members, issued a

Afternoon Concert at the Hollywood Bowl, 1924
(Courtesy Hollywood Bowl Museum Archives)

statement of purpose in 1919. They announced the creation of "a park and art center and kindred projects of a civic nature, . . . not for personal individual or corporate gain or profit." Their aim was: "To encourage and develop, through a community spirit and civic patriotism, the finest forms of arts and crafts and individual talents, and to promote appreciation of and inculcate love for artistic and beautiful creations and productions of every sort and nature."

In the early days of its history, the Hollywood Bowl was the scene of community pageants and informal concerts. In 1922 a makeshift stage was created by volunteer labor, wood was donated for informal bench seating, and a season of concerts by the Los Angeles Philharmonic was inaugurated. In 1926 a formal stage was created, and in 1929 a permanent shell was built. The community, through committees and volunteer leadership, made most of the decisions about presentations. The management brought in international artists and presented local artists who were considered to have equivalent reputations. The Hollywood Bowl during the 1920s and 1930s seated over 20,000 people and the entrance fee was 25 cents. The civic leaders considered dance important and did not limit their choices to any particular genre.

The result of their policies was that choreographic works of widely divergent aesthetic visions were presented. Audiences coming to the Bowl were exposed to a range of dance activity. They were exposed to the traditional arabesques and pas de bourrés of Kosloff's *Chopin Memories* and to Horton's modern hip thrusts and angular movements of *Le Sacre du Printemps*. The audiences included a broad segment of the Los Angeles population—students, artists, workers, bankers, and merchants. Anything that happened at the Bowl became an important part of the total cultural experience of the community. Families were in the habit of coming two and three times a week, carrying picnic baskets— as they still do. If you missed a performance, you would be sure to read a lengthy review in any one of the several newspapers circulating at the time.

Since the stage was big, often large group dances were presented. Many young performers were needed for each production, and cast lists for the various choreographers show them using the same dancers. Here are some examples: In 1931 and 1932 Robert Bell performed with Adolph Bolm, and in 1933 he performed with Harold Hecht and Benjamin Zemach. Jessica Spitzer is listed on the programs in 1933 for Benjamin Zemach's *Fragments of Israel*, Harold Hecht's *Skyscraper Ballet*, and Francesca Braggiotti's *Tales from the Vienna Woods*. Betty Pease appears on the 1933 program presented by Harold Hecht and on the 1936 cast list for the Martha Deane evening. Waldeen Falkenstein was a soloist in 1933 for both Harold Hecht and Benjamin Zemach. Thelma

Babitz was in the chorus of Adolph Bolm's *The Spirit of the Factory* in 1932 and in the chorus of Benjamin Zemach's *The Victory Ball* in 1933. Edith Jane in 1932 performed with both Adolph Bolm and Jose Fernandez. In 1935 Bella Levitsky (program spelling) and Paul Godkin performed in Agnes de Mille's *Three Dance Scenes;* in 1937 Paul Godkin appears on the cast list for Theodore Kosloff's *Petrouchka,* as Bella Lewitzky does for Horton's *Le Sacre du Printemps.*

The Hollywood Bowl has a fascinating history as an institution that grew out of a belief in the power of art for the spiritual benefit of the entire community. The early history of the Bowl is related to the development of the American Pageantry Movement, which from around 1910 to 1925 formed an important chapter in new ideas in American theater and dance, in the Americanization of new immigrants, and in the integration of the arts with the life of the community. Dance in Los Angeles would not have had the same opportunities in the 1920s and 1930s without this important institution.

Dance requires substantial patronage and leadership from individual benefactors. In 1937, when Los Angeles dancers wanted to form a year-round ballet company parallel to the Los Angeles Philharmonic with a summer home at the Hollywood Bowl, no one came forward to lead this venture financially. All attempts to have a major ballet company in Los Angeles failed during the 1940s through the 1960s. In the 1970s John Clifford created a Los Angeles Ballet, and it lasted for a few years to mixed reviews.

Considering the enormous wealth in the city, the arts in general did not receive a great deal of private support in Los Angeles during the 1940s and 1950s. In 1964 the Music Center opened due to the successful efforts of Dorothy Chandler of the *Los Angeles Times* family. She mobilized some of the money in the community, and a large cultural facility with three performance spaces was created. The Los Angeles Philharmonic and the Civic Light Opera Company became resident organizations, and the Mark Taper Forum began to produce regular seasons of high-quality theater. There was still no Los Angeles dance company in residence at the Music Center, nor was dance a significant part of the programming.

By the 1980s patronage for the arts in Los Angeles had increased considerably. Money was raised to have the Joffrey Ballet as a resident dance company at the Music Center; the arrangement was that they would have a dual home base—New York and Los Angeles. The Hollywood Bowl Museum was created in 1984, and two new museums opened in 1986: The Museum of Contemporary Art and the Anderson Wing of the Los Angeles County Museum. There are plans for a new Getty Museum and research complex. Ground was broken for Bella

Hollywood Bowl, 1932
Franklin Delano Roosevelt speaking during the presidential election campaign.
(*Courtesy Hollywood Bowl Museum Archives*)

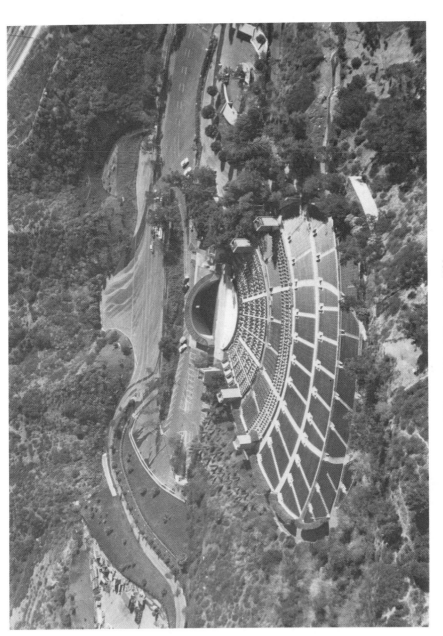

Hollywood Bowl Overview, 1930s
(*Courtesy Hollywood Bowl Museum Archives*)

Lewitzky's Dance Gallery in 1986; this will be a facility exclusively for dance.

In 1985 a Performing Arts High School opened, and in 1986 money was raised for an impressive season of a new Los Angeles Opera Company. In 1987 planning was ongoing for an addition to the Music Center that consists of three additional theaters. It will be interesting to see what the future holds for dance in Los Angeles, and what patronage and leadership there will be to encourage local talent to stay and to attract artists from elsewhere. Los Angeles is a young, growing, and very wealthy city interested in developing the image of an international capital.

Is it possible that the individuals who brought their artistry to Los Angeles in the 1920s and 1930s are responsible for laying the groundwork for today's burgeoning dance activity? There are certainly strong linkages with the past. The most noticeable example is Bella Lewitzky, whose mentor was Lester Horton. Many leaders in the dance community were trained either by the artists discussed in this book or by their students. The rich dance heritage of the past was prevented from a full flowering in the 1940s through the 1970s because there were no imaginative arts patrons and the dance community did not provide dynamic leadership. Other factors prevented growth: the prevalence of commercial entertainment values in performance due to the pervasive influence of the movie industry; rapid, chaotic geographic sprawl; and the red baiting and McCarthyism of the 1940s and 1950s. There is no excuse needed to enjoy history, but it is particularly interesting to look at the work of the eight artists in this book and to hope for a bright future emerging from the groundwork they established.

Part One

Early Pioneers:
Norma Gould and Ernest Belcher

Introduction to Part One

In 1915 Ruth St. Denis and Ted Shawn began the famous and widely documented Denishawn School in Los Angeles. By 1924 the school was being run by other people, and the two founders had moved their base of operations to New York. Ruth St. Denis and Ted Shawn were flamboyant, charismatic self-promoters whose originality was supplemented with superb marketing techniques. Their choreography was theatrical, and they were powerful performers. St. Denis and Shawn, even when they had a base in Los Angeles, chose to tour a great deal—both in this country and abroad. In 1930 they published "six original Denishawn dances" under the aegis of G. Schirmer and made them available at $25 for the set or $5 for one. They franchised schools throughout the country and kept their names and the Denishawn name alive in the public eye.

The careers of Norma Gould and Ernest Belcher were developing simultaneously with those of Ruth St. Denis and Ted Shawn in Los Angeles through 1924, but then they diverge geographically. Norma Gould first started teaching in her Los Angeles home in 1908. Beginning in 1908 she performed as a soloist and then, from 1912 through 1914, as part of a duet with Ted Shawn. She traveled to New York with Shawn in 1914 and returned to Los Angeles in 1915 to resume her teaching and performing. From 1915 on she stayed in Los Angeles, performing often with large groups of her students and teaching extensively. Ernest Belcher opened his first Los Angeles studio in 1915 and soon was teaching thousands of students, creating dance sequences for movies, and concertizing with his groups throughout the city.

What is the relationship of the Denishawn School to the work of Gould and Belcher? Why is the work of St. Denis and Shawn analyzed so often and very little mention made of the other two dancers? During the time all four were in Los Angeles, Gould and Belcher received as much press and acclaim as St. Denis and Shawn, and their schools were larger than Denishawn. By the 1920s and 1930s Gould and Belcher were nationally known. They were asked to teach master classes, students came from all over the country for their summer classes, and their students were achieving acclaim on their own. All four artists knew each other in Los Angeles, shared students, and even performed with each other on occasion. In *One Thousand and One Night Stands* Shawn wrote about the pioneering spirit prevalent in Los Angeles at that time, and this feeling encouraged all four artists to explore and gave them the courage to produce.

St. Denis, Shawn, Gould, and Belcher choreographed dances that look very similar in retrospect, both in theme and style. They all created dances based on Greek, Spanish, Japanese, and Oriental themes. They all developed a similar use of torso, arms, and feet patterns based on "national" dances. Gould, much like St. Denis and Shawn, sought the spiritual essence of dance. Belcher shared with the Denishawn founders a firm belief in entertainment values, although he was also a strict believer in emphasizing dance as a serious art form. Belcher sold his dances, and Denishawn titles for sale look similar. Denishawn sold the following dances: *Bakawali Nautch, Idyll, Scarf Plastique, Schubert Waltz, Tales from the Vienna Woods, Sonata Pathétique.* Among the dances for sale by Belcher were: *Veil Dance, Nautch Dance, Valse Caprice, The Incense Bearer, American Indian Dance,* and *Sting of Death* (Serpent Dance). It is interesting that in July 1915 we find Norma Gould lecturing on "Music Made Visible" for the annual convention of the Music Teachers Association of California. Stephanie Jordan, in "Ted Shawn's Music Visualizations" (*Dance Chronicle*), notes that Shawn's first music visualizations appeared in 1916 and 1917. St. Denis began experimenting with the idea around 1918.

Developing in the same environment of time and place, the four artists could have shared many ideas without necessarily copying from each other. Yet there is no attempt in this book to analyze Ruth St. Denis, Ted Shawn, or Denishawn because so much has already been written about them. Gould and Belcher made their own important independent contributions to dance in America, and the next two chapters seek to explore their work in a way that will shed light on their place in dance history. Very little has been written about either one, and their work has been largely unknown. There are several reasons for this. Both Gould and Belcher were reserved, self-effacing personalities. Both deemphasized their own performance; neither was interested in touring extensively. Nonetheless, each in his or her own way explored pathways new to American dance and influenced future dancers and audiences.

1

Norma Gould (1888–1980): Spirited Freedom

Norma Gould's parents encouraged their daughter's early interest in the arts. Her mother, who taught music at home, combined for the young child formal instruction and the opportunity for creative expression. Dance classes in ballet were provided when available in the community, and ballroom dance lessons were also part of her background. Norma's father, by profession a milliner, was proud of his daughter's dramatic and musical abilities. Active as a Mason, he was happy to have his daughter perform, often as part of an evening's program for his group.

The Goulds' interest in allowing their daughter to develop her talents led to her participation in an educational experiment that was to prove a formative influence in her life. In 1905 Norma was among the first group of students to enroll at the new Los Angeles Polytechnical High School. The basic premise of the school was the development of a curriculum that equally emphasized college preparatory academic classes and vocational courses—a radical idea for that time. The school was coeducational, and women were trained alongside men in a variety of business and commercial skills.

There was serious study of math, literature, science, and language; the courses in music and art were exceptionally complete and advanced for that time. Piano, organ, and all orchestral instruments were taught as well as voice, music composition, music history, and appreciation. Art work included illustration, house decoration, and costume design. Self-government was another unusual feature of the school. Students managed the lunchroom and the bookstore and staged their own productions. Every boy and girl was expected to do work of some kind to earn money and keep accurate books. In one year the students handled and accounted for more than $45,000.

Norma was active in various facets of school activities. She was class historian and also president of the Girls Club, a group that staged productions and shared in teaching their peers various things that interested them. Several clippings in her scrapbook indicate that she studied in New York while in high school.[1] Her family was reasonably well off and this is a likely possibility.

When Norma graduated from Polytechnical High School in 1908, she started teaching at home, 1615 Georgia Avenue. The high school yearbook described her: "Well groomed appearance and superior air / Tall stunning figure and copper hued hair."[2] Her "superior air" and striking appearance were valuable assets. At age twenty she was embarking on a precarious and uncharted course. Armed with a strong sense of possibilities created through parental support and a rigorous, multifaceted, independent-minded education, Norma began to acquire a reputation in Los Angeles as a dance teacher.

In 1911 Ted Shawn arrived in Los Angeles. He had studied ballet with Hazel Wallack in his native Denver but became restless in search of new adventures and more dance. His search for studios and teachers in the new city led him to Norma Gould. Shawn was just beginning to think in terms of dance as a career, and Gould had been running her own school since 1908. The two joined forces and entered into a partnership that was to prove valuable and stimulating for both during the next three years. It is intriguing to wonder how many of Shawn's ideas were developed during the process of working with Gould and what her contribution was to his development.

Both young artists were interested in developing ideas beyond classical ballet and decided that working as a ballroom team would finance other creative work they would do. Shawn noted that "she was as little interested as I in a ballroom dancing career, but neither she nor I could resist the easy money which helped to support . . . our serious dance projects."[3] Gould and Shawn danced at tango teas at the Angelus Hotel in the late afternoon, and later in the evening they danced in the Alexandria Hotel for the after-theater set. Both artists kept busy dancing for various clubs and groups in the city, where they persisted in exploring their own ideas in dance. Shawn wrote:

> With Norma, I created duets for programs we gave for clubs and other organizations in the area. We pooled pupils to form a modest supporting company which gave me my first chance to experiment with group choreography. . . . Everybody in California was pioneering in business or the arts. The movies, themselves experimental, were exciting to imaginations geared to accept the creative process wherever it mushroomed. No serious minded innovator was sneered at or ridiculed, and, for more than a year, I worked with freedom and encouragement.[4]

In the summer of 1913 Gould and Shawn made a movie for the Thomas Alva Edison Company in their Long Beach studio. These two adventurous, eager artists, with a limited background but with large imaginations, made a short movie in two weeks that portrayed the entire history of dance as they knew it. The movie was called *The Dance of the Ages,* and, as Shawn wrote, they began "in the Stone Age, progressing through the glorious ages of Egypt, Greece, and Rome, into Medieval Europe"; they made sure that the dancing ended "with contemporary dance of the United States"[5] in which they could show their skill with the current ballroom hits.

The next major venture of Gould and Shawn was an engagement in San Diego at the Majestic Theatre, once called the Mirror Theatre. When these artists had their two-week engagement there, the theater had been leased for five years to produce Orpheum acts. The engagement of Shawn and Gould was considered something of a coup, and Norma Gould's scrapbooks contain a newspaper article, undated, about the performances.

> San Diego playhouses will include after July 7, a theatre of classic dancing and musical specialties. The Mirror Theatre building at Third and C Streets has been leased for a term of five years and will be reopened as "The Majestic" on that date as the home of the stellar attractions in these lines by C. Stanley Rogers of Portland. "It is my object to make The Majestic a strictly high-class theatre," said Mr. Rogers, "and only the highest class attractions I can secure will be brought here. I believe the finest offering in a vaudeville way at the present time are musical specialties and classic dancing with soloists of note, and I have a long booking of acts from Oscar Hammerstein's New York Theatre and the Orpheum's Vaudeville circuit."

Pictures accompanying this article about the Majestic Theatre show Norma Gould and Ted Shawn in *Oriental Love Dance* and in *Marsovia, A Panier,* which is called in the picture caption "a modern waltz." The pictures of these two young artists show costumes and poses ranging from ballroom dances to Oriental interpretations to Greek numbers complete with loose tunics, flowers, and draperies across Gould's bosom, torso, and hips. Gould and Shawn performed five shows daily, "dances of every nation, dances of every age, with a change of program every Monday, Wednesday, and Saturday."

In 1914 Gould and Shawn set out on a trip to New York on the Santa Fe Railroad. They were hired as entertainers to play employee recreation centers along its line. They were signed to play 19 performances for the Santa Fe in return for round-trip tickets, Los Angeles to New York, for the company of six: Shawn, Gould, Adelaide Munn, and Otis Williams, dancers; Blanche Ebert, pianist; and Brahm Van Den Berg, soprano soloist and violinist. They billed themselves as the "Shawn-Gould Company of Interpretive Dancers . . . in the rendition of classical and historical works of the Masters."[6] Shawn included the announcement of their Santa Fe program in his autobiography.

Norma Gould and Ted Shawn, 1912
(*Courtesy Karoun Toutikian*)

Ted Shawn, ca. 1914
(*Courtesy Karoun Toutikian*)

In the past few months the names of Ted Shawn and Norma Gould have become household words in Los Angeles and Southern California. Their appearances have been hailed with delight by the educated and refined, and the results of their entertainments, from a classical and literary standpoint, have been very satisfactory. . . . Some people may object to an entertainment of this character because it is dancing; but please do not commit an error here. It is a portrayal of perfect development by the most exacting labor and much self-denial. It is the drama acted and illustrated by music and the graceful movement in artistic forms of the human body guided by pure hearts and active brains. It is an attempt to personify history. It is an effort to make a past age live in the present.[7]

The dances they performed were listed on the bottom of the announcement: *Dances of Henry VIII; Diana and Endymion;* and *The Cycle—Winter, Spring, Summer, Autumn.*

Before coming to New York, Gould, Shawn, and Adelaide Munn went to New Canaan, Connecticut, to study at the Unitrinian School of Personal Harmonizing and Self-Development. The school was run by the Canadian poet Bliss Carman and a woman named Mary Perry King, who had founded the school in 1911 at Moonshine, Twilight Park, in the Catskills. Their method of education was a combination of Delsarte exercises, free gymnastics, and movements based on expressive use of the voice and body. The month that Gould and Shawn spent at the school was to influence them both in their later work and in their artistic perspectives.

Norma Gould kept a copy of the 1911 speech made by Bliss Carman to the first graduating class of the school. The copy, autographed to Gould by Mary Perry King, is dated 1914. Excerpts from this speech reveal the idealistic tenor of the Unitrinian School, its emphasis on the importance of the spiritual nature of the arts, and the role of the teacher in fashioning new personalities.

But here in the establishing of a school for the education of personality, our feet are on the foundations of the world, partial aims are merged in those which are universal and we become co-workers with the Lord of Life. We are no longer merely students acquiring knowledge for our own gratification, no longer merely artists proud in the perishable achievements of our skill, but seers and prophets of a new day, taking part in the creation of that better world which is to be. . . . Unitrinianism has truly its religious note, as well as its philosophic and artistic . . . it concedes and inculcates the primacy of the spirit in all things, in conduct, in growth, in art. . . . Your particular field of teaching is the training of the growing body into harmony with the growing mind and spirit. You are to reach to the inmost recesses of moral being, to arouse, to encourage, to strengthen human nature at its source, and by offering it beautiful things to think about, to do, and say . . . and by freeing the natural avenues of expression, motion and speech, you will stimulate the mind to clarify and express whatever thought and reflection life may have engendered. In this, your making of personality, you will use chiefly the three great rhythmic arts of music, poetry and dancing.[8]

After Gould and Shawn left the Unitrinian School in New Canaan, they went to New York, where they both studied and performed. Shawn wrote in his book: "Friends made it possible for Norma and me to appear now and again in New York recitals." They had a reasonable degree of success and publicity. "At the MacDowell Club we appeared on one program with two well-known dancers, Lydia Lopokova and Eduard Maklif, and were no end set up to receive equal applause with those established performers."[9]

It was in New York that Ted Shawn and Norma Gould went their separate ways. Ted Shawn met Ruth St. Denis, and they became not only husband and wife but also dancing partners. Norma Gould returned to California and became active once again as a teacher and performer. She resumed her work at her Georgia Avenue studio and proceeded to choreograph and develop performances for herself and her students. In April 1915 she gave a performance at the Little Theatre (Pico and Figueroa Streets) in Los Angeles, but the summer was to bring two even more important professional assignments.

During the summer of 1915 Norma Gould embarked on two trips, one to San Francisco and one to Texas and Louisiana. The San Francisco trip came first, for she was asked to present a performance of "music made visible," an idea also developed by St. Denis and Shawn with their music visualizations. The occasion was the fifth annual convention of the Music Teachers Association of California, which was holding meetings from 12 July through 17 July at locations in San Francisco, Oakland, and Berkeley. A report in a San Francisco paper *The Bulletin*, dated 14 July, singled out Gould's presentation as a special feature of the conference. The writer helps give a feeling of the nature of her dancing.

A special feature of the fifth annual convention of the Music Teachers Association of California now in session in the ballroom of the Hotel Oakland, in which great interest is being taken in the classic interpretive dances to be given tomorrow morning at 11 o'clock on the grounds of the Faculty Club at the University of California. This will be the first time at a convention of music teachers that the dance has been used to interpret the great themes of music. It will be "music made visible." Miss Norma Gould, a classic dancer of Los Angeles, will present the interpretive dances. Miss Gould will interpret to the following numbers: *Humoresque*, by Dvorak; *To a Wild Rose*, by MacDowell, showing how a rosebud opens into a full rose, only to be torn and thrown to the ground by the cruel winds, and dying, it sends out its fragrances; *The Spirit of the Rain* (dagger dance from *Natoma*), by Herbert, in which is shown the appeal of the earth to the sky for rain, the coming of the rain and the instant response of vegetation; *The Broken Tryst* (serenade), by Drigo, the story of the maiden whose delight at finding a flower at the old trysting place is turned to anguish by the discovery of her lover's name linked with another on the tree trunk; *Diana* (the huntress goddess), from *La Source* ballet, by Delibes. The Lombardi woodwind quartet will accompany Miss Gould.

Immediately after her performance for the Music Teachers Association, Norma Gould toured with the Don Philippini Symphony Band. The tour began on 20 July and lasted through mid-August. Gould took as her partner a young man of 17; Ted Lehman, one of her students. His mother, Suzanne, was a featured singer with the band. Philippini, his 40-odd musicians, Suzanne Lehman, Gould, and young Lehman performed in Galveston, Houston, and Dallas, Texas, as well as in Shreveport, Louisiana. The Texas and Louisiana newspapers reported that this was the first time there had ever been interpretive dancing to a symphony band, and the reviews of the band concerts all noted favorably the dancing of Gould and Lehman. The *Galveston Daily News* of Friday, 23 July, had this to say of one of the performances:

> Miss Norma Gould and Lehman presented a really classical event of the evening, dancing classical and interpretive numbers. Miss Gould appeared alone in the first number and in the second was accompanied by Lehman. Miss Gould is very good. Her dancing is marked by strict observance of technique, and the work of Mr. Lehman, while still rather unfinished, gives promise of a fine future. Miss Gould is one of the most popular dancing instructors in the West, conducting the largest dance studio in Los Angeles. Many of her classes and groups of dancers have been used in moving picture films.

Norma Gould was soon in great demand as a performer for the numerous clubs in and around Los Angeles. She gave performances by herself and with her students at many clubs, among them the Ebell Club, Gamut Club, Philanthropy and Civics Club, Hollywood Women's Club, Wa-Wan Club, Matinee Music Club, Los Angeles and Pasadena Chapters of the Drama League of America, MacDowell Club, Friday Morning Music Club, Shriners, Elks, and others. These clubs played a major role in bringing the arts to the community and in making possible a forum for presentation and discussion. It may be that in Los Angeles the clubs played an even more important role than in some eastern cities because of the lack of established tradition in presenting the arts. These clubs, many led by women, helped the community come together to share ideas and to build an interest in civic and cultural affairs. It is also possible that the clubs in Los Angeles were attempting to combat the scandal, commercialism, and false values they felt were emerging in the movie community.

Norma Gould's performances for these clubs consisted of short solo and group numbers often in a variety of styles, which would ensure interest on the part of the audience. They were also designed to propagandize her ideas about dance as a simple, meaningful, expressive form of art closely allied to and first among the other arts. Her dances were meant to display the beauties of spirit and intellect.

The flavor and importance of these programs is captured in an unidentified newspaper article from Gould's scrapbooks, dated 27 March 1920, "Dancers Appear in Original Roles—Artistic Program Enjoyed by Ebell Members and Their Guests."

> The Norma Gould Dancers, coming to Pomona under auspices of the Ebell Club, charmed a capacity audience of club members and their guests with their program of interpretive Oriental classic and character dances Friday afternoon. . . . Holding a unique place in the artistic world of Southern California and becoming every season more widely known and admired, the Norma Gould dancers had something distinctly original to offer, something entirely different from the ordinary dancing specialty that it stamps itself at once as a new departure in this field of art. Every dance on the program—and the dances were widely varied in character—had a particular meaning which the dancers interpreted not merely with the feet but with the entire body and arms as well as with the facial expression and the costuming in every case was designed to accentuate their art.

This article went on to praise the individual dances and dancers on the program: *La Problème* (Dorothy Lyndall, Elizabeth Schrieber, Dorothy Harris); *Ancient Greek Frieze* (same trio); *Hungarian Czardas* (trio plus Josephine Spates); *Spanish Dances* (Louise Velasco); and *Daffodil and Larkspur*, "a charming minuet" (Velasco and Spates). Two dances were singled out for special praise: Lyndall's dance, *Moth and Flame*, "was wonderfully suggestive of the frail creature of the air as it fluttered in ecstasy about the light and at last fell broken and spent." In the dance *A Wild Rose*, by Dorothy Harris, "she suggested a rosebud, pale and pink, with the joy of life in gesture and facial expression. Slowly opening, the bud is torn and thrown to the ground by the cruel winds as the soul in the guise of fragrance escapes to the breezes and so, lives on."

To what degree were Norma Gould's activities of a professional nature? Did she ever work to develop dance material that went beyond many of the shorter dances she presented in her numerous programs for the Ebell Club, the Hollywood Women's Club, the Drama League, the Friday Morning Music Club, and the others? The answers would have to be that she was considered a professional performer, and that, although her activities in more formal professional settings were limited, presentation of concert dance in Los Angeles in such settings during the years 1915 through the early 1920s was in general limited.

In Los Angeles the Pantages Theatre and the Orpheum Theatre were part of the vaudeville circuit. The Philharmonic Auditorium, at Fifth and Olive Streets, was used by the impresario L. E. Behymer for the occasional visiting ballet company or for stars he considered really significant. In 1921, for example, he presented "Pavlowa and her 'Ballet [*sic*] Russes'"[10] as well as the Bolm Ballet at the Philharmonic Au-

Norma Gould Dancers, Early 1920s
(*Courtesy Karoun Toutikian*)

ditorium. One of the theaters that functioned as a professional theater for small groups, or for those somewhat less known internationally, was the Egan Little Theatre at Figueroa and Pico, usually referred to as just the Little Theatre. It was here that Ruth St. Denis and Ted Shawn performed their concert programs in 1919, 1920, and 1921. Trinity Auditorium (later called the Embassy Auditorium) and the Ambassador Hotel Ballroom were also considered professional performing spaces. In 1921 St. Denis and Shawn performed at both of these alternative spaces.

Norma Gould's career was in full swing in 1915. It was in 1915–16 that she came under the management of the all-powerful and all-important L. E. Behymer. In Gould's 1921–22 winter school brochure, Behymer is quoted as making these comments in a letter to her: "I have watched in the press your recent success and am doubly your admirer for the standard you have set and what you are doing to help elevate, entertain, and particularly add to the artistic influences of this city." Behymer was an impresario who only took on recognized artists. No other dancers in Los Angeles came under his sponsorship at the time he took Norma Gould under his wing.

On 27 April 1915 Norma Gould presented an evening of dance at the Little Theatre, where she was to present dance evenings for the next few years. In her 1915 performance was Ted Lehman, soon to tour with her to Texas and Louisiana with the Don Philippini band. The other major participants in that evening were Ned Bolles, Bertha Wardell, and Louise Velasco; they were accompanied by a six-piece orchestra under the direction of Helen Tappe. There were two suites on the program, each with quite a few dances. One was *Suite Fantastique*, the other *Suite Orientale*. Gould performed, aided by a total of 20 of her more advanced students. The *Los Angeles Tribune* in an article dated 27 April suggested that its readers could look forward to this evening of dance: "Exquisitely simple, artistic in conception, and entirely original, the entertainment to be given this evening by Miss Norma Gould and her dancers at the Little Theatre promises to be of exceptional beauty and interest."

In 1916 Gould presented her ballet, *Jeanne d'Arc*, at the Little Theatre. A preopening report in the *Los Angeles Evening Express* of 1 June 1916 noted that Gould had worked on this ballet for six months. The reporter, Dorothy Willis, attended a dress rehearsal and commented that "even at the dress rehearsal last night spectators were moved to frequent applause and exclamations of admiration." An even earlier report on the ballet in the Sunday *Los Angeles Tribune* of 21 May 1916 emphasized the scholarly thoroughness of Gould's approach to the ballet: "The difficulty and delicacy of this story can better be

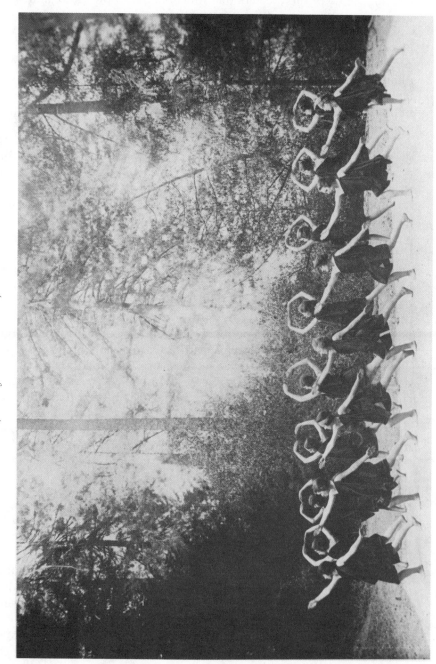

Norma Gould Students, Early 1920s Summer school at Idylwild. *(Courtesy Karoun Toutikian)*

realized when it is known that for three months Miss Gould has been studying the history of the famous maiden as treated by half a dozen well-known historians from various points of view." Gould made her own costumes and used 40 of her students in this production. In Gould's scrapbook a review of 2 June 1916 is accompanied by a picture that shows her in midthigh tunic with a cape and neck-ruff. The review commented that the costumes were indeed "different in every way from the ordinary dance attire." The review, unsigned, was extremely favorable, noting that the evening had met with "unprecedented success" and that in the audience were drama students and professional dancers.

The ballet scenario noted three scenes: a forest scene in Domremy (scene of Joan's childhood), a battlefield near Orleans (a scene of victorious battle), and a prison cell in Rouen (where she is to be burned as a witch). Dorothy Willis in her 1 June report of the dress rehearsal in the *Los Angeles Evening Express* was impressed. "The entire ballet is singularly clear-cut and beautiful and reflects the greatest possible credit upon its young creator, who is still in her twenties." This reviewer also saw the ballet in performance and was pleased. "The highly artistic standard of the work excels anything of the kind heretofore exhibited in Los Angeles."

The year 1916 marks Gould's first involvement with a university, although it is still peripheral at this point. There is a clipping in one of her scrapbooks that notes a "wonderful program of interpretive dancing" given by the Physical Education Club at the University of California, Los Angeles (then a normal school). This program featured four dancers—Dorothy Lyndall, Ann Walter, Bertha Wardell, and Mildred Burns. The first three were listed as students of Norma Gould, and the fourth (Mildred Burns) was listed as a student of Ernest Belcher. It appears that the program was a collaborative effort between Gould and Belcher, and each teacher choreographed their own students' presentation.

The following year Norma Gould presented another program at the Little Theatre. This time, with herself in the leading role, it was a ballet called *Naia*. Naia was the ruling spirit of the undersea, and the story is of her love for a handsome prince. Dorothy Willis in the *Los Angeles Evening Express* commented on this presentation in an extensive article on 3 June 1917 accompanied by a large picture spread.

> With consummate artistry Miss Gould has woven into the dances the story of passion and gladness, sorrow and joy that comes to the spirits of water folk, and each of her fifty dancers will express by movement and by costume of exquisite design the character she portrays. . . . Her students are taught the art of dancing from the standpoint of the truly beautiful and artistic and every dance created by her bears the mark of simple portrayal of truth and purity of movement.

Two other performances at the Little Theatre were to follow. In 1919 Gould presented *The Golden Bough,* and in 1921, *Diandra.* In 1918 she moved her studio out of her home to an adjacent space at 1633 Georgia Avenue. It is hard to know what kind of interaction there was between Gould and the Denishawn School, but in 1918 Gould, St. Denis, and Shawn performed together in a large Red Cross Pageant. It is unfortunate that all we have of this event is a picture in Gould's scrapbook, with no information as to how they interacted in terms of students, ideas, and collaboration.

The years 1915 through 1920 marked a period of great activity for Gould. Here was clearly the establishment of her career in Los Angeles. Sometime between 1919 and 1920 she went to New York to study, according to an article dated 1920 in her scrapbook. The article indicates that this was not her first trip, supporting evidence in the scrapbook that she studied in New York while still in high school. The article does not have a source or a specific date, but notes that Gould was in New York "gathering material for the advancement of her school." The writer goes on to report more specifics:

> This season Miss Gould made a close study of the Dalcroze system of eurythmics, which she considers an essential factor in dance, not only because it is the basis of musical understanding and interpretation through bodily expression, but stimulates development in mental alertness and poise. She took additional training in Russian, Hungarian, Polish and Czecho-Slavic dances from Chalif, an authority on the Slavic, made an accurate study of the French period dances, such as Pavan, Sarabande, Passepied, Minuet, etc. with Rosetta O'Neil, and was a member of the advanced classes in the Unitrinian School of Personal Harmonizing, where she graduated in 1914.

In 1919 Norma Gould began teaching at the University of California, Southern Branch (now UCLA),[11] and in 1920 she began teaching at the University of Southern California. Probably one of the first professional dancers to become involved in higher education, she was also a pioneer in training her own students to become university teachers. During the years 1919 through 1924 she functioned in a dual capacity at these two institutions—as a faculty member in the Physical Education Department and as director of pageantry.[12] Gould's involvement in pageantry is provocative and important for understanding the relationship between early American modern dance and the American Pageantry Movement. She has left behind extensive documentation on the pageants she created and produced, her complete syllabus for the pageantry course she taught, and two pageants she sold commercially. It is clear in Gould's work that her interests in expressive dance and pageantry were mutually reinforcing. In the framework of the pageants

Norma Gould, 1920s
(*Courtesy Karoun Toutikian*)

and courses she was able to experiment with movement and to reach a large audience of students and onlookers.

It is not possible in the context of this material to provide a full study of the American Pageantry Movement and its relationship to the development of modern dance.[13] A brief background, however, is helpful for an understanding of the way in which Norma Gould's work in this area illuminates an important but relatively unexplored movement in early twentieth-century theater, dance, and education. The development of the American Pageantry Movement resulted from many changes in American society. Educators, social workers, political reformers, innovators in the fields of theater and dance used the pageant as a vehicle for social and artistic reform. They were responding to the largest influx of immigrants ever experienced in the United States, new patterns in urban/rural living, increased industrialization, the growth of the Labor and Progressive Movements, changes in schools and curriculum, and the strong belief that the right environment could help mold a society. From 1913 through the 1920s as many as 100 pageants were produced each year in various communities, but the American Pageantry Movement began to diminish in importance by the late 1920s.

What were these pageants? The word has been used to describe all manner of events—parades, processionals, floats, festivals, ceremonials, and even swimming exhibits. Yet the pageant should not be used loosely in the context of twentieth-century American history for it refers to a theatrical form of expression that is identifiable and can be defined. The American pageants that developed during the early part of the twentieth century were usually outdoor historical, dramatic spectacles consisting of independent, loosely connected episodes with a unifying theme.

Norma Gould's unpublished lecture notes for her 1924 course in pageantry at the University of Southern California show what she did in each lecture, what kinds of assignments she gave, and how she led her students toward a final production. She was concerned that students understand expression through movement and wanted them involved in the practical aspects of dance composition as it related to actually staging a production. She lectured on lighting and costuming as well as the meaning of dance. The use of historic material for a pageant was both didactic and artistic. The intent was to teach a community or group about a particular event; at the same time the pageant provided a way to celebrate that event together and create a cohesiveness through artistic activity. Quality and form were important, and thematic material allowed for the exploration of a variety of ideas in dance that produced new forms of creative expression. The pageants in-

Norma Gould, 1920s
(*Courtesy Karoun Toutikian*)

cluded dances derived from Indian folklore or dances concerned with sacred ritual and feelings of nature, to mention just a few. Pageantry courses in colleges emphasized expression, exploration, performance, and production.

Norma Gould wrote an introduction to her course, in which she gave an overview about the meaning and development of the pageant. Following are a few excerpts:

> The pageant is the lowest form of dramatic expression but it is a form which is deeply rooted in the hearts of the people. It appeals strongly to a characteristic we all share, the love of display, and it is only recently that a serious effort has been made to harness this instinct to higher status. The emphasis of the older pageants was an aim to entertain by means of lavish display, while the purpose of the modern pageants is to instruct by means of entertainment. My first desire to combine the study of pageantry with my original work in the Art of Dancing, grew out of a love for the nature-worship and ritual of the ancient peoples of all countries, and the contribution of these to Art. It has been the study of these ancient rituals, the origin of the Dance and Drama, which has fascinated me and aroused a desire to reproduce these great ceremonies in our lovely Southern California. The Greek word for a rite is *dromenon*—"a thing done." The Greeks realized that to perform a rite you must *do* something, you must not only feel something but express it in action. . . . There are two types of pageants: local and historical pageants; pageants dealing with impersonal forces, or pageants of ideas. These may have a strongly historical character but would be more general than specific.
>
> Each community has its own individuality. Beautiful myths and poetry may be woven about its symbolic representation. The industrial town—the seaport—the literary center—the artistic center . . . all have distinctive individualities. The movement (or action) is the most important factor in a pageant. . . . The form can scarcely be separated from the movement . . . and should be studied for its psychological effect.[14]

We do know that other pioneers in dance were involved in pageants. Ruth St. Denis and Ted Shawn staged a pageant at the outdoor theater in Berkeley in 1916, and Gould, St. Denis, and Shawn were involved in the 1918 Red Cross Pageant in Los Angeles. Gertrude Colby, a pioneer in dance education at Columbia Teacher's College, is listed as the director of dances for the *Pageant of Schenectady* in 1912, and she was dance director for later pageants. Lester Horton's first major theatrical and dance experience was in the pageant *Hiawatha*, initially staged in Indianapolis in 1926. Horton came to Los Angeles in 1928 to perform in the *Hiawatha* pageant, presented at that time in the amphitheater at Eagle Rock. Pageantry classes began at colleges in 1912, when the first such course was offered at Dartmouth.

Norma Gould worked at the University of California, Southern Branch, for three years as director of pageantry, and in that role she composed and produced three pageants. In 1920 she created *Dionysia*,

Norma Gould, 1929
(*Courtesy Karoun Toutikian*)

a pageant in honor of Dionysus. An article dated 6 May 1920 in the *Los Angeles Evening Express* said the pageant would tell the story of "the god of vegetation and of the newborn year, especially as manifested in the vine and juice of the grape." The pageant was produced on 7 May, but an article in the *Pasadena Star News* of 1 May 1920 gave a preview. The writer noted that Dr. Moore, in charge of the events, wanted to "make this entertainment known throughout the state and for this reason has made it free from any admission charge."

> The theme of the pageant has an educational value as well as being of great beauty, for it deals with "The Dionysia," one of the most important of ancient Greek festivals held in the spring in honor of the god, Dionysus, regarded as the spiritual form of vernal life. It was a festival of the fruits of the whole earth and was the origin of drama. The large and beautiful garden of the university will serve as the stage and it is expected that the true spirit of an ancient Greek ceremony will be incarnated.

The cast of *Dionysia* was made up of university students and some of Gould's advanced dancers. Among these was Bertha Wardell, who joined the faculty of the University of California, Southern Branch, as an associate in Physical Education in 1921–22. In 1921 Gould directed a pageant on a Spanish theme, *Andalusia,* commemorating the anniversary of the circumnavigation of the globe by Ferdinand Magellan. In 1922 she composed and directed *Children of the Sun,* a pageant depicting ceremonies in celebration of spring as practiced by the ancient Egyptians, Japanese, Aztecs, and Russians. This pageant was performed on 5 May and 6 May, and an admission fee of 50 cents was charged for the performance on Vermont Avenue. The university orchestra was conducted by Mr. Kraft; Gould was assisted by Bertha Wardell.

In addition to her work as director of pageantry, Gould was part of the Physical Education Department. She is listed in the 1919–20 bulletins as being on the faculty of the women's physical education program in the role of "assistant in gymnastics." She was listed in the same way in the bulletins for 1920 through 1923; after that her name no longer appeared as a faculty member. Dance courses offered during those years were rhythmic dancing, natural dancing, aesthetic dancing, folk dancing, and pageantry.

In 1924 Gould taught during the summer session at the University of Southern California (USC). An announcement in the 18 April 1920 edition of the *Los Angeles Times* noted that beginning 28 June, for six weeks, Norma Gould would lecture and conduct classes in "esthetic interpretation" of the art of dance. Another undated article treated the summer session as very important, noting that it was the first time a course in "esthetic dancing" had been taught at USC. The course was being met with "genuine enthusiasm," and the enrollment was proving to be larger than for the other physical education classes. An article in the August issue of the *California Graphic* said that in Gould's class one could receive credit toward a master's degree.[15]

A reporter wrote that Gould would be "teaching dance courses in connection with some of the most advanced work in physical education." The article also noted that her courses would have the same academic respectability as Greek and Latin and that students could now get a master's degree with an emphasis in dance. During her 1924 teaching assignment at USC, these press announcements made a point of emphasizing that Gould was to be associated with Dr. William Skarstrom of Wellesly College, Dr. Leroy Lowman of the Los Angeles Orthopaedic Hospital, and Dr. Baird Hastings of the Rockefeller Institute. The association of Gould with these eminent men was important; it meant that dance was a serious endeavor and that she as a dancing teacher had academic respectability. The press reiterated many times that Norma Gould's dancing and teaching had spiritual and aesthetic components. There was no question that her form of dance made a connection between art and education and stood apart from and above dance that was mainly entertainment.

An article titled "Norma Gould to Be U.S.C. Dance Director" stated that Gould's course would include dance technique and composition, musical interpretation, composition, and an introduction to dance dramas, pageants, and pantomimes. Another undated article quoted Gould directly, printing her first address to the class at USC: "This training, which deals with dancing as a fine art, is both formative and recuperative. It aims to produce a harmonious use of the entire body, to develop character and the natural powers of expression and above all to establish poise and a body freed and attuned to the finest uses of thought and feeling."[16] Gould's appointment to the two universities as a teacher of aesthetic dance, interpretive dance, and pageantry was in keeping with her philosophy of teaching in her studio. She never felt that she was teaching her students only for the purposes of their becoming professionals. Her 1921–22 brochure had the heading "Norma Gould School for Science of Good Motion and Art of Dancing."

She taught dance to fulfill a variety of goals for the students. She wanted to prepare them if they were to be professionals. She also had courses designed specifically for those who were already teachers or dancers. She taught her students so that they could themselves prepare to teach and offered special teachers' courses in the summer. Many of her Los Angeles students went on to become teachers either in educational situations or in their own studios. From 1917 through the late-1920s, three teachers of dance at what is now UCLA had been trained by Norma Gould—Marion Wallace, Bertha Wardell, and Ina Thach. Marion Wallace also taught dance in a summer session at Stanford University, and Bertha Wardell taught in a summer session at Pasadena Community Playhouse. Helen Mathison went on to teach at the University of Southern California; Mary Carroll at Santa Monica High School; Leah Wooton and Lillian Hayes with the Los Angeles Playgrounds; Martha Gill at Marymount School for Girls; Dorothy Misner in the Physical Education Department of the Covina Schools; and Violet Guthrie with the Santa Monica School System. Dorothy Lyndall opened her own studio and became the teacher of Myra Kinch and Yuriko. She assisted the latter in leaving Los Angeles when Japanese were being interned. Marion Morgan was a performer on the Orpheum circuit and may have studied with Gould. An article about her is in the Gould scrapbook noting that Morgan took up interpretive dancing while she was teaching in a Los Angeles school.[17]

If financial success is any indication, Gould was doing well by 1923. It was then she moved into a studio built to her own specifications at 460 Western Avenue. The structure consisted of seven auxiliary studios and a main studio designed to be used as a theater, with special lighting equipment. The building was low-lying in the style of old Spanish architecture and was approached through a patio and a courtyard with a small pool and water plants. The press was interested in reporting on this studio, saying it was the first such specially designed building for dance in Los Angeles.

Gould's classes were popular during this period; several articles report that there were waiting lists for her classes. She had some of her advanced students teaching in branch schools in Santa Monica, at the Beverly Hills Hotel, and at several girls' schools, such as Westlake. Her summer courses for teachers were popular, and in this studio she produced evenings of dance, pageantry, and dance pantomime. It was during this period that she sold two pageant scripts: *Diandra* and *A Desert Nocturne*. Gould was also popular as a lecturer for women's clubs on three major topics: dance as an educational factor, dance and pageantry, and the development of dance.

The years 1926 through 1929 signified widespread public acceptance of Norma Gould as a major choreographer in Los Angeles, and it was during this period she appeared in two major performance spaces—Philharmonic Auditorium and the Hollywood Bowl. In 1926, on 11 June, Norma Gould appeared in Philharmonic Auditorium in *The Pearl of Kashmir* accompanied by 75 dancers and Adolph Tandler's Little Symphony. On 30 August 1927 and 4 September 1928 she appeared on the Hollywood Bowl stage in two postseason evenings called "California Night of Music." In her 1928 Hollywood Bowl appearance she was accompanied by Adolph Tandler's Little Symphony in the premiere of her new ballet, *The Shepherd of Shiraz*. The story was by Alice Pike Barney and the music by Sigurd Frederickson. On 15 June 1929 she presented a dance drama, *The Twilight of the Gods*, at the Windsor Theatre.

On 30 August 1929 Norma Gould and her group were asked to appear at the Hollywood Bowl as part of the regular summer concerts. She was the first native California dancer to be given this honor. The Hollywood Bowl program notes for Gould's performance relay the regard in which she was held:

> Hailed as one of California's distinguished native daughters among the arts, Miss Gould has long occupied a position of esteem in the community. Her artistry as a dancer is matched by her skill as a teacher and many of her pupils have won acclaim in the artistic field of their choice. This Bowl engagement, therefore, comes as a fitting reward for her long endeavor in upholding the best traditions of her art in the West.

The program consisted of two dances. The first was set to Schubert's Symphony No. 8 in B minor (the "Unfinished") The program listed two movements: Allegro moderato and Andante con moto. The second dance was to Tchaikovsky's *Nutcracker Suite*, for which the program listed eight sections: "Miniature Overture" (orchestra), "March," "Danse de la Fée Dragée," "Trepak," "Danse Arabe," "Danse Chinoise," "Danse des Mirlitons," and "Valse des Fleurs."

Bertha McCord Knisely in a *Los Angeles Saturday Night* article dated 7 September 1929 reported on Norma Gould's performance at the Hollywood Bowl.

> Color and rhythm, utilized with taste and skill by Norma Gould in the ballets of Friday, delighted the largest audience of the season. Sylvain Noack directed the Schubert *Unfinished Symphony* and Tschaikowsky's *Nutcracker Suite*, to which Miss Gould adapted her interpretations. For the symphony, a dignified, serious conception of humanity's vacillation between faith and doubt was carried out by two groups of dancers, and a solo dancer, Norma Gould, representing the human soul.

The pictures of the dancers suggest a simplicity and an emphasis on grouping and plastique, as opposed to complex steps and virtuosity. In one typical picture the arms are loose and the bodies, though lifted, give a natural feeling. The feet are relaxed, although Norma Gould herself has her front foot turned out and her back foot in an extended formal ballet tendu. The knees of all the dancers are gently bent; their torsos reach back slightly or turn. The feeling imparted is of simple, harmonious movement, with emphasis on simplicity and strong visual im-

Ballet to Schubert's *Unfinished Symphony*, Hollywood, 1929
Choreography by Norma Gould.
(Courtesy Karoun Toutikian)

Norma Gould and Dancers, Early 1930s
This shows the dancers in the Larchmont Boulevard studio.
(*Courtesy Karoun Toutikian*)

ages created by various kinds of unison groupings. The group consists entirely of women clothed in tunics. In another picture the tunics are covered by capes.

The performance at the Hollywood Bowl was the end of an era for Norma Gould. By that time she was no longer as strong a performer as she had been. In 1980 Karoun Toutikian, an associate of Gould's in the twenties, recalled how Gould was "sensitive and magically ethereal."[18] Bella Lewitzky, on the other hand, who saw her perform in the 1930s, remembered "a dreamy eyed lady who put her to sleep."[19] It is likely that by 1929 Gould's simple, meaningful dances looked outdated and simplistic to audiences. As a pioneer in developing choreography that moved away from classical ballet, she relied on imagination, musical knowledge, and dramatic flair rather than a highly developed technique. She herself never went beyond a certain level in her movement vocabulary, but she was training people who did, and those individuals (such as Dorothy Lyndall) were now exploring on their own.

Gould received national recognition in 1931. She was hired as a master teacher for the national meeting in Los Angeles of the Dancing Masters of America Association. She continued through the 1930s as she had before, teaching and offering annual summer courses. She also continued performing and choreographing, but from this time on her major contribution was of a totally different nature. Gould became an impresario in 1932 when she opened a new studio at 118 North Larchmont Boulevard, one that she designed herself to include a stage and good lighting facilities.

It was on Larchmont Boulevard that she created her Dance Theatre, an institution that was to have repercussions for Los Angeles dance and young artists who went on from Los Angeles to work and perform elsewhere. The Dance Theatre that Norma Gould founded was an umbrella unit for a wide array of guest performers and teachers. It was based on her advanced vision that all kinds of dance should be encouraged and seen, that audiences have to be developed, and that young dancers need exposure to many different kinds of technique from masters of various forms.

When she established the Dance Theatre Gould created a Board of Directors to help her as a decision-making and fund-raising group, an uncommon idea in those days. The initial board included Muriel Stuart, Anna Duncan, Lester Horton, Marjorie Dougan, Wanda Grazer, L. E. Behymer, and Philip and Odetta Newberg. Norma Gould was the guiding force and created an atmosphere of freedom and exploration. It was most unusual in the 1930s for an individual artist to create a space where people of different aesthetic persuasions in dance would come together so that they could perform, teach, and learn.

The announcements about Dance Theatre over the years explained its nature and purpose:

> The Dance Theatre of Los Angeles is a movement rather than an organization. It is non-profit and . . . its purpose is to form a nucleus for a large and appreciative audience for the concert dancers that they may eventually enjoy the support and following which attends symphony orchestras, art galleries and theatres of the drama. It presents only professionals and has no connection with any school. The present home of the Dance Theatre is the auditorium of the Norma Gould Studios. When funds are available, a special theatre will be constructed for this movement. Dancers interested in being presented by the Dance Theatre will be granted an interview at any time with Miss Gould. Suggestions for interesting dancers and groups who might be invited to appear are welcome at all times.[20]

Gould did not just use her studio as a place for artistic exchange; she also created an attitude of openness for young artists struggling to make their own statements. Dancers who performed in the space were also engaged to teach there. The list of dancers and dance groups Norma Gould presented over the years as teachers and performers is impressive, among them: Carmelita Maracci, Tina Flade, Waldeen, Teru, Tom Youngplant and Hopi Indians, Angna Enters, Detru and Aztec-Mayan Dancers, Harold Kreutzberg, Grace Borroughs, Han and De Negre, Jack Reinhart, Hasoutra, Charles Teske, Okajima, Lester Horton, Luz Garoes of Mexico, Sumita and Lilivati Devi, Frances and Rosemary Stack, Prince Modupe and the Nigerian Ballet, Helen March, Melissa Blake, Dorothy Jarnac, and David Thimar and the Red Gate Players. Two pianists (Verna Arvey and Francisco Avellan) gave special programs of dance in music such as "The Oriental Heritage of Spanish Dance Music." A 1936 program listed a course in Martha Graham technique taught by Bonnie Bird as well as a series of lecture teas with David Edstrom, Leo Katz, Dane Rudhyar, and Norma Gould. In 1937 Ann Mundstak gave a lecture on "Laban Dance Notation."

In 1935 Gould moved her studio and Dance Theatre activities to 831 South La Brea and continued to be a presenter and impresario through 1942. During the ten years that the Dance Theatre functioned, it played a vital role in the technical and artistic development of many young dancers. It was a crucial factor in the career of Lester Horton, who began teaching classes at Norma Gould's studio in 1932. Gould and Horton shared several programs presented by Dance Theatre. The most interesting occurred in 1935 when they joined forces for an evening called *Sun Cycle*. The program note read as follows: "Sun worship, one of the earliest forms of emotion to inspire dance will be the motif of the program. Four groups will contribute compositions to this Cycle, so that a great diversity of choreographical tradition will be represented by the various groups." Participants were the Norma Gould dancers,

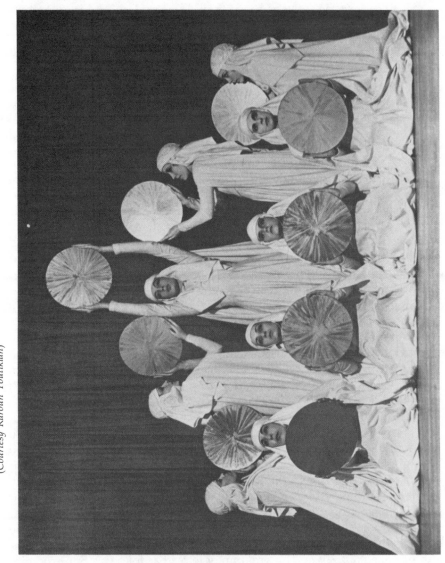

Norma Gould Dancers in *Sun Ritual* (Portion of the *Sun Cycle* Evening), 1935
(*Courtesy Karoun Toutikian*)

Lester Horton's group, a group of Hopi Indian dancers, and the Rudolf Abel dancers. Percussion accompaniment was used by all except Gould, whose work was accompanied by piano and flute. Aside from performing, Lester Horton attended master classes and was on the Board of Directors of Dance Theatre.

Where else in Los Angeles (or very many other places at that time) could young dancers present their work at no expense? Gould arranged that profits would be shared if there were any. Various members of the Board of Directors would assist in taking tickets, sending out mailing, doing publicity, and lighting. Artists were presented in Los Angeles who might not have been seen if they had to depend on a commercial arrangement. Young Los Angeles artists had a chance to present programs in an intimate setting, testing their ideas, and an opportunity to share and learn at the same time. The various special programs and lectures provided another unique opportunity for learning and growing and the chance to think in new directions or reflect on special issues. For a while, in connection with the Dance Theatre, Gould also published a small newsletter. Its purpose was to list dance activities in the city and provide a forum for activities and information.

In 1938, probably as a result of the activity she had generated as an impresario, Gould was ready to try a new direction in her own choreography. To the music of William Grant Still, now recognized as an important Black composer, Gould choreographed *Lenox Hill* to the accompaniment of the Hall Johnson Choir. The music and dance followed a scenario written by Verna Arvey and dealt with "The Adventures of the Man from Down South" (played by Charles Teske) who comes to Harlem. There he experiences various aspects of Harlem: the sidewalk characters, the rescue missions, night clubs, and rent parties—all shown in a choreographic montage. Preceding the ballet were five divertissements tracing the transition of the African dance to its current character in Harlem: "Primitive Rhythms," "Cakewalk," "Salute to Damballa," and two rhythm and buck dances. *Lenox Hill* was so popular after its first performances on 1 May and 2 May that it was repeated on 22 May to serve those who were turned away. To coincide with the production an exhibit was mounted of Negro cultural life: books by Negro authors and those concerning Negro life; manuscripts and printed scores by William Grant Still; photographs of Sargent Johnson sculpture, well-known as an Afro-American artist; photographs of Negro dancers; and handicrafts by Florence Russell Phillips, a Negro craftswoman.

One of the last programs given at the Dance Theatre was a benefit for the British War Relief Association on 26 and 27 May 1941. The evening was called *Present Pagan Primitive* and ranged far and wide in terms of style and content. Listed on the program were: Jose Cansino and Carmela (Spanish); Nico Charisse Group (ballet); Gene Cole and Partner (jitterbug); Leela Devi (Hindu); Jac and Laura Dieger (tap); Eliner Hague's Jarabe Dancers (Mexican); Martin Herrara (American Indian); Virginia Hall Johnson (modern American); Thurston Knudsen (jungle drums); Lani (Hawaiian); Joe Stevenson (African); Julia Taweel (Syrian); The Dancing Velascos (ballroom dance in the modern mood); Allan Cook, Sally Dick, Julia Ann Reynolds, Anastine Powell, Lester Shafer, John Stanley, Charles Teske (Western cowboy dancers); and a Scotch Highland dancer and piper.

In the late 1940s Gould moved out of her La Brea studio. She continued teaching until 1967. By then she had very few students and was only teaching sporadically. By the 1960s she was already ill with what we might now diagnose as Alzheimer's, and she was institutionalized in a nursing home in 1968. She had lost contact with the world, and the world had lost contact with her.

Norma Gould's accomplishments and her interactions with other artists help add to our understanding of the complex and multifaceted roots of American modern dance. She was an important teacher in Los Angeles for many years, and her lineage through Dorothy Lyndall, Myra Kinch, and Yuriko is a significant one. Her influence on dance in education created a base for the development of dance at UCLA and USC. She was a potent force in creating interest in contemporary dance with her numerous lectures and articles, and her classes for nonprofessionals gave many an appreciation of dance.

It may be that her most important contribution was the creation of the Dance Theatre—a place where her spirited belief in the freedom of expression encouraged many artists to perform and develop their own ideas and gave them an opportunity to consider the ideas of others. At a time in New York where the modern dance artists were each fighting to stake out their own territory, Los Angeles may have provided an atmosphere of freedom that allowed for greater crossover. It may also have been that dancers in Los Angeles felt a stronger need to join together, as the city was small and resources were limited. The early support from the community that Norma Gould received in Los Angeles was probably also a factor in her development in the creation of Dance Theatre and in her work at both UCLA and USC.

In an unpublished article by Norma Gould dated October 1926, she wrote:

> The dance is not a lonely art. In its most complete manifestation it bears the proportion and balance of great temples; it dramatizes the emotions of mankind; it embodies the color and richness of great paintings; it makes live the beauty of line and

form of statues; it charts the measures of poems; it traces the beautiful melodic patterns and visualizes the harmony of music. Dancing is the loftiest, the most moving, the most beautiful of arts because it is no mere translation or abstraction from life; it is life itself.

2

Ernest Belcher (1882–1973):
Early Visionary of American Ballet

As a youth in his native London Ernest Belcher had no exposure to the worlds of dance and theater. His father was a butcher, and childhood and adolescence were spent helping in the shop, singing in the church choir, and attending meetings of the Boy Scouts. No one in the family exhibited any musical or dramatic talents; in high school painting and architecture were Belcher's major interests. He did, however, develop a feeling for music and began attending orchestral concerts at Royal Albert Hall while still in high school:

> During these concerts I would sit enthralled with the beauty of the music. I seemed to see vague forms swaying and waving about in soft undulations, without definite plan or result. I felt myself striving to control these movements and bring them to a specific sense of order, but something within me was lacking, and afterward when I had learned the technique of the dance and the proper control to the body, I realized that knowledge was what I had lacked when attending the symphonies.
>
> When the music had ceased and I again found myself, I would realize that I had been living through a great sensation of rhythmic form, and thus seemed to move a step forward in the linking of music and rhythm.
>
> About this time there was a sudden realization that this expression of myself in gesture and movement was to be the great dominating force in my life and I was immediately ready to sacrifice almost anything and everything to attain success in this art.[1]

In 1898, 16 years old and determined to find out about dance, Belcher began searching for a teacher. A young person wanting to study dance seriously was at a great disadvantage in England during the late nineteenth century and early years of the twentieth. No school or permanent company existed where ballet traditions were nurtured and handed down from generation to generation, as was true in Russia, France, and Denmark. Mary Clarke in *The Sadler's Wells Ballet* wrote that by the middle of the nineteenth century "in England ballet moved to the music hall where it remained quite happily enjoying a quarter-

The Go-Bang-Girls, ca. 1900
Ethel Payne, a member of this music-hall troupe, was Ernest Belcher's first dance teacher.
(*Courtesy Department of Special Collections, University Research Library, UCLA*)

century of fantastic popularity at the Empire and Alhambra."[2] Teachers were primarily interested in preparing the students, most of them women, for the popular theater.

Ernest Belcher began his study of dance with Ethel Payne, a member of the Go-Bang-Girls, four women who performed in music halls. He went to her home in Mecklenburg Square for lessons; at the same time he worked as an architecture apprentice in the office of Maxwell Maberly Smith. This arrangement continued for about two years, until Belcher decided that a more intensive study of dance was necessary. Belcher's family disapproved of the new direction his life was taking. They were against a career in the theater and refused to support any further activity. However, Belcher began intensive study with Francesca Zanfretta, who danced at the Empire Theatre for many years and, according to G. B. L. Wilson, "taught many of the great dancers of the younger generation."[3] Belcher left home and took odd jobs, often spending most of the money for food, car fare, and laundry on lessons. This period remained painfully vivid even in later years:

> It became necessary to deprive myself of everything except the barest necessities in life in order to pay for my lessons, which even then were few and far between, and were to be had only by the exertion of walking a distance between nine and ten miles (sometimes each way) to the studio. This I did for two years, with little or no encouragement from anyone except a few close friends and even they doubted that anything of any value would be the outcome of my efforts.[4]

In addition to the intensive work with Zanfretta, Belcher began taking lessons with Alexandre Genée, the uncle and teacher of the Empire Theatre's Danish ballerina Adeline Genée. Realizing that survival as a dancer would mean the ability to perform in music halls and on vaudeville circuits, Belcher sought out other teachers to gain expertise in a variety of dance forms. By his own account he studied period and national folk dances with Louis d'Egville and Cormani; Spanish dances under Caroline Otero, Lopes and Tortola Valencia, and Malaganita; Indian and Eastern Oriental dances under Roshanara.

It is not clear how long Belcher studied with Zanfretta or Genée, much less the transitory other teachers. Information about many aspects of his career comes from radio programs in 1935, some interviews taped in 1969, and unpublished typed autobiographical notes—all housed at UCLA in the Special Collections. However, these reminiscences are not always reliable. For example, Belcher always claimed that his debut at the Alhambra took place in 1902 in *Sal-Oh-My*, a parody of Maud Allan, but it is clear that the date is inaccurate. The program from the Alhambra, recently found by his daughter, Marge Champion, gives the date as 20 September 1909—and Allan's London

Playbill of the Alhambra Theatre, London, 20 September 1909
This evening's performance included Ernest Belcher's debut in
Sal-Oh-My, part of the revue, "On the Heath."
(*Courtesy Marge Champion*)

debut was in March 1908. Belcher was part of a revue called "On the Heath," produced by Elise Clerc, and his skit, *Sal-Oh-My*, was the last portion of the revue. Belcher as *Sal-Oh-My* took the part created the year before by La Belle Leonora, and the substitution of a young man may well have strengthened the revue. For these performances the opening spectacle was a ballet called *Les Cloches de Corneville* starring a Danish ballerina, Britta (Britta Petersen). The program notes that this was "the complete Ballet d'Action invented and presented by Alfredo Curti to Robert Planquette's original music" for the popular operetta of the same name. Also on this typical Alhambra mixed bill was the London debut of the popular American comedienne Ethel Levey, who had been George M. Cohan's first wife.

After the Alhambra engagement, around 1910, Belcher got a job in the Haymarket Theatre production of Maurice Maeterlinck's *The Blue Bird*. He played the role of "Fire" and was required to speak as well as dance. According to Belcher's recollections, he stayed with this production about 17 months, touring the entire British Isles. He then went on to head his own acts on the Moss and Stoll music hall circuit, and through 1914 he had performing partnerships with several women— Nora Walker, Dorothy Graham, Dorothy Edward, and Gertrude Atherton.

Belcher was unclear and often contradictory about the specific dates and lengths of his various partnerships. There are several pictures captioned "Ernest Belcher and Norah Walker in the Tango Waltz" but there seems to be no further information about their performances. His next association was with Dorothy Graham; their partnership featured "The Apache Dance," which Belcher claimed he learned from Max Dearly in Paris. Dorothy Edward was his next partner, and there are several pictures of the two of them in ballet and ballroom poses. Soon after becoming partners they took a stage name, "The Celestes." A document recently found by Marge Champion shows an agreement dated 13 November 1913 between Ernest Belcher and Max Brunell. It states that "in consideration of the sum of five pounds Ernest Belcher . . . is given sole performing rights for the dance *Tango Celeste*." One of the places The Celestes performed was at the Royal Automobile Club. According to Belcher this was then a prestigious private club where he had the opportunity to dance for King Edward, Queen Alexandra, and the Prince and Princess of Wales, among others. In their advertising card The Celestes listed their repertory as four kinds of tangos, a maxixe, three waltzes, and operatic dances. The *Daily Express* called The Celestes "as fascinating a pair of Tango experts as are to be seen in London."[5]

Ernest Belcher in *Sal-Oh-My*, 1909
In this skit, Belcher did a parody of Maud Allen. The part was originally performed by La Belle
Leonore, but the substitution of a young male dancer was felt to have strengthened the
parody—and the revue.
(*Courtesy Marge Champion*)

Among Belcher's other activities between 1910 and 1914 was an early involvement with films, a facet of his career that was to become very important when he settled in California. For the Selsoir Motion Picture Company of London he created a series of dance scenes. Special music was written to be played by an orchestra; although none was shown on the screen, the conductor appeared in the foreground of the picture.

Ernest Belcher's last partner in England was Gertrude Atherton, whose specialty was comic and acrobatic dancing. They were booked by Ernest Rolls, known at that time as the "Ziegfeld of London." Engaged for a revue at the Oxford Theatre, the couple was contracted for two years but left after six months. As Belcher recalled their performances: "The act consisted of three segments: an orthodox ballet surrounded by the company in revue; the *Yankee Tangle*—a heavy character dance of the Bowery type with some good tricks in it; and a very difficult acrobatic ballroom number which used twenty-three tricks in two and three-quarter minutes. It was much too hard and we both soon grew tired of it."[6]

Ready for new adventures in dance, Belcher joined a troupe called The Golden Dancers that was preparing to tour America. He recalled, "I don't remember exactly what I did, but I know I was not a part of their company; rather, I was a special number between their acts."[7] The group arrived in the United States sometime in August 1914, just as World War I was breaking out in Europe. A piece of paper among his memorabilia lists a permanent address in America as c/o Paul Tausig and Sons, 104 East Fourteenth Street, New York City, and is dated 22 September 1914. Belcher seems to have made the decision not to return to England shortly after arriving in this country.

After leaving The Golden Dancers, one of Belcher's first jobs in New York was as a dancing partner at Bustanoby's restaurant, where "it was his pleasant duty to dance with ladies unescorted or with non-dancing partners. Fat ladies. Thin ladies. Young ladies. Old."[8] It was for this job that he created the name "Eddie York," a name he was to use years later when he spent his Sunday mornings cooking for fun at the coffee shop in the Beverly Wilshire Hotel. One night the management of Bustanoby's was short an entertainer, and Belcher danced for the crowd. Becoming popular, he acquired the title "The Dancing Busboy." He soon achieved recognition and was even invited to dance for President and Mrs. Woodrow Wilson at the Waldorf-Astoria Hotel at the President's request.

In that same year Belcher also had a very different kind of audience—performing for the inmates at Sing-Sing prison. There were two groups of about 800 men, and he remembered dancing a hornpipe and

Advertising Card for "The Celestes," ca. 1913
Belcher joined Dorothy Edward in this dancing partnership. The card listed their repertoire.
(Courtesy Marge Champion)

The Celestes

(Miss DOROTHY EDWARD)
(Mr. ERNEST BELCHER.)

Will dance a selection from the following Repertoire

Tango Argentine
    "   Parisien
    "   Two-Step
    "   Espana
Maxixe Bresilien
Valse Variation R A C
    "   "   Celeste
Valse Tango

Operatic Dances
   { Mazurka Russe
    Adagio
    Valse
   { Solos, &c.

Communications to

Oxford Lodge,
4n, High Road,
    Gunnersbury. W

Ernest Belcher, ca. 1913
(*Courtesy Marge Champion*)

Ernest Belcher in Apache Dance, ca. 1912
(*Courtesy Marge Champion*)

Ernest Belcher and Dorothy Edward, ca. 1913
(*Courtesy Marge Champion*)

a "French Acrobatic Dance." He noted that this was "one of the most novel experiences" that he ever had. Aside from these special experiences, Belcher's main source of employment toward the end of 1914 and during part of 1915 was an engagement with the Keith-Orpheum circuits to present his own act. It is hard to determine whether it was the rigor of the touring schedule, the climate and living conditions, or the emotional difficulty of adjusting to new experiences, but Belcher became ill and decided to leave New York. His doctor found that he was suffering from tuberculosis and said that he had only one year to live. Southern California was the place he chose to go—motivated certainly by the weather and probably also by the attraction of the movies, which had recently become settled there.

Belcher arrived in Los Angeles in September 1915 and rented a room on the second floor of a small apartment building. Here, according to Marge Champion, he decided to cure himself.[9] He built a platform from the window to a tree in the yard and slept outside every night. After a short time he felt cured, and he opened his first school in Los Angeles in May 1916 with five students, "two who paid and three who did not."[10] This first studio was at Fourth and Hill Streets. Two years later a larger one was opened at 1500 Figueroa Street.

When Belcher arrived in Los Angeles at the age of 33, it is likely that he began to dream of a more stable existence, for body and psyche were weary of constant shifts and pressures. His experience in New York had led to the feeling that teaching might be an answer. Belcher knew many forms of dance, including more ballet than was usually taught to American performers. He wanted "to give the American people the dancing as it was given in Europe."[11] A certain sense of adventure was being generated in Hollywood, and the little town of Los Angeles was seen as a land of opportunity with a new, slightly crazy industry. Belcher's creation of the synchronized dance scenes for London's Selsoir Motion Picture Company in 1911–12 had intrigued him, and he began to imagine the further possibilities of dance in film. Furthermore, he had nothing to lose—life had not been stable in either London or New York, and here he could always draw on his background for vaudeville if necessary.

It was in Los Angeles, now his permanent home, that Belcher began to formulate his vision for American ballet: systematic graded training, respectability for male dancers, an educated lay public, careful training and refresher courses for teachers, the possibilities for ballet in movies, and a ballet company of American dancers. Belcher shortly acquired a large following and a reputation as a good teacher. He began to work for the movies in 1918 and soon was doing well financially. By 1922 he was able to build his own studio building. This facility, located at 634 West Fifteenth Street, housed a large studio of 3,600 square feet as well as a balcony for stage mothers. There were an adjoining hall with a stage and excellent dressing rooms and costume facilities. Finally, in 1931 Cecil B. de Mille built Belcher a three-story studio of 36,000 square feet, which he was to occupy until 1955. Belcher had worked on many films with de Mille, and the school was valuable as a source of dancers and as a place to send actors for coaching and training.

There were many reasons for Belcher's success and the large following he attracted as a teacher. For serious students he offered the opportunity of systematic graded training and the financial incentive of movie work. Directors turned to him with great regularity not only to create the dance sequences for films using his own students, but also as a source of dancers for a variety of production numbers as well as for extras, stand-ins, and occasionally stunt performers.[12] Movie stars came to his classes and hired him for private lessons as he had the ability to train them quickly both in ballet fundamentals and in the specific requirements of a particular movie or dance sequence. Men were encouraged to come to Belcher's studio for ballet training because he held special men's classes and because he was able to find them employment in films and movie prologues.

When Maria Tallchief was interviewed by Marion Horosko in 1964 for a WNYC radio program, she credited Belcher with giving her the careful training and awareness that formed the true foundation for her career. She had come to him at age eight after having attended ballet classes everywhere, and he made her start again from the very beginning. Tallchief's mother had heard that Belcher was the best and most rigorous teacher in Los Angeles. The young Maria was his student from 1933 to 1937, before going on to Bronislava Nijinska for another level of training. But first, she commented, "it was a good thing I ended up with Ernest Belcher."[13] June Roper, a Belcher student who went on to a career as a performer first in movies, then in clubs and revues, and who later became an important teacher in Canada, noted that Belcher "was an expert purveyor of the Cecchetti ballet method, approaching dancing as a scientist."[14] Carmelita Maracci, one of the most important dance figures in Southern California and the teacher of Allegra Kent and Cynthia Gregory, received her early training with Belcher and performed with him in 1926 at the Hollywood Bowl. In addition to Maria Tallchief and her sister Marjorie, well-known dancers who studied with Belcher included Rod Alexander, Cyd Charisse, Nanette Fabray, Paul Godkin, Rita Hayworth, Loren Hightower, Matt Mattox, Rosita Moreno, and Gwen Verdon.

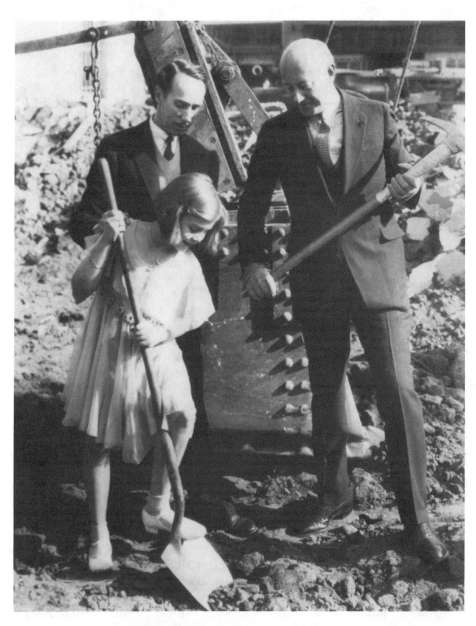

Groundbreaking for New Studio, 1931
With Belcher are his daughter and Cecil B. de Mille.
(*Courtesy Marge Champion*)

The silent movies were demanding in terms of bodily expression, since movement and gesture had to relay meanings that would normally be expressed in words. Many actors came to Belcher for training in movement and assistance with dances, among them Mary Pickford, Pola Negri, John Barrymore, Ramon Novarro, John Gilbert, and Marion Davies. In the sound era he continued to teach both dancers and dramatic performers, including Ruby Keeler, Betty Grable, Ida Lupino, and Yvonne de Carlo. In 1924 Belcher's school catalogue featured a letter signed by Pola Negri:

My dear Mr. Belcher:

It is with warm appreciation that I write these few lines of a happy association with Mr. Belcher while planning the dances which are so in evidence in my latest picture "The Spanish Dancer."

Quiet and unassuming, yet an artist showing strength and decision in his work backed by a technique of unusual excellence, a studio reflecting refinement and happiness, one can easily find the reason for his popularity and success both in the theatrical and picture world, developing talent which in a short time is undoubtedly going to place Los Angeles in the front ranks as "Mecca of the Dance."

A continued success for such a conscientious effort is the wish of

[signed] Pola Negri[15]

Carol Dempster, Lillian Gish, Colleen Moore, and Loretta Young were movie stars who studied at both the Denishawn and Belcher studios. In an article on 5 June 1932 about Loretta Young, the *New York Times* reported that "her earliest ambition was to be a dancer and she twisted and turned under the professional eyes of Ernest Belcher and Ruth St. Denis." There were probably more who did the same, particularly in the period from 1916 through 1923. In the mid-thirties Belcher gave dance lessons to Shirley Temple.

In 1916 a beautiful, ambitious stage mother, Gladys Basquette, a widow, brought her nine-year-old daughter Lina to Ernest Belcher's studio for training. Lina studied with Belcher until 1923 and became one of his best pupils, performing with him on several occasions. She then became a featured dancer in the Ziegfeld *Follies of 1923*. After her marriage to Sam Warner she made a number of movies, including Cecil B. de Mille's first sound film, *The Godless Girl* in 1929. Gladys Basquette and Ernest Belcher fell in love and were married in 1917. Lina Basquette commented on the marriage:

Few men would have had the temerity to bind himself in marriage to a beautiful widow with two offsprings, a live-in mother-in-law and a wayward younger brother. My mother, certainly a charmer from all outward appearance—a superb cook, housekeeper and affable hostess—BUT—no wonder, after about 25 years of

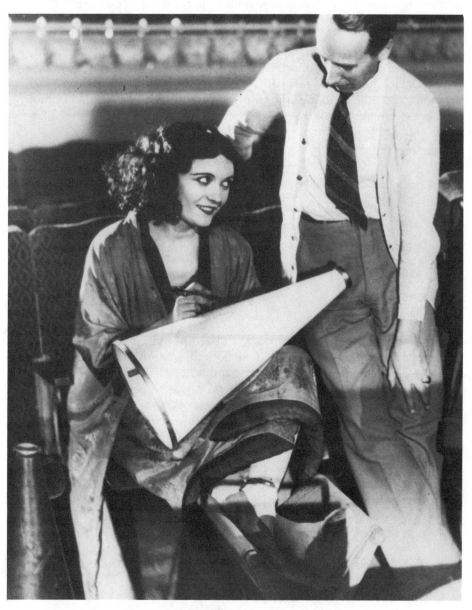

Pola Negri with Ernest Belcher, 1925
Negri was a student of Belcher, and Belcher also helped her
prepare the dances she used in the film *The Spanish Dancer* (1923).
(*Courtesy Marge Champion*)

quietly tolerating her harangues about everything from accusations of infidelity, lack of luxuries and sexual neglect, Ernest Belcher walked out of the home at 1323 Orange Drive and never returned. He accomplished this without resorting to violent behaviour—just one day, packed up his wardrobe and a few "mementos" and took off. . . . By this time, it was obvious that Gladys, my mother, suffered from a debilitating mental disorder and was more to be pitied than condemned.[16]

Lina's younger brother became ill and died shortly after Belcher and Basquette were married, but two children were soon born of the marriage—Marjorie in 1919 and Richard two years later. Belcher was happy being a father, a husband, and homeowner who enjoyed working in the garden and having tea at four. He also loved his teaching, the many students he guided, and the studios he created. Lina wrote of the man who played a dual role in her life: "I always had a deep affection and high respect for my teacher and loving step-father, Ernest Belcher. . . . So many of his pupils have passed on or are sadly incapacitated like Rita Hayworth, I fear that there are only a handful of us left to furnish memorabilia of a truly fine human being and extraordinary mentor and teacher."[17]

After Belcher and his wife separated in 1942, he continued devoting himself to teaching and family. Until 1946 he still presented advanced students in occasional performances. By the early 1950s Belcher had cut back on his teaching and enjoyed spending time with children and grandchildren—Richard's three daughters and Marge and Gower Champion's two sons. He also took great pride in the various professional activities of the Champions, their performances in clubs or stage and in movies. Marge and Gower had met in Belcher's studio and were married from 1947 to 1973; although performances often took them away from California, Los Angeles remained their home base. By the 1960s Belcher had retired, except for giving a few rare private lessons.

In 1965, when he was 83, Belcher was honored at a special ceremony, joined by Ruth St. Denis and Marge and Gower. At that time he presented his 45-year collection of *The Dancing Times* to James Doolittle, manager of the Greek Theatre. His last years were spent with the many people he loved. After Ernest Belcher's death on 24 February 1973, Alice Perissi—mother of Ersilia, Richard Belcher's wife—wrote to Marge Champion: "I had known Mr. Belcher for years and he visited us often and was always gentle and kind. When my husband Odolindo was so ill, he came and talked with him and me with such excitement, and the days seemed brighter for him having been there; and Odolindo looked forward to his visits which were many. We all loved your Dad very much. He brought us great comfort with his beautiful thoughts."[18]

Ernest Belcher and Lina Basquette, ca. 1920
(Courtesy Department of Special Collections, University Research Library, UCLA)

After a memorial service for Belcher, Marge Champion received many letters from those whose lives he had touched. Although he taught many movie stars, he was not as interested in fame and glory as he was in reaching out to the thousands of students and friends and the family who were part of his life. Certainly Gower Champion never forgot the man who was his first teacher, became his father-in-law, and was the grandfather of his two sons. Some time later, looking backward over his career, he recalled how Belcher had changed his life—as he had changed the lives of many dancers:

> I first met Mr. Belcher when I was thirteen years old. He had seen me do a ballroom dance in a school production at Bancroft Junior High. He said to my mother at that time, "That boy should study seriously. He has 'It.'" And for the rest of my life to now and beyond I have had "It" and him as two of the touchstones of my life. Proud, erect, autocratic, mischievous I can see him now. In movement. In dance. In my heart.[19]

When Belcher came to Los Angeles and started teaching in 1916, ballet performances were a rarity and good training was virtually nonexistent. He insisted on ballet as a formal discipline, knowing that it required time and application. He refused to accept instant success in a town full of get-rich-quick schemes in both real estate and films. Movies were made quickly and in quantity; movie stars were created overnight. But in a career that spanned 50 years of teaching, Belcher never changed his emphasis on slow, careful training and the comprehension of ballet as an art. This was true whether he was training professionals or amateurs: in 1944 Ann Barzel wrote that "Ernest Belcher has been the most prominent 20th century English teacher in America."[20]

By 1928 Belcher had over 2,000 students; a faculty teaching tap, acrobatics, physical culture, "moderne" dance, hula, ballroom, and Spanish dance; and a business manager. Among the better known associates at the Belcher studio over the years were Elisa, Eduardo, and Gabriel Cansino, who taught Spanish dance and enrolled the youngest member of the family, Margarita (later known as Rita Hayworth), in Belcher's ballet classes. These often had as many as 60 to 100 students in the lower levels; possibly the less talented escaped attention, but Belcher kept close watch on those who showed promise. June Roper, who took her best students down to Los Angeles for special classes with Belcher, remembered how "Maria and Marjorie Tallchief would tremble under his exacting tutelage . . . his perceptive eye could single out the weakness of the individual, and the personal correction he offered was invaluable."[21]

Ruth St. Denis, Ernest Belcher, James Doolittle, Gower and Marge Champion, 1965
This photo was taken at a ceremony in which Belcher donated his complete collection of *The Dancing Times* to the Greek Theatre in Los Angeles.
(*Courtesy Marge Champion*)

Lina Basquette is convinced that "his knowledge of anatomy and musculature became as much of an asset to his training as his excellent background as a ballet dancer and choreographer. I firmly believe that the reason I have maintained strong and healthy limbs and am still agile at 79 can be attributed to the careful training I received from Ernest Belcher."[22] Marge Champion, who studied exclusively with her father from the age of five until she left for New York, credits him for her long professional career: "I never suffered any serious injuries nor any hint of the back problems that plague so many dancers."[23] She credits her good health and long career to her father's teaching principles: careful, strict progression of activity, emphasis on correct alignment, precise placement of the body, attention to detail and to the totality of dynamics and phrasing. Belcher was especially proud of the fact that when Anna Pavlova performed in Los Angeles in 1921 and 1922, she watched classes at his studio and used some of his students in her performances.

Marge Champion recalls that her father never held recitals but instead arranged for the best dancers to perform in regular concerts. Belcher himself performed only rarely, at the beginning of his years in Los Angeles. From the accounts in Belcher's school catalogues, articles, and autobiographical notes, the productions at the Hollywood Bowl played the greatest role in his concert work, and he considered them the most prestigious—he created more programs at the Bowl than on any other stage. Indeed, in 1922 he was the first choreographer to present dance there. At that time the Bowl was a makeshift facility with primitive benches for seating and temporary wooden boards with a canvas awning that formed a stage. On 8 July Belcher was asked to stage the dances for the preseason presentation of *Carmen,* a prelude to the official opening of the first season on 11 July that used a hundred dancers. In the 9 July *Los Angeles Times* report of the evening, the reviewer wrote: "One of the prime attractions was the ballet, which not only visualized the dance numbers of *Carmen* itself, but also interpreted the fascinating *L'Arlésienne Suite.*"

In 1923 Belcher staged the dances for the opera *Aida* at the Bowl. After the stage and grounds were renovated in 1926, he presented a revised version of the ballet sequences created the year before for the movie *The Phantom of the Opera.* A picture in the Hollywood Bowl program shows six women dancers on pointe in tutus reminiscent of the Romantic period. The ballet included an adagio section utilizing eight men and eight women. The other dancers were divided into "corps de ballet" (18 women and one man) and "coryphées" (60 dancers, among them (Carmelita Maracci). Music for the first two sections was from Gounod's *Faust* ballet and the third used Chopin's *Grande Valse,* op. 18.

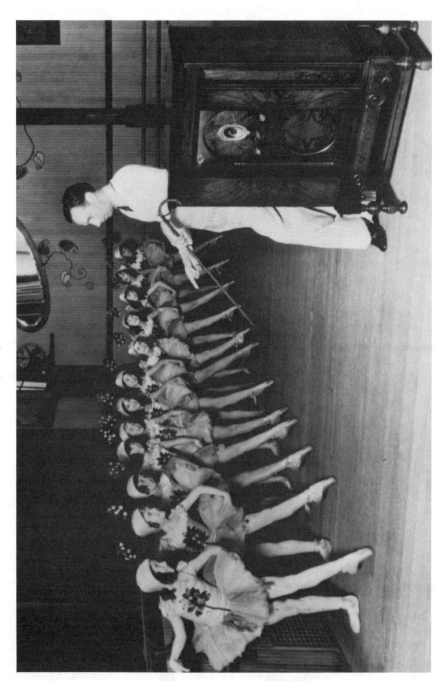

Belcher with Students, 1920s
(*Courtesy Marge Champion*)

On 17 and 18 July 1931 Belcher presented two evenings of dance at the Bowl, the program including dances to the second entr'acte from Schubert's *Rosamunde*, a *Grande Valse de Concert* by Glazunov, the "Hopak" from the *Nutcracker Suite*, a "Gavotte Royale" by Massenet, "Valse Viennese-Wiener Blut" by Strauss, and five dances to the ballet music from *Le Cid* by Massenet: "Castillane," "Aragonaise," "Aubade," "Madrilène," and "Navarraise." Belcher had studied Spanish dance extensively and was an accomplished Spanish dance teacher and performer. Marge Champion recalled that although members of the Cansino family were hired as instructors of Spanish dance in the school, she was taught this material by her father. The costumes for both these 1931 evenings were made in Belcher's studio; he also designed the lighting. Seventy advanced dancers from the studio were utilized. Over 15,000 people were reported in attendance for each concert. The second evening was reviewed in the *Hollywood Citizen News* on 19 August:

> The Belcher Ballet was ingeniously presented. The picture presented was throughout one of charm and grace. The Massenet "Gavotte Royale" had an old world atmosphere enhanced by powdered wigs and billowy costumes in which the dancers tripped the stately measures. The Strauss Wiener Blut followed with a corps of small dancers who pirouetted like wind blown powder puffs in well trained ensemble. The final Ballet Suite was colorful with Spanish costumes.

On 29 July 1932 Belcher presented an evening-long ballet at the Hollywood Bowl called *Elysia* (*A Grecian Divertissement*). The public reacted very favorably, and it was produced again on 6 August, which Belcher conceived of as a tribute to the Olympic games being held in Los Angeles that year. The *Los Angeles Times* contained only a short comment on 8 August: "The spectacle proved one of the most successful productions of its kind ever attempted in the Bowl." *Elysia* was in three scenes. The music to scene 1, "Eve of the Olympics—The Beautiful Galatea," was by Franz von Suppé. Diana was the major figure, supported by four groups of dancers: Hand Maids of Diana, Flora's Flower Girls, South Winds of Zephrus, Hestian Virgins. Scene 2, "The Enchanted Hour," was to music by Tchaikovsky (Op. 27, no. 14). This section, which used the most advanced dancers, featured more duet and solo work. "Lovers" were portrayed by Billy Baker and Iola Cochran; "Statues" by Caroline Lloyd and Billie Brown; "Spirit of Life" by Marjorie Belcher; and in the "Fountain Group" the soloist Margaret Westberg was flanked by four women—Dorothy Winebrenner, Ida Mae Sephenson, Elfriede Evertz, and Gertrude Knowlton. Scene 3, "The Festival," to music by Leo Delibes, had three sections: "March and Procession of Bacchus," "Festive Dancers," and "Maidens of the Temple." The grand finale, it used a large number of dancers.

Ernest Belcher produced two more evenings of ballet at the Hollywood Bowl. On 27 August 1932 he presented *"A Ballet Divertissement in Two Scenes"* to Saint Saens's *Samson and Delilah:* "The Dance of the Priestesses" and "Bacchanale." The soloists included Margaret Westberg, Elfriede Evertz, and Adelia Moulton, with a mixed corps of 40 dancers. His last ballet for the Bowl, presented on 20 July 1934, was called *Carnival of Venice* and had a score specially composed for it by Albert Hay Malotte, a composer associated with the Fox, RKO, and Disney studios, but now best known for his setting of "The Lord's Prayer." Malotte had been working with the studios since 1932 as both organist and composer.

The elaborate scenario for this ballet, as was usual for Belcher's works, had three scenes: "Venice by Night," "Beneath the Adriatic," and "The Carnival." The scenario gave ample opportunity for a wide variety of short dances and probably gave Belcher a chance to use many of his pupils. The "Synopsis," which covers several pages in the program, was written by Marshall Stedman, who "translated into words" the music and dance.

> It is the night before the Carnival, The Adriatic—blue topaz, silvered by pale moonbeams—lies quiet save for the occasional sound of some sleepy wave as it kisses the marble of pillars of a noble palace. Fabriano, a wanderer, a stranger in Venice, the embodiment of the Spirit of Adventure—(he may well be you)—takes a stroll under God's blue canopy of velvet set with diamonds. As he stands by the Grand Canal, his thoughts are all of the great Carnival of the morrows. He pauses, enraptured, as a woman's glorious voice floats out upon the evening air. She is singing "The Carnival of Venice"—the while she drifts over the moonlit waters, reclining among soft cushions in her golden gondola. He crosses the water's edge and gazes down into the limphid depths; there he sees strange life—weird fish with golden tails and slender silver bodies; there, too, he sees the Spirits of the Adriatic—three beautiful young girls, as they disport themselves in the purple waters. Suddenly, a look of horror comes into Fabriano's eyes as he discovers a hidden Octopus. It slides its slimy tentacles from beneath a mottled rock . . . the strange creature is about to wind its snaky arms about the three beautiful Spirits when suddenly, from out of the sea forest rushes a great Sea Dragon—spitting bubbles and roaring.

The remainder of scene 2 recounts how the Octopus and the Sea Dragon, "two horrid monsters," fight a fierce battle, each one hoping to slay the other and win the prize, the lovely maidens of the sea. But "instead of conquering, these beasts are conquered, and the Octopus and the Dragon glide into the shadows and disappear." We are not quite sure how these creatures are conquered, but it is possible that in the dance the lovely maidens of the sea were able to work some magic. The scene closes with the question: "Was this a dream—as life is?" The audience was thus prepared for scene 3 and the carnival:

Fabriano wonders if he has seen a vision. . . . Suddenly night has gone and Fabriano hears the blare of silver trumpets ushering in the day of the Carnival. The square is filled with a jostling laughing crowd—Peasant and Prince, Poet and Pilgrim—dressed in gay costumes. Youth-Happiness-Joy—and Laughter fill the sparkling air, and the sound of music and of many dancing feet floated over the blue waters. Down the promenade ambles a performing bear. Then some acrobats, they tumble, and roll their big eyes, their painted faces shine with the joy of living. Joy reigns supreme.

The scenario then introduces a number of characters who dance out their roles: ponies, a ringmaster, a clown (played by Gwen Verdon), a poodle, an Egyptian princess, Egyptian slaves, a Javanese dancer, a Spanish maiden, a Chinese dancer, a dance of mirrors, puppets (Pierrettes, Pierrot, harlequin, clown), a gypsy boy and girl, and fireflies. The carnival scene also has two character dances—a waltz-minuet and a tarantella. In addition to the ballet dancers, the program lists the participation of the Swedish Folk Dance Club of Los Angeles.

Audiences for Belcher's Hollywood Bowl presentations were large and enthusiastic. He was not a major choreographer, but he was musically sensitive, and his work consisted of movement combinations that were graceful, well phrased, and varied in dynamics. He created effective mass groupings, and his movements were never overly complicated but always well suited to the capabilities of the dancers. In solo and duet sequences pirouettes were a basic virtuoso step and there were also spectacular and beautiful lifts.

When Belcher first began creating ballets for the Hollywood Bowl, he wrote about the need for a company of American dancers. In 1931 he expanded on this idea and made several statements to the press upon opening his opulent new 36,000-square-foot studio. An article in the 12 May issue of the *Hollywood Citizen News* was headlined "Belcher Tells Dream of Organizing Truly American Ballet." The report enlarged on what that dream meant:

Ernest Belcher today considers himself nearer the realization of a dream. The dream, as he expressed it, is organization of an American ballet—something that will have a national color and texture, that will become an institution and that will tour not only this country but Europe and other lands as well. . . . The time for this is ripe, in Belcher's belief. He recalled that, not many years ago, American "wild west" shows and similar exhibitions made quite a hit in Europe. They were regarded as typical of American life, and the people were anxious to see them and got a thrill out of the rough riding, the shooting and other melodramatic episodes and perils of existence in wild America. All that is gone now as everybody knows, said Belcher. Is it not time that we start here the nucleus of an American ballet that will carry to Europe a new and different picture of ourselves.

It might have been exciting if Belcher had been able to form an American ballet company, bringing in other choreographers and teachers to help him and building on the solid technical base he had established. However, Belcher's new school was extremely successful, and he enjoyed teaching enormously. The creation of ballets for the Bowl seemed to have fulfilled both his choreographic urge and the need to present his advanced dancers before an audience.

During the 1930s Belcher was also attempting to regain his place as a dance director for films. His involvement with Hollywood films began in 1918, when he worked with Cecil B. de Mille on *We Can't Have Everything* (Famous Players-Lasky), and according to newspaper articles on Belcher written when his large studio was opened, by 1931 he had been involved in over 200 movies. Belcher's film work ranged from instructing actors on how to behave in a way appropriate to the period—such as how to bow in Regency style for *Beau Brummel* (1924), starring John Barrymore—to extended dance sequences—as in *The Phantom of the Opera* (1925), with Lon Chaney. Belcher also staged the dance numbers for *The Jazz Singer* (1927), the movie that spelled the end for silent films and revolutionized the industry. After 1930 the only films on which he is known for certain to have worked were the Greta Garbo-Fredric March *Anna Karenina* (directed by Clarence Brown, MGM, 1935) and Shirley Temple's *The Little Princess* (directed by Walter Lang, Twentieth Century-Fox, 1939). Although for Shirley Temple he staged a full dance sequence, for *Anna Karenina* he may have served primarily as a movement coach, since the ballet scene at the Moscow Opera was credited to Margarethe Wallman and a mazurka to Chester Hale. Since coaches seldom received screen credit then, Belcher may well have worked with actors on other films of this period.

Whether as movement coach or choreographer, Belcher's varied theatrical background could be drawn on effectively for many different situations. Thus his memories of *Sal-Oh-My*, the Alhambra Theatre's satire on Maud Allan, may have been useful for Mack Sennett's *Salome vs. Shenandoah* in 1919, one of the earliest films on which Belcher worked. Presumably parodying the Theda Bara *Salome*, issued the previous year, this two-reeler called on the comic Ben Turpin to play simultaneously John the Baptist in a version of *Salome* and a Confederate spy in the old Civil War melodrama *Shenandoah*. Phyllis Haver played Salome and Charles Murray was Herod. Unfortunately, as with so many of the films on which Belcher worked, no copy of this comedy seems to have survived.

Two years later Belcher worked again with the Sennett company, on the much more elaborate *Small Town Idol* (directed by Earl Kenton, 1921). In this episodic seven-reel comedy Sam Smith (Ben Turpin) is

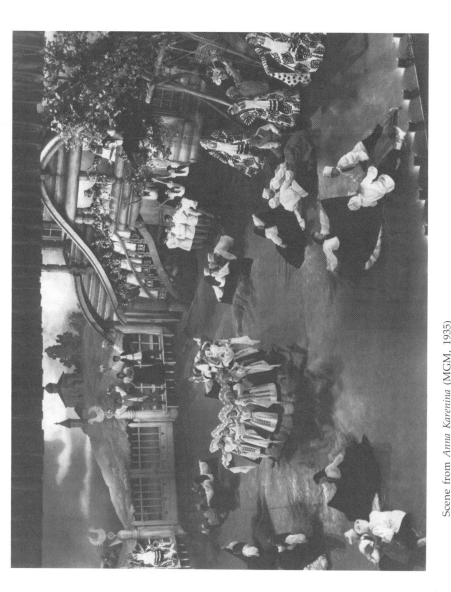

Scene from *Anna Karenina* (MGM, 1935)
This film was directed by Clarence Brown and starred Fredric March and Greta Garbo.
(*Courtesy Department of Special Collections, University Research Library, UCLA*)

Salomé vs. Shenandoah (Mack Sennett Studios, 1919)

This parody of Theda Bara's *Salome* (1918) was one of the first motion pictures on which Belcher worked as a choreographer.

(Courtesy Department of Special Collections, University Research Library, UCLA)

Salome vs. Shenandoah (Mack Sennett Studios, 1919)
(Courtesy Marge Champion)

driven from his small-town sweetheart (Phyllis Haver) by false accusations and ends up in Hollywood, where he costars with Marcelle Mansfield, "the queen of the films" (Marie Prevost), in an exotic spectacle before returning to his hometown to bask in his new-found glory and reclaim his girl. Belcher's contribution came during the parody of a Hollywood extravaganza and was praised by the reviewer for *Variety* (15 April 1921), who found that this film-within-a-film had

> "production features" worthy of a serious spectacular affair. It shows the studio of the Soandso Film Co., where an oriental story is being filmed. Some of the ballets would pass at the New York Hippodrome for size and scenic effect and the camera shots of an enormous palace throne room are striking in their magnificence.
>
> These incidents fill in the interest which usually goes with the Sennett Bathing Girls, for there were half a dozen dancing groups in the extreme of undress and several solo and small group dancing numbers of real beauty.

Belcher was an important influence on the acceptance of dance in the film industry and the way in which it developed. He set a high technical standard for the dancers and insisted that the camera capture the movement in a way that would preserve the integrity of his concept. The Belcher Collection at UCLA has a list of 40 films for which Belcher created the dance sequences, most of them from the early to the mid-twenties. It is not clear who drew up this list, and more research needs to be done on locating these films as well as on finding documentation of Belcher's work on them. To date, only a small number of the movies on which he worked have been located.

Although none gives Belcher any credit, his involvement with many of them is documented through publicity pictures or newspaper references and the list at UCLA. So far, only one film has been identified that gives Belcher credit for choreography—*Heroes of the Street* (Warner Brothers, 1922). Although in 1925 Belcher was given the title "Dance Director of Movieland" by the Western Association of Motion Picture Advertisers, he never fully capitalized on his own success by insisting on more recognition. Lina Basquette's comments are revealing:

> [It is] not difficult to remember that my step-father, Ernest Belcher, was one of the gentlest human beings I have ever known. He hardly ever raised his well-modulated voice and spoke with a British accent that matched his impeccable manners and was rather an "oddity" in those early days in raw and rowdy Hollywood during the first quarter of this century. . . . Because Ernest was not the type to "push and shove"—would not play the "Tinsletown game" of chicanery and "underworld" tactics, he never achieved the renown that he richly deserved as a choreographer and producer of magnificent dance sequences. . . . I firmly believe that if Ernest had taken on an exotic RUSSIAN label and played the "social scene" of the "Golden Age"—wild life of "Gower Gulch" and "Burbank Bacchanales," he would have become more famous and monetarily successful.[24]

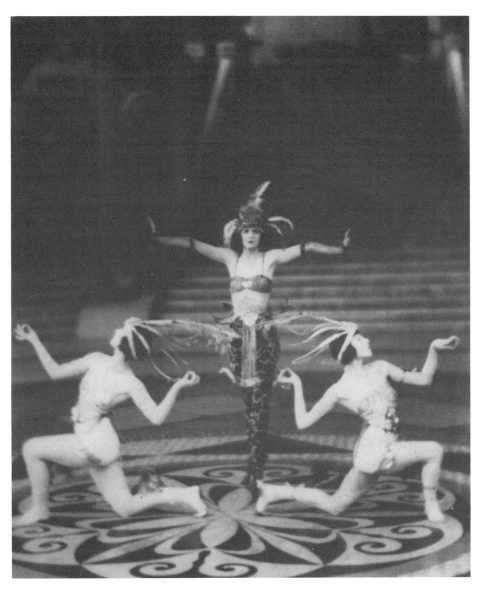

Small Town Idol (Mack Sennett Studios, 1921)
Choreography by Ernest Belcher; the dancers shown here include
Isabelle Clark, Ann Heloise, and Naomi Black.
(*Courtesy Marge Champion*)

Raymon Novarro and Derelys Perdue in *Small Town Idol* (Mack Sennett Studios, 1921) (*Courtesy Marge Champion*)

Belcher Rehearsing Lois Moran in Charleston for *Padlocked* (Paramount, 1926)
(*Courtesy Department of Special Collections, University Research Library, UCLA*)

Many films called on Belcher to show a nondancing star coping effectively in a show business setting. For supporting dancers Belcher could draw on the advanced students from his school and in front of them arrange steps that the star could do effectively. Two films from 1926 are typical of this kind of work. Of *Padlocked* (directed by Alan Dwan, Paramount), which starred Lois Moran, *Variety* commented on 8 August that it was "a mush story of the country girl going to the big city to become a dancer in a cabaret and be saved in time." A publicity photograph shows Belcher standing next to Moran, who is practicing a Charleston in a rather seedy cabaret. Although *Variety* found the film full of clichés, the critic praised Moran for "a corking good performance as the girl." *Twinkletoes* (directed by Charles Brabin, First National) showed Colleen Moore in a music hall setting, quite a change from her usual flapper roles. Belcher was apparently asked to set the dance numbers for the stage sequences, although Moore may not have been one of his pupils: in her autobiography, *Silent Star,* Moore includes a picture of herself in this film as part of a group of dancers, along with the caption that "Theodore Kosloff, the local dancing teacher, finally got me up on my toes."

The dances in the silent films *Souls for Sale* (Goldwyn Pictures, 1923) and *The Phantom of the Opera* (Universal Studios, 1925), in *The Jazz Singer* (Warner Brothers, 1927), and in *General Crack* (Warner Brothers, 1929), John Barrymore's first sound film, provide examples of the range and style of Belcher's movie work. In all of them the dance sequences are relatively short but important in terms of advancing the action of the movie. The dancing is technically high in quality and filmed to get the maximum impact. Belcher's versatility is clearly in evidence, but at no time is there a sacrifice of integrity or historical accuracy.

For *Souls for Sale* (directed by Rupert Hughes) Belcher created three dance sequences that show the wide variety of dance numbers he was called on to stage for films. The first takes place in a music hall. The few women seen on the stage are somewhat seedy but do their kicks and turns quite competently. The three watching the show are all crooks trying to outwit one another by each claiming to be something they are not, and the music hall scene illuminates their shabbiness. The next dance scene in this movie takes place in an elegant restaurant where there is social dancing. Eleanor Boardmand as the heroine, whose first name is Remember, has just become a famous movie star. As the fashionably dressed dancers foxtrot, the importance of the occasion and the social status the heroine has achieved are established. In the last part of *Souls for Sale*, Remember is seen playing a circus performer, doing a sequence of back bends, turns, and promenades appropriate to her role.

Colleen Moore in *Twinkletoes* (First National, 1926)
(*Courtesy Department of Special Collections, University Research
Library, UCLA*)

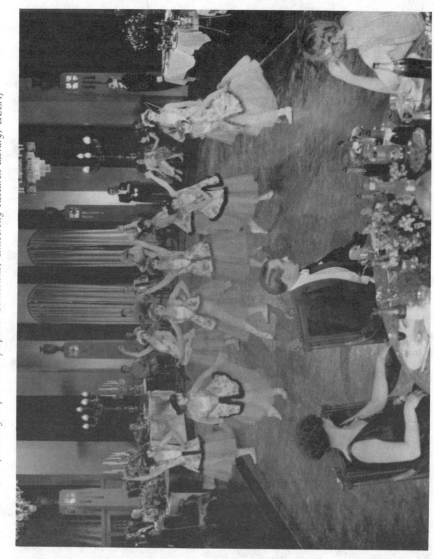

Twinkletoes (First National, 1926)
(Courtesy Department of Special Collections, University Research Library, UCLA)

Ernest Belcher Rehearsing the Cast of *Beau Brummel* (1924)
This film starred John Barrymore and Mary Astor.
(*Courtesy Department of Special Collections, University Research Library, UCLA*)

In one of the most famous films in which Belcher worked, *Phantom of the Opera* (directed by Rupert Hughes) starring Lon Chaney, there are two ballet sequences. These occur on stage at the Paris Opéra as the action is seen unfolding in both the auditorium and behind the scenes. Each time the large corps de ballet is shown, it helps to establish the sense of the Paris Opéra as a large and fashionable theater. The dancing is not complicated, consisting mostly of the corps doing simple unison movements either side to side or forward and backward. But the camera has captured all of the bodies and the effect is strong. In 1925 the newspaper publicity about the film heralded these sequences as the most spectacular ballet dancing ever seen in movies. Given the history of dance in Hollywood films at this point in time, the presentation of a formal ballet segment with no excuses and no frills was important. When Belcher restaged these dances for the Hollywood Bowl in 1926, he made the sequences longer and included a series of solos and duets as well as an adagio section.

Belcher made other contributions to *Phantom of the Opera.* There is a great deal of group movement and exceptionally telling gestural activity. The young women who danced in the ballet appear in various parts of the film, helping to further the story. They are participants in an extended scene in which the Phantom of the Opera is being chased through the opera house and the catacombs, and their movements are "choreographed" to convey a wide assortment of emotional qualities— fear, hope, excitement. Belcher's trained eye for movement is very much in control here, and he was also responsible for a subsequent scene when the Phantom reappears in the opera house. Large groups of people mill around the grand staircase: groupings are carefully choreographed, and there are even well-placed segments of dancing revelry that provide much of the feeling the director wanted to convey.

For the silent version of *La Bohème* (directed by King Vidor, MGM, 1926) Belcher not only staged an impromptu polka for the stars, Lillian Gish and John Gilbert, but also a short ballet sequence for the scene in which the young viscount takes Mimi and Musetta (Renee Adoree) to the theater. There they watch a "white ballet," which Belcher has set in appropriate period style. Although filmed in 1925, the same year as *The Phantom of the Opera* was released, *La Bohème* was actually made two years later, so its ballet scene is less important in the history of film dance; it is also less integral to the story.

The moving force behind *The Jazz Singer* was Lina Basquette's husband, Sam Warner. Based on Samson Raphaelson's Broadway success, the 1927 film version starred Al Jolson as the Cantor's son who leaves home to break into show business and May McAvoy as the vaudeville star who helps him to get his big chance on Broadway. Although most of the film is "silent," with titles, it had a prerecorded score (as in the earlier John Barrymore film *Don Juan*) as well as the revoluntionary sequences when Jolson bursts into song and occasionally speaks a few lines, notably in a scene with his mother, Eugenie Besserer. Belcher's dance numbers fit naturally into the show business scenes, the first a vaudeville routine and the other three, all of them brief, part of the Broadway show *April Follies*.

The vaudeville routine, showing a girls' kickline on a shallow stage set, featured McAvoy in a short solo on pointe, ending with a Harriet Hoctor-like backward bourrée on pointe, which clearly establishes the character's talent but also the rather shabby conditions of vaudeville. Although beginning with a conventional chorus rehearsal routine, the Broadway show numbers are more elaborate. In a rehearsal sequence, McAvoy does high kicks in front of a line of kicking chorus girls, then leaps into the arms of the chorus boys, who lift her triumphantly. The last number shows the chorus in a "tennis anyone" routine which they reprise with croquet mallets. Throughout the film Belcher follows conventional vaudeville and Broadway styles, but he is also helping to establish the pattern for stage dance and rehearsal scenes in the flood of backstage musicals that followed the introduction of sound in *The Jazz Singer*. As a result of such imitations, these numbers look more routine to modern audiences than they would have seemed to audiences in 1927.

General Crack (directed by Alan Crosland) shows Belcher working with very different material, this time using both humor and satire. During the first dance scene in the movie, set in a cafe, John Barrymore, as Prince Christian (known as General Crack), meets a future love—a fiery, sensual gypsy called Fidelia and played by Armida, a Mexican actress. He sees her dance and falls in love. Here Belcher has Fidelia effectively performing a Spanish dance, which helps reveal her character. The steps of this solo are designed to show her wit, elegance, sensuality, and passion and thus give credibility to the ensuing scenes of love, betrayal, and revenge. The action in *General Crack* later moves to the Archduke's ballroom in Brussels, and we are given a sense of the grand late-eighteenth-century environment through Belcher's staging of a large number of couples dancing the minuet. Marion Nixon as the General's other love, the Archduchess Maria Luis, and Lowell Sherman as Ludwig are shown in their aristocratic milieu. In a second ballroom scene Belcher wittily focuses on a stout, elderly couple who, as they dance, show us their slyness and delight in intrigue by their gestures and the way they perform the steps, revealing the true character of the court. Although Barrymore is not involved in any actual dancing, it seems probable that Belcher coached him in the

Scene from *Phantom of the Opera* (Universal Studios, 1925)
(Courtesy Academy of Motion Picture Arts and Sciences)

Scene from *Phantom of the Opera* (Universal Studios, 1925)
(Courtesy Academy of Motion Picture Arts and Sciences)

correct ways of walking, bowing, and standing in a style appropriate to the period—as he had done earlier for Barrymore's first Warner Brothers film, *Beau Brummel* (1924).

In 1938 Belcher's school catalogue had a long article about his private lessons with Shirley Temple at her home.

> Significant of the high esteem in which Ernest Belcher is held by the Motion Picture Industry is the fact that Mr. Darryl Zanuck, chief executive officer of the 20th Century-Fox Film Corporation, has entrusted to his careful guidance the professional dance training of the delightful little star, Shirley Temple. . . . Mr. Belcher arrives at the Temple residence at 8:30 each morning, and ballet claims Shirley's immediate attention. Bar work, center practice, positions of the hands and feet, graceful movements of the hands, and back bends comprise the first half of the lesson, gradually developing into little dance steps which she adores. . . . There is one approving spectator always in attendance at Shirley's lessons, and he is Ching Ching, her pet Pekinese, who sits sedately on his chair, his eyes following every movement of his little mistress with doggish concern. On one occasion when he seemed particularly engrossed in her work, Shirley smiled at Mr. Belcher and said, "Ching Ching is fascinated with my feet."

Another school catalogue from 1938 featured a drawing by Shirley Temple of a dancer executing a pirouette and the information that Shirley was awarded a certificate upon her successful completion of the third-grade work in the Belcher School. Apparently Belcher felt little Shirley's training required more than just teaching her steps, and we are told: "An increased enthusiasm about her dancing was displayed by Shirley after she accompanied her parents and Mr. Belcher to a performance of the Ballet Russe last season." The first time Shirley Temple's ballet work was shown on screen was on 17 February 1939 in the press preview of her first Technicolor film, *The Little Princess.* In the "Dream Fantasy" sequence, in which the impoverished and ill-treated Little Princess visualizes herself dancing with the ballet, 16 of Belcher's students functioned as the corps around her, dressed in filmy white, with gold wigs and bouffant skirts.

It was no accident that Belcher's dance sequences were effective, for he had given a great deal of thought to the differences between stage and screen. Special attention had to be paid to movement that was to come under the scrutiny of the camera. Although dance seemed an exciting medium for film, at the beginning of the growth of the Hollywood film industry, many dancers made only sporadic attempts to use the medium inventively. Belcher stuck with it for over a decade— perhaps because of the determination that came from his early background and temperament. It was not always easy working with the various movie directors; as Lina Basquette noted: "Many of them thought they were the reincarnation of Jesus."[25] Movie-making condi-

Belcher Rehearsing Marion Nixon in Dance from *General Crack*
(Warner Brothers, 1929)
(*Courtesy Department of Special Collections, University Research
Library, UCLA*)

Scene from *General Crack* (Warner Brothers, 1929).
This film featured John Barrymore and Marion Nixon.
(*Courtesy Department of Special Collections, University Research Library, UCLA*)

Ballroom Scene from *General Crack* (Warner Brothers, 1929)
(Courtesy Department of Special Collections, University Research Library, UCLA)

Yvonne De Carlo, 1940s
Signed: "To the best ballet instructor in the United States barring
none! With deepest gratitude for what you have taught.—
Yvonne De Carlo"
*(Courtesy Department of Special Collections, University Research
Library, UCLA)*

tions in those days were also very primitive—long hours, dirty bathrooms, less than perfect space, and often impatient and antagonistic attitudes on the part of the directors.

Belcher stuck with it and learned. Although he would never lower his standards, he was able to ignore the bombastic outcries and demands and to pursue his ideas. Belcher could afford to refuse work he did not want since he was the only dance director who kept a ballet school going on a consistent basis. The directors were happy to have him available, as were his students, who could be used not only as dancers but also in small parts as stand-ins or extras who knew how to move. From the beginning Belcher saw that there was an enormous difference in the placement of the dancers within the dancing space for the movies in contrast to live performance. The ensemble lines in film had to remain in the foreground of the picture for a total effect. On the stage more depth was available and the soloists could be brought forward, leaving the ensemble in various groupings in the background. Certain movements that were good for the stage had to be eliminated for films, since they would cause a flickering or jumping effect in the early movies. Belcher was quoted in an interview in *The American Dancer* in 1929 as follows: "Four steps done one way will photograph perfectly, while the identical four steps taken another way will produce a flicker. . . . The camera does not lie. And that is why particular attention must be paid to the angle of the arms and body of the screen dancer, and also to the casual position of the arms and face of the screen actor. . . . The angle from which the camera shoots must be a perfect one."[26]

The question arises as to why, if Belcher was so productive, was he not better known in later years for his movie work, and why did he not go on to create for the movie musicals in the 1930s? There are several reasons for the shift away from Belcher, even though according to newspaper accounts of the early 1930s he had created 70 percent of all dance sequences for the movies up to that time. According to Lina Basquette and Marge Champion, he was not a publicity grabber. He was not involved in sordid affairs, in Hollywood partying, or in egotistical displays, and he refused to "claw his way to the top" or to play political games.

After Lina Basquette's husband, Sam Warner, died unexpectedly in 1927, she became involved in a vitriolic battle with the Warner family over the estate.[27] This was at the time when Warner Brothers, after a difficult period, was just beginning to make a fortune because of Sam Warner's foresight in obtaining the newly invented Vitaphone process for their production of *The Jazz Singer*. Although the brothers soon were heavily involved in movie musicals, they became hostile to Bas-

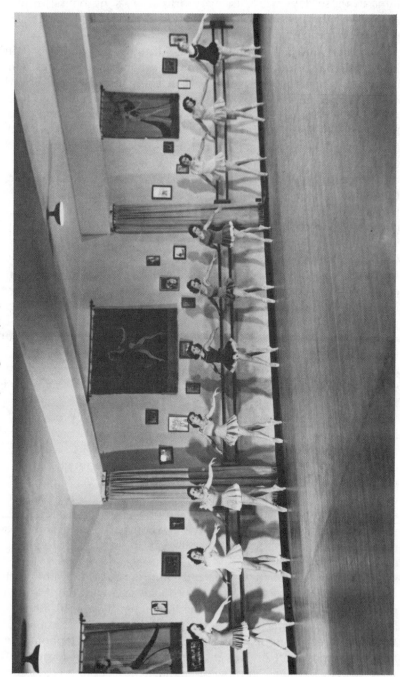

Belcher Students in Rehearsal, 1930s
(*Courtesy Marge Champion*)

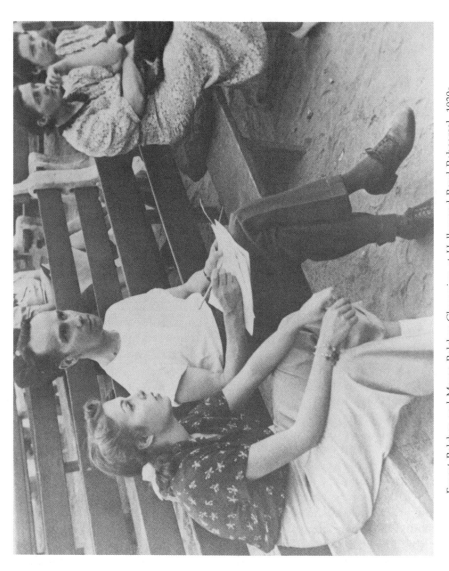

Ernest Belcher and Marge Belcher Champion at Hollywood Bowl Rehearsal, 1930s
(*Courtesy Marge Champion*)

quette and Belcher because of the legal fight over the estate; eventually, Lina Basquette was blacklisted in Hollywood and returned to New York for a time. It is her strong feeling that Belcher was also blacklisted at about that time.

Also, the studios began hiring Broadway dance directors like Albertina Rasch, Busby Berkeley, and Sammy Lee for their musicals, and Belcher had no interest in expending the energy necessary to compete against these people. By the 1930s he was happily settled in a comfortable routine. It is also possible that if the movie directors no longer wanted his services, he was even happy not to be involved with the enormous egos and autocratic demands of the volatile and increasingly commercially oriented movie producers. As a teacher he had to answer only to himself and could set his own standards.

Despite the large numbers of students who flocked to his studio, throughout his teaching career Belcher maintained a consistently high level of expectations. By 1922 he was already known for the disciplined and sequential training offered through his "Eight-Grade System." Based loosely on the Cecchetti method, it relied on repetition of the same material until a certain level of proficiency was attained. Young dancers were classified as beginners or upper-classmen, and there were four grades for each. Pointe work was not allowed until students had the required strength. If the student came to take class several times a week, the eight-grade course could be finished in four years. There was also a "postgraduate" course that was meant to take a year and give professional finishing touches. Students in this course learned performing material, knowledge about costumes and makeup, and business and stage management.

The lower level of training provided a thorough grounding in basic technique, correct body placement, musicality, and the learning of simple dances. A simple barre consisted of pliés in first, second, and fifth positions. The center portion of the class emphasized échappés, simple ports de bras, and elementary combinations using pas de basque, glissade, polka steps, and arabesques. For the upper levels the barre lasted about fifteen minutes. The students then did another barre in toe shoes and worked on échappés, relevés, pirouettes, and fouetté turns. Center work in toe shoes followed, and the students would learn an extended and more complex dance than in the first part of the lesson. For the end of the class the toe shoes were removed, and jumps and allegro combinations were practiced. Class ended with either a character or a Spanish dance.

Belcher was strict, not allowing progress to the next level until material was mastered. Placement was continuously emphasized, but never for its own sake, as performance was of the utmost importance.

Presenting oneself to the audience was drummed into the students, and pupils at all levels were always to keep in mind that they were dancing. Belcher developed a particularly fluid, full use of the arms and upper torso: never straining, always harmonious, but particularly poetic. He would give any men in the class special combinations with a great deal of elevation, but he considered jumps significant for women to practice as well. Belcher was known for teaching students multiple pirouettes and turns of all kinds. Allegro and adagio work were considered equally important.

Ann Barzel wrote about Belcher that "although he has arranged his school in definite grades, his work is not so pedantic as that of most English, nor as free as that of the Russians."[28] Technique in his classes was always a means to an end, and an important component of his vision about American ballet was the necessity to train dancers who would be expressive as well as competent. In conversations with former students the joy of their training is emphasized, as is the feeling of always dancing. According to Renee Dunia Hawley, who wrote a thesis on Belcher: "Even in his last years of teaching, when he was in his seventies, a student might pass his discerning eye without a comment if a leg was not high enough or a turn was not finished perfectly, but no one could ever expect to leave the classroom without severe criticism if he did not put his entire 'self' into whatever he attempted."[29] Belcher himself wrote about the importance of expression and the necessity to have an awareness of what was being done: "Technique is a mental form of structure, giving the mind control over the body, so that the body will readily move and act as the thoughts or mind desires."[30] Belcher was quoted in an August 1928 article as saying: "Dancing comes from the mind as do all the arts. . . . The emotion a dancer feels in his mind is transmitted to the audience, though the source of the emotion is unknown to them. It is an authentic emotion and they get it . . . it is a matter of timing—psychic timing, for want of a better expression."[31]

Teachers were not neglected in Ernest Belcher's campaign to improve and develop ballet in America. A very important part of the work in his schools were the "Teachers' Normal Courses" held every summer for one month, from the beginning of July to the beginning of August, always starting right after the 4 July holiday. Ballet classes met every morning at 10:00 for two hours, and other classes were given during the rest of the day: tap, acrobatics, Spanish, ballroom, and in the 1930s he added "moderne." Fridays in the ballet classes were given over to review, and at the end of the course the teachers were given a written and a practical exam; afterward, they received a certificate of completion. There were two sections of written material on the exam.

Belcher Students, 1940s
Front row: Barbara Williams, June Edwards; second row: Marjorie Tallchief, Maria Tallchief, Diane Alden; third row: Mitzi Kenyon, Nadine Fischer, Myra Seeley.
(*Courtesy Marge Champion*)

Section 1 consisted of general questions: What is ballet? What comprises a ballet lesson? What are five of the commonest errors in a student's work? What means would you use to correct these faults? Section 2 consisted of "Theory." Students were asked to describe the five positions of the feet, arms, and head. They were asked to explain specific positions: en face, croisé, effacé, épaulé. They were asked differences between attitude and arabesque, between grand and demiplié, between adagio and allegro movements. In section 3 they were asked to demonstrate various movements such as battement tendus, grande battement, ronde de jambe par terre and en l'air at the barre, and a large number of center movements (50 in all).

The announcements for the "Teachers' Normal Courses" indicate that teachers came from all over the country. There were also many admonitions to the prospective students in the school catalogues over the year about what was considered important in these courses. "Special attention is given to proper training of muscles and general development of the body. . . . The instructor should be able to discern immediately any discrepancy in the pupil's execution of the barre and center exercises and make corrections, which if not given immediately will often lead to physical defects. Each part of the body is considered and the correct position of the feet, knees, thighs, back, shoulder and neck muscles are shown and explained and the teacher's daily practice gives ample time for the corrections."[32]

A significant facet of Ernest Belcher's pedagogical work was his concern with making dance an acceptable vocation or avocation for men. He had special classes for boys and men and allowed them to take part in the women's classes when they were ready. In the 1924–25 school catalogue Belcher wrote: "Erroneous thoughts have crept into the minds of the public that the male dancer shows effeminacy in his carriage and demeanor. The properly trained male dancer is a perfect specimen of manliness, both physically and mentally, and does not tend towards the effeminate."[33] Belcher was in a good position to fight the battle of making dance for men acceptable. He was able to give the better ones jobs in the movies and also served as a good role model: successful dance maker, teacher, and family man, a person of quiet strength, regal bearing, warmth, and kindness. He exemplified discipline and hard work, as well as a stable, conventional personal life. In a 1935 radio interview Belcher told his audience that "men have a definite place in the artistic world. . . . We find them musicians, singers, painters, sculptors, etc., so why not dancers? In Europe you will find that the he-man, if you want to describe him, understands the art of dancing, and is encouraged in developing it."[34]

Ernest Belcher Rehearsing, 1940s
(*Courtesy Marge Champion*)

Ernest Belcher Teaching Angela Cartwright, 1950s
(*Courtesy Department of Special Collections, University Research Library, UCLA*)

In the 1920s Belcher wrote an article titled "Male Dancers Are Never Effeminate."

> The other day a great truck, heavily loaded with gravel, pulled up before the Ernest Belcher School of Dancing in Los Angeles. . . . Its driver, a big husky in overalls, climbed down from his gasoline steed and entered the chief's office without knocking. Mr. Belcher looked up with a grin. He knew what was coming. "Well John," he laughed, "what's on your mind this afternoon?" John drew a soiled sleeve across his face and hesitatingly remarked that a stiff neck would prevent his attending class that evening. . . . "Stiff neck nothing," roared Belcher, ". . . Come into class and work it off." And John was present that night, pulling applause from the gallery of students' mothers.[35]

There does not seem to have been any special emphasis on men's classes among the dancers teaching in Los Angeles in the early years—Ruth St. Denis, Ted Shawn, Norma Gould, Theodore Kosloff, or Serge Oukrainsky. But there were sometimes enough men attracted to Belcher's studios to fill as many as three or four special boys' and men's classes. His large dance productions, such as those at the Hollywood Bowl, had substantial numbers of men in the cast, and in the 1935 radio broadcasts he emphasized the validity of dance for men.

Belcher felt that if he could combat the ignorance about ballet in general, he would eliminate the notion that ballet dancing was effeminate, only for women, or "unfitting for a he-man," as he put it. Men should take dance classes for their general well-being, even if their goal was not to be professional dancers. "It is my opinion that men have as much right to enjoy and appreciate the dancing and rhythm, and build and use their physical strength this way as they have to run, wrestle, pole vault, play tennis, etc."[36] He was able to convince the movie directors he worked with, certainly not a group particularly informed about ballet or male dancing, that his classes would benefit their stars and in no way challenge their virility. Apparently, he was even able to convince doubtful mothers to enroll their sons, providing the boys not only with technical training but also with a special feeling about the art form.

Ernest Belcher's vision was not only of well-trained American ballet dancers—men, women, and teachers—but also of an educated lay public. With this in mind he published ballet lessons both in a daily newspaper and in a small book of his own. In 1924 the Los Angeles *Record* published 21 consecutive lessons for the interest of the general public. In 1927 Belcher published his own *Basic Principles of Dancing*, a book of 23 progressive lessons. The introduction to the book reads: "This book has been prompted by the apparent lack of literature for the person who has had little or no training in classical dancing. . . . While

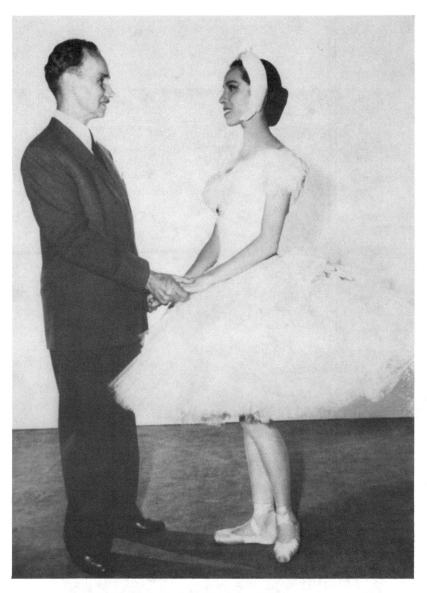

Ernest Belcher with Maria Tallchief, ca. 1960
Tallchief, an outstanding ballerina who danced for years with the
New York City Ballet, and was married to George Balanchine,
now serves as Director of the Chicago City Ballet.
(*Courtesy Department of Special Collections, University Research
Library, UCLA*)

Marge and Gower Champion in Dance Scene from the Film *Everything I Have Is Yours* (1952)
The two dancers met in Belcher's studio, became a famous dance team, and, after they married in 1947, appeared in numerous films and on television in the 1950s and 1960s.
(*Courtesy Marge Champion*)

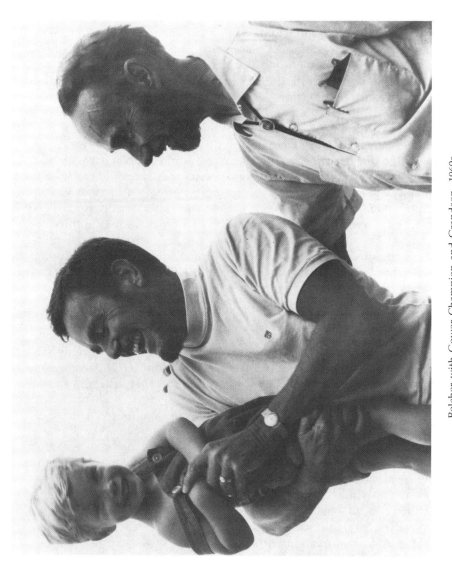

Belcher with Gower Champion and Grandson, 1960s
(*Courtesy Marge Champion*)

the basic principles in this book are absolutely legitimate for one expecting to become a professional dancer, the book was essentially produced for the thousands more than the individual."[37] In the 1935 radio interview Belcher emphasized teaching the general public about ballet and invited questions from the audience. An interesting product of these interviews were the letters written by listeners requesting information about exercises, correct placement, and injuries. Belcher's missionary zeal about his methods also led him to write an article about his technique in the April 1929 *Dancing Master* and a monthly series with pictures in *The American Dancer* from January 1931 through September 1932.

Belcher's prominence began to decline in the late 1930s, at a time when new ideas in dance were beginning to emerge in Los Angeles. In 1928 Lester Horton came from Indiana. He formed a company in 1932 and began to explore movement and thematic concepts with striking originality. Teachers as varied as Benjamin Zemach, Albertina Rasch, Adolph Bolm, Michio Ito, Serge Oukrainsky, and Theodore Kosloff worked intensively in Los Angeles at various times from 1928 through the late 1930s, and Bronislava Nijinska taught there from the mid-1930s. Each introduced new elements in training and choreography. In 1940 Belcher was 58 years old and apparently not prepared to incorporate new ideas into his school or productions.

The Hollywood environment in which Belcher operated was a mixed blessing. Although it provided a stable financial base for his teaching and gave him a performing outlet through his movie and concert work, this environment did not encourage him to develop his choreographic talents beyond a certain level. Without the strong film link he might have sought to ally himself with other artists in music and theater and to experiment more with new ideas. But apparently there was never sufficient incentive for him to take these chances.

Ernest Belcher had a firm commitment to the development of excellence in American ballet. Although he did not become a distinguished concert choreographer nor found an American ballet company, he should be given a place in the history of American ballet because of the work he did in Los Angeles from 1916 through the late 1930s. He cleared a path for those who came later. For many who went on to successful dance careers, he was their first teacher, giving them a solid technical foundation and a strong sense of the expressive powers of dance. His work in emphasizing the possibilities of dance for men is important. He was given credit for only a small portion of the 200-odd movies he made, but judging from what is available, he made an important contribution in raising standards of expression and technique in early films. Ernest Belcher believed that ballet had a future in America at a time when those with such a vision were few in number. He dedicated his life not to fame and fortune but to teaching and guiding others in sharing his love of dance and the beauty of expression possible with training, discipline, and understanding.

On 22 June 1986 at Jacob's Pillow there was an evening of tribute to the genius of Gower Champion, but it was also a celebration of Ernest Belcher's life and work. Marge Champion—Belcher's daughter, trained exclusively by her father until the age of 17—performed with her son, Blake Champion. In Marge Champion's words: "It was a trip down memory lane, and a special testimony of my father's contribution to American dance . . . a continuing heritage of three generations."[38]

Part Two

The Russian Heritage: Theodore Kosloff, Serge Oukrainsky, and Adolph Bolm

Introduction to Part Two

Three Russians played major roles in the development of American dance from 1917 through 1937—Theodore Kosloff, Serge Oukrainsky, and Adolph Bolm. All three came to Los Angeles after they had already established reputations as artists and teachers. They had several things in common: training in the traditions of the Russian Imperial Ballet, knowledge of the work of Diaghilev's Ballets Russes, active careers in the Hollywood movies, involvement in the formation and development of the San Francisco ballet, and choice of Los Angeles as a city of residence in the last phases of their careers.

While Kosloff, Oukrainsky, and Bolm used and relied upon their Russian Imperial backgrounds to varying degrees and had much in common, there were also distinct differences in their backgrounds and their approaches to choreography. Their work in Los Angeles sheds light not only on their common background but also on the elements that made each one distinct. Each responded to his stay in America and in Los Angeles with different artistic results.

Kosloff relied upon his ability to restage the early Fokine masterpieces. Oukrainsky relied upon an aesthetic developed early in his life—one that favored exotic Orientalism plus sensual stagings and extensive use of plastique. Though Bolm never totally relinquished his involvement in the Fokine masterpieces, he seems to have been the only one of the three who used his transplantation to America to explore beyond what he had experienced before. Because of Bolm's background, it was natural for others to call on him to restage the classics, and this may have been a hindrance in his own development as a choreographer. The teaching of all three artists was always related to what they were doing in performance. Students working with each of them received superb training and absorbed the individual's particular style and artistic vocabulary.

Most of the major choreographic activity of Kosloff, Oukrainsky, and Bolm in Los Angeles was centered around the Hollywood Bowl.

Their productions were presented on that stage for thousands of people, and over the years they used many of their own students in these performances. Their work at the Bowl was reported in detail in the press and provides an excellent way of studying their choreography and teaching in Los Angeles. The work that the three artists did during the late 1920s and the 1930s in Los Angeles was representative of what they did in other cities during their American careers.

There is definitely more that needs to be written about Kosloff, Oukrainsky, and Bolm. It is hoped that an analysis of their careers in Los Angeles will provide future researchers with more insight and information in formulating extensive critical biographies. In this book each of the three artists will be discussed separately in the order in which they arrived and settled in Los Angeles. General biographical information is provided relating to activities prior to arrival in Los Angeles, including data not available in any other published documentation. Activities in Los Angeles from 1915 through 1937 are emphasized; also provided is some information beyond this time frame where it provides an important perspective to their work, careers, and contributions.

When they came to Los Angeles, Kosloff, Oukrainsky, and Bolm brought a rich tradition with them. Adolph Bolm was the most well-known and inventive choreographer of the three. Although *The Spirit of the Factory* (1931) and the three pieces created to the music of Bach (1936) were in the contemporary vein, Bolm did not continue in this direction in his choreography during the 1930s and 1940s. After working to develop the San Francisco Ballet from 1932 to 1937, he became active in 1940 with Ballet Theatre in New York and thereafter primarily restaged Fokine's work. For most of their careers in Los Angeles, Kosloff and Oukrainsky restaged works they had done elsewhere.

Kosloff, Oukrainsky, and Bolm had come to Los Angeles toward the end of their careers. The fact that they did not develop their choreographic talents much further after they came to Los Angeles is unfortunate, for they might have been able to mobilize the talent in that city toward a permanent company. As it is, their influence was felt in two spheres. They exposed audiences to a tradition that emphasized strong technique and superb theatricality. They also exposed young dancers to this same tradition and gave many of them a basis for their own work.

3

Theodore Kosloff (1881–1956): Diaghilev Revisited

Theodore Kosloff graduated from the Moscow Imperial Ballet School in 1898. After graduation, he was sent to the St. Petersburg School for one year to attend what was called "the class of perfection" taught by the great master teacher, Nicolas Legat. His wife, Baldina, explained his year of study at St. Petersburg: "Theodore Kosloff was a promising male dancer from the Bolshoi. And as sometimes occurred, promising dancers from other companies were sent to St. Petersburg for advanced study and performing."[1] Theodore Kosloff did well in St. Petersburg and was chosen by ballerina Matilda Kchessinkaya to be her partner. He was apparently not just talented but charming as well. Alexandra Baldina was a young artist in the company and years later recalled his charm and her successful attempt to become his wife: "When he came as guest to our company, I thought him fascinating, as did many of the other girls . . . and we all hated to see him go. I knew that in Moscow I would have much more opportunity to perform leading roles, so I requested a transfer and it all worked out the way I had hoped. I became a ballerina, and I married Theodore Kosloff."[2]

Both Theodore Kosloff and Alexandra Baldina were invited to go to Paris by Serge Diaghilev in 1909, when he presented his first Russian season of ballet and opera there. The season took place at the Théâtre du Châtelet in May and June. The ballets choreographed by Michel Fokine, *Le Pavillon d'Armide*, *Cléopâtre*, *Les Sylphides*, "Polovtsian Dances" from *Prince Igor*, and *Le Festin*, premiered in Paris on 19 May and 2 June. The Paris season ended on 18 June, and on 20 June a group of the Diaghilev dancers, under the leadership of Karsavina, gave a series of performances at the Coliseum in London.

The Russian dancers who performed at the Coliseum for six weeks in 1909 included (in addition to Tamara Karsavina) Alexandra Baldina, Theodore Kosloff, Alexis Kosloff, and George Rosay. Nesta Macdonald, in *Diaghilev Observed*, comments on the London performances:

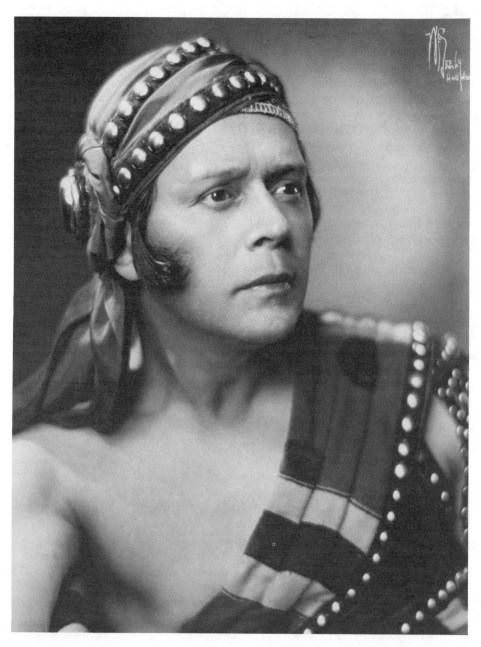

Theodore Kosloff, ca. 1920
(*Courtesy Hollywood Bowl Museum Archives*)

"It would appear . . . that the repertoire was hastily concocted from items in the ballets just given in Paris. . . . As there was no time for preparations, one may surmise that Diaghilev helped by lending Karsavina the necessary costumes."[3] The Coliseum program announcement heralded these dancers as "Russian dancers—from the Imperial Opera House, St. Petersburg, recently the rage of Paris at the Chatelet Theatre."[4] Karsavina's dancers were very successful in London. The *London Daily Mail* of 29 June heralded their performance: "A new sensation is provided for London by the appearance, which began last night, of the famous Russian dancers at the Coliseum. . . . It is the old classical school dancing which they illustrate, but raised to such a pitch of dexterity and grace which has never been surpassed here in our generation."[5]

The program at the Coliseum in 1909 consisted of a series of short dances.[6] In May 1910 Karsavina, Kosloff, and Baldina appeared at the Coliseum with a larger group of dancers and a more ambitious program. Theodore Kosloff played an important part in this London engagement, restaging the ballet *Giselle* with himself, Baldina, and Karsavina in leading roles. The ballet was listed on the Coliseum program as *Gisella or La Sylphide*. The original music by Adolphe Adam was used, but the scenario shows that Kosloff had created a condensed and rearranged version of the original *Giselle*. His version emphasized a series of divertissements by the principals rather than the developed and extended story line and balletic action of the original choreography.

In May and June of 1910 Diaghilev presented a second season of Russian ballet in Paris, this time at the Grand Opéra. Among the ballets that attracted attention during that season were two new ones by Michel Fokine: *Schéhérazade*, with music by Rimsky-Korsakoff, and *L'Oiseau de Feu*, the first ballet score written by young Russian composer Igor Stravinsky. Tamara Karsavina received a leave from the London Coliseum engagement to perform with the Diaghilev group in Paris in June and returned to the Coliseum in July.

Kosloff's success in London brought him to America, where he sought a career as producer and performer. In 1911 he became involved with an American attempt to present a season of Russian dance based on the artistic triumph of the Diaghilev dancers in Paris. Kosloff became the choreographer for the *Saison des Ballets Russes*, which opened in New York on 14 June 1911 at the Winter Garden. Three of the titles listed in the Winter Garden program were identical to ballets that had been premiered by Michel Fokine in Paris in 1909 and 1910: *Cléopâtre*, *Les Sylphides*, and *Schéhérazade*. In each case the credits given read "staged by Theodore Kosloff, Director of Choreographie."[7]

The New York *Saison des Ballets Russes* at the Winter Garden was the brainchild of Gertrude Hoffman and Morris Gest. Hoffman, born in San Francisco in 1886, "became the first of many female stage managers/dance directors on Broadway in the early years of this century. Her first New York production was *Punch and Judy,* which she staged for the Hammersteins' Paradise Garden Roof Theatre in 1903."[8] Hoffman made a career "based on imitations of the iconographies and performances of her contemporary colleagues."[9] She became a celebrity in late 1908 with her imitation of Maud Allan's *Salome.* She and her musician/producer husband, Max Hoffman, had gone to England in 1908 to study a production of that piece. In 1909–10 she presented an act, *The Gertrude Hoffman Review,* in which she did imitations of Isadora Duncan, Annette Kellerman, Ruth St. Denis, Eddie Foy, Ethel Barrymore, George Cohan, and Eva Tanguay.

The 1911 souvenir program of the Hoffman *La Saison Russe* tells of her ambition to bring Russian ballet to America.

> From the night, two summers ago, when Miss Gertrude Hoffman first saw the Russian dancers perform at the Châtelet Theatre, Paris, the one presiding, dominant thought in the ambitious young Californian's mind has been: "How can I ever succeed in bringing such a wonderful corps of artists to America?" . . . Including the orchestra of seventy-five musicians and the working staff behind the scenes, Miss Hoffman's company numbers over two-hundred persons. . . . It is especially noteworthy that all of the scenery, costumes, and properties, even down to the smallest details, have been specially imported from St. Petersburg, Moscow, and Paris.[10]

Gertrude Hoffman joined forces with Morris Gest, who in later years was to become an important impresario on his own. In 1909–10 he was employed by Oscar Hammerstein to "keep the vaudeville bills at his Victoria Theatre and Paradise Roof in the public eye, but also to help him sustain the sleepless rivalry between his Manhattan Opera and the Metropolitan."[11] Gest saw the Diaghilev company in Monte Carlo in 1909, after their Paris season, on one of his trips abroad for Oscar Hammerstein. He was immensely impressed and wanted to bring the company to the United States, but in 1909 Hammerstein was not interested. A year later Gest watched the success of Anna Pavlova, Mikhail Mordkin, and their small company at the Metropolitan Opera, and he felt the time was right for another presentation of Russian ballet. When Hoffman and Gest teamed up, they decided their season would be quite different from that of Pavlova and Mordkin.

> Story-ballets would dominate the repertory, challenging with their passionate intensity the varied divertissements in the Pavlova-Mordkin program. *Cleopatra,* a stabbingly erotic tale of the whims of a night with the Serpent of Old Nile, with

music by Arensky, Rimsky-Korsakov and Glazunow. *Les Sylphides*, for emotional breathing space. And finally, to send the audience home breathless and speechless with its tornado of love, suspicion and jealousy and revenge— *Scheherazade*. . . . Strictly speaking, Gest and Miss Hoffman had "stolen" their repertory and their choreography from the parent company in Paris and Monte Carlo, for no copyright laws prevailed with Russia then any more than they do to this day. All doubts as to the authentically Russian character of the production, however, were set at rest later in the week when the Imperial Russian Consulate General in New York and the embassy in Washington joined in banqueting Miss Hoffman and her associates.[12]

Theodore Kosloff, the "director of choreographie" for the Hoffman-Gest venture, naturally chose to stage the Fokine ballets that he knew intimately from the 1909 and 1910 Diaghilev seasons: *Cléopâtre* and *Les Sylphides* from 1909 and *Schéhérazade* from 1910. Alexandra Baldina, Kosloff's wife and principal dancer in the Paris production of *Les Sylphides*, along with Anna Pavlova, Tamara Karsavina, and Vaslav Nijinsky, supplemented Kosloff's knowledge of the other two ballets in the Hoffman repertory. Anything that Kosloff or Baldina did not remember, Lydia Lopoukhova, Alexander Volinine, Alexis Boulgakov, or Alexis Kosloff—the other Russian dancers—could help to reconstruct.

After the Hoffman tour ended in 1912, Kosloff taught in New York and then formed his own small group to play the Keith vaudeville circuit. A program dated 9 July 1916, from the group's performance at the Orpheum Theatre in San Francisco, headlined their performance as the "Season's Greatest Engagement, Russia's Supreme Dancing Stars."[13] Theodore Kosloff is listed as "premier danseur of the Imperial Russian Ballet of Moscow and Petrograd," even though by that time he had resigned from that institution. The other artists on the program were also listed as being from the Imperial Russian Ballet.

The program presented by these Russian artists, headed by Kosloff, consisted of a series of divertissements to music by Strauss, Delibes, Brahms, Glazunov, and Tchaikovsky. The inclusion of music by Rimsky-Korsakoff and by Stravinsky leads to the possibility that among these divertissements there were once again excerpts from the Fokine-Diaghilev repertory. A note at the bottom of the printed program in San Francisco reinforces the probability that Kosloff's Imperial Russian Dancers in 1916 were bringing to the public the exotic and spectacular elements of the Diaghilev Ballet seasons of 1909 and 1910 as well as duplications of the choreography. In a duet that Kosloff performed with Vlasta Maslova to music by Delibes, *Ecstasie* [sic] *d'Amour*, his legs were painted. About this the program note says: "Mr. Kosloff's legs painted in oils represent the element of Asiatic extravagance present in the Imperial Russian Ballet. The designs are painted twice a day for his dance, *Ecstasie d'Amour,* by John Wenger, the Russian apostle of the advanced school, who recently arrived from Petrograd."[14]

The San Francisco engagement was followed by one in Los Angeles; there Kosloff met Cecil B. de Mille, who was impressed by the Imperial Russian Dancers. De Mille offered Kosloff a role in a film and thus began Kosloff's association with Los Angeles. Kosloff appeared in the unsuccessful 1917 movie *The Woman God Forgot.*[15] In 1919 he opened a school in Los Angeles and in 1920 appeared in two films: *Why Change Your Wife* and *City of Masks.* He appeared in several other films during the next few years: *Forbidden Fruit, Affairs of Anatol, Fool's Paradise* (all in 1921); *The Lane That Had No Turning, The Green Temptation, The Dictators, To Have and To Hold* (all in 1922); *Law of the Lawless, Children of Jazz,* and *Don't Call It Love* (all in 1923). His film activity decreased but continued for the next few years: *Triumph* (1924), *Feet of Clay* (1924), *The Golden Bed* (1925), *New Lives for Old* (1925), *Beggar on Horseback* (1925), *The Volga Boatman* (1926), and *The King of Kings* (1927).

By 1925 Kosloff had become heavily involved in live dance production in Los Angeles. In that year he was appointed ballet master of the newly formed California Opera Company, which had been organized by Gaetano Merola of the San Francisco Opera and was being managed locally by L. E. Behymer and Rena MacDonald. The season, from 5 October through 12 October, took place at the recently completed Olympic Auditorium. For the 12 October evening Kosloff created a ballet called *The Romance of the Infanta,* about which John Sanders, in an article on Los Angeles opera from 1924 to 1926, wrote: "Theodore Kosloff, who was getting much publicity for his ballet depicting 'Old Spain' . . . was a familiar face in Los Angeles society. By opening night he was a favorite of the crowd."[16] Kosloff's ballet shared a double-bill with the opera *The Love of Three Kings* by Montemezzi. On 13 October Gilbert Brown's review in the *Los Angeles Record* was headlined "Kosloff Ballet Is Triumph": "Los Angeles has seen in many years no ballet offering so richly staged nor one performed so thoroughly in the tradition of the Russian Imperial Ballet of happy memory as this fantasy which might have been a novelette of Spain by Cabell come to life." The ballet, which was 45 minutes long, featured Vera Fredowa as Kosloff's partner.

The years 1925 and 1926 marked the beginnings of Kosloff's most active period in Los Angeles and in San Francisco. In 1925 he opened a studio in San Francisco at 466 Geary Street, where he was assisted by Estelle Reid and Vera Fredowa. In 1926 he was once again ballet master for opera in Los Angeles—this time for the Los Angeles Opera Company, formed from the Los Angeles segment of the California Opera Company and the existing Los Angeles company.[17] In 1926 Kosloff was also appointed the new director of the San Francisco Opera Ballet, a post he held through 1927. In 1925 and 1926 he staged movie prologues.[18]

The year 1926 also marked the beginning of Kosloff's association with the Hollywood Bowl, for which he was to create dances through 1939. In 1926 Kosloff presented the ballet *Schéhérazade* at the Bowl on the evenings of 24 June through 28 June, sharing the program with the West coast premiere of *Shanewis*, an Indian opera by Charles Wakefield Cadman. The double-bill was a preseason concert celebrating the newly renovated seating and rebuilt stage at the Hollywood Bowl. In the 1926 program for *Schéhérazade* the writer of the unsigned synopsis acknowledged that Kosloff's ballet was derivative: "The symphonic suite, *Scheherazade*, is a tonal narration of some of the stories which the Sultana told the Sultan Schariar during the Thousand and One Nights, and thereby saved her life. . . . Mr. Kosloff's scenario is that of the Imperial Russian Ballet, with touches of his own invention."[19] It could be that this was an oblique way of giving credit to Michel Fokine, since when *Schéhérazade* was first created, the artists who came to Paris with Diaghilev were still on leave from the Russian Imperial Ballet. But it is more likely that it was a reference to and a reminder of Kosloff's roots in Russian Imperial traditions.

In 1927 Kosloff once again presented *Schéhérazade*, this time at the Philharmonic Auditorium under the sponsorship of L. E. Behymer. He discussed this presentation with Bertha Wardell, who wrote about it in a 1927 article for *The Dance*, "Scheherazade in Hollywood—The Spirit of Rimsky-Korsakoff Is Carried to a Prominent Manufacturing Town in Southern California." In this article there is no acknowledgement that the ballet had any roots in earlier productions.

> Theodore Kosloff was rehearsing *Scheherazade*. The huge bare room where the rehearsal was being carried on hummed with vitality; the life of the fiery ballet, its story of the Eastern soul coming to itself again; the disturbing music of Rimsky-Korsakoff being pounded on the piano; the desperate faces of the dancers as they dashed about, bodies streaked with dirt from squirming on the floor, faces and bodies shining with sweat; Kosloff, his square body with feet apart planted on the sidelines, every wave of movement running through him, his baton stumping on the floor. . . . Mr. Kosloff told me as he rested, "Last night I stayed up until midnight making the formation of this ballet with colored papers. This morning I got up at half-past four because we rehearse at quarter-to-seven. I quit my classes here in the studio, I leave my work in the moving pictures with Mr. Cecil De Mille, for whom I am technical art director, to do this ballet.[20]

Kosloff talked about knowing Rimsky-Korsakoff when he was a student at the Imperial Russian Ballet School in Petrograd. He acknowledged that he had produced *Schéhérazade* in London and told Bertha

Wardell: "Mrs. Rimsky-Korsakoff gave me permission. The settings were by Korovin." He also told Wardell he had produced the ballet in 1911. "I do the ballet in New York for Morris Gest, David Belasco advising, with Gertrude Hoffman as 'Scheherazade.' Now I do it again here for Mr. Behymer."

Theodore Kosloff's next production for the Hollywood Bowl took place on 15 July 1932 when he presented *Chopin Memories*. The program noted that this ballet was "a choreographic tribute to the pure beauty of classical music and dancing." An extensive article by Mary Mayer on Kosloff in the *Los Angeles Times*, 12 June 1932, was meant to serve as an introduction and preview of Kosloff's thought and work prior to the Hollywood Bowl performance. In that article, titled "Kosloff Declares New in Repetition of Old," Kosloff gave credit for the genesis of his ballet based on the music of Chopin. "The first arrangement of Chopin for ballet and orchestra was made twenty-two years ago by Diaghilev for a ballet presented in Paris."

The 12 June article provided clear statements on the part of Kosloff as to how he felt about the creation of ballets and choreography. Mary Mayer quoted Kosloff as saying: "Some of the loveliest ballets ever written were presented some twenty-two years ago—and yet, if those same ballets unaltered were offered today, people would laugh at them." Kosloff had great reverence for the past. His work was rooted in the dances he experienced as a student and artist at the Imperial School and later with the Russian artists in Paris and London. He did not feel he could trust the old works to exist on their own merits for American audiences. He relayed these thoughts to Miss Mayer for her *Los Angeles Times* article: "The American audience must be startled—it must be treated to splendor on a large scale—it must have motion, intricate trickery, subtle lighting. . . . America is moving so rapidly. That is why we have the so-called jazz and the peculiar types of entertainment. It is the cry for something new—always something new. But the new is only a revival of the old."

Kosloff had easy access to the original Fokine version of *Les Sylphides* through his wife, Alexandra Baldina. But he did not present the original Fokine version either with the Hoffman group or at the Hollywood Bowl. Barbara Naomi Cohen, in an article on Hoffman and her Russian season, concludes that the evidence points to Kosloff's use of Fokine's first version of the Chopin ballet done in 1907 in Russia called *Chopiniana*. "It has been theorized that the Kosloff version is based on the discarded *Chopiniana*."[21]

Kosloff's *Chopin Memories* at the Hollywood Bowl was a combination of the different versions that he knew, the *Chopiniana* from 1907 and *Les Sylphides* from 1909.[22] Kosloff made an unusual decision about the visual aspect of his choreography. He decided to place the orchestra in front of the dancers instead of behind them. For the 1932 version at the Bowl he used the following 10 Chopin pieces: *Mazurka,* op. 50, no. 3; *Nocturne,* op. 32, no. 2; *Mazurka,* op. 33, no. 2; *Valse,* op. 64, no. 1; *Nocturne,* op. 9, no. 1; *Polonaise,* op. 40, no. 2; *Valse,* op. 70, no. 1; *Mazurka,* op. 7, no. 1; and *Grand Valse Brilliante,* op. 18. Perhaps to please the American audience, he gave each of the sections a name to help the audience understand and feel the music: "Moonlight Dream," "Flight of Gladness," "Echoes of Romance," "Spring Idyll," "Tears from the Heart," "Pomp and Pleasure," "Whimsical Caprice," "Daisy Chain," and "Moonlight Festival."

After creating dances for the opera *Carmen* (which was performed at the Bowl on 15 July 1937), Kosloff's next work for the Hollywood Bowl was presented on 2 September 1937, when he staged the ballet *Petrouchka,* music by Igor Stravinsky. In the Hollywood Bowl program notes for this ballet, Kosloff specifically gave credit to Fokine for the original version.

> Igor Stravinsky wrote music for several of Diaghileff's most famous ballets and as an inspiration came the idea for *Petrouchka*. The artist Alexander Benois created the decor for the ballet, and Michel Fokine, the choreography. Fokine, always the innovator, did an unusual thing in this ballet. He gave the effect of an informal carnival. He did not set any choreographic movements for the corps de ballet, but permitted them to move about as they wished. . . . The formal choreography of the central characters against this background made them stand out with greater clarity.

Referring to the original 1911 version, the program notes stated that "Theodore Kosloff knew that Stravinsky had never been happy over the way 'Petrouchka' was performed." According to these notes, Kosloff started a correspondence with Stravinsky when he decided to create his own choreography to the music.

> He found that their ideas of the story coincided perfectly. *Petrouchka* is a children's tale. He is a child's character, with the soul of a baby! Kosloff found that Stravinsky had never played for the Russian ballet. When Mr. Kosloff was preparing the ballet for presentation at the Shrine Auditorium last spring, Stravinsky was acting as a guest conductor with various orchestras throughout the country. *Petrouchka* was played on three of these programs which were broadcast over the radio. Mr. Kosloff noted the time of the broadcast . . . and had his company waiting in his studio, and when *Petrouchka* was played the dancers went through the ballet, in that way setting the tempo correctly.

On the evening of 17 September 1938 Theodore Kosloff presented a postseason evening of ballet at the Hollywood Bowl. The program read: "First of a series, Theodore Kosloff presents Midsummer Night

Ballet and Symphony." There is no record at the Hollywood Bowl of any ballet and symphony evening presented by Kosloff after this event, despite Kosloff's stated plans, which appeared on a separate page in the printed program devoted to both his picture and the following statement: "Ever since my staging of Stravinsky's *Petrouchka* in the Hollywood Bowl last summer, I have planned to present the world's foremost ballets in this community." On that September evening, which was to be the first of a master series, Kosloff staged four ballets. Two of them had been presented by Kosloff on previous occasions in Los Angeles, both at the Bowl and elsewhere: *Schéhérazade* and *Chopin Memories.* The other two ballets were new ventures for Kosloff. One was *Le Spectre de la Rose,* the original choreography for which had been created by Fokine for the 1911 Diaghilev season in Paris. The fourth ballet on the program was *Shingandi.*

Shingandi was certainly a departure from anything Kosloff had previously done and perhaps was an attempt on his part to move in a new direction. The program called it "A Symphony of Primitive Africa"; the music by David Guion was conducted by Constantin Bakaleinikoff, who was in charge of the orchestra for all four ballets. The characters in the ballet were listed as: M'Talaka (Voodoo Queen), Wetta, Kalombwan, Nkozo (Voodoo), Medicine Man, Chizongo (Chief of the Batongas), and Praja. The corps de ballet took the roles of the men and women of the two tribes that Kosloff had created in his ballet—the Batongas and the M'Tetes. There were several witch doctors—not attached specifically to either tribe.

The synopsis of *Shingandi* gives some idea of the flavor and form of the ballet.

> War between the two tribes in darkest Africa had drained them of their strongest and best men. At last, after much ceremonial and procrastination, peace was declared imperative. A human sacrifice must be given to the Spirit of Peace to seal the bond. It is only the power of M'Talaka, the Voodoo Queen, to choose a warrior suitable for the sacrifice. The handsomest and strongest men strive for the honor, but M'Talaka has already determined upon Kalombwan, strongest of his tribe. M'Talaka, with a ceremony of the black horn, points out Kalombwan to be burnt on the pyre. Wetta is prostrated, but in spite of her frantic efforts to halt the ceremonial, the pagan festival continues. Finally, after the torches have been lit, Wetta becomes crazed and rushes to the funeral pyre and lights it herself. M'Talaka, exultantly, leads the procession around the pyre. Wetta, in the depths of despair, gives a final appeal to Kalombwan to renounce the honor of being the sacrifice. He steadfastly refuses and starts toward the fire, but Wetta embraces him and clings to him and together they leap to death.[23]

If the picture on the program is any indication, the ballet *Shingandi* used the same movements and groupings that Kosloff had derived from Fokine with additional posturing and theatricality. The picture shows two women (very Anglo-Saxon) in position on their knees. Torsos are bent and twisted, arms outstretched, and fingers spread. The effect is similar to the many Oriental bacchanal scenes in ballets such as *Cléopâtre* and *Schéhérazade*. Two men are in shallow second position plié with arms outstretched, with another man on his knees on the floor. The libretto, with its pseudoprimitive convolutions, and the movement, with its Western ballet version of Africa, give the feeling of a Cecil B. de Mille movie spectacular—a story of Africa from the viewpoint of the Hollywood Hills.

Theodore Kosloff's gradually diminishing activities as a choreographer for the Hollywood Bowl were probably directly related to the appearances in Los Angeles of the ballet companies that emerged from the remains of the Diaghilev organization after his death in 1929.[23] In 1935 Sol Hurok, the New York impresario, began an association with L. E. Behymer, the Los Angeles impresario. Together they sponsored the Ballet Russe de Monte Carlo at the Philharmonic Auditorium in Los Angeles during the week of 27 January in the 1935–36 season. In 1935–36 they also announced in an advertisement in the Hollywood Bowl programs, "the return of Col. W. de Basil's *Ballet Russe* from January 15 to 23 at the Philharmonic." In 1937–38 this company appeared at the Philharmonic from 21 to 26 January.

During the 1938–39 season, from 26 January to 4 February, the "New and Enlarged Ballet Russe de Monte Carlo" (as noted in the advertisements) appeared at the Shrine Auditorium in "9 Gala Performances," and for the 1939–40 season Behymer advertised the Ballet Russe's appearances at the Philharmonic Auditorium from 9 to 17 February. In the summer of 1941 the Ballet Russe de Monte Carlo, directed by Leonide Massine, appeared for the first time at the Hollywood Bowl on 29 July, 30 July, 2 August, and 16 August. Their repertory at the Hollywood Bowl included the following ballets: *Les Sylphides, Schéhérazade, Le Beau Danube, Swan Lake, Prince Igor,* and *The Nutcracker.* The company presented the original choreography by Michel Fokine, danced by Leonide Massine and a star-studded cast consisting of Alexandra Danilova, Igor Youskevitch, Tamara Toumanova, André Eglevsky, and Frederick Franklin.[24]

Theodore Kosloff brought with him to Los Angeles the technical and artistic traditions of the Russian Imperial School and the aesthetics of reform that had grown from within those traditions to encompass new ideas of expression, form, and content. Kosloff was the first bearer of these traditions to settle in Los Angeles as a permanent exile. His teaching, which began in 1919, was always an important aspect of his activities in Los Angeles. In 1922 he advertised in the Los Angeles City and County Directory as follows: "Theodore Kosloff—Imperial Russian Ballet School."[25]

In an interesting series of articles in the *Los Angeles Times* in both 1926 and 1927 it was noted that Kosloff's school was most unusual. The reporter, who was not identified in any of the articles, wrote that Kosloff's school was modeled after the Imperial Russian Ballet School; students could take not only their ballet classes but also their regular academic subjects. The article said that the school had the approval of the Los Angeles Board of Education and was "under the supervision of that August body." Dance classes started at 8:00 in the morning and were followed in the afternoon by the regular school curriculum. Often Alexandra Baldina, Kosloff's wife, taught with him in their various studios in Los Angeles. They brought to their work the professionalism, technical expertise, and artistic strength embedded in the teaching of the conservatories in both Moscow and Leningrad. Among the many distinguished artists developed by Kosloff and Baldina are Agnes de Mille, Nana Gollner (first American ballerina of Ballet Theatre), Flower Hujer (founding ballerina, San Francisco Opera Company), and Dimitri Romanoff (regisseur, Ballet Theatre).

Kosloff did not settle permanently in Los Angeles during the 1920s and 1930s the way Belcher did, establishing a studio that had continuity, day in and day out, year in and year out. Kosloff had done well financially, particularly when the stock in Paramount Pictures that he had been given in 1917 began to become more valuable. He had also purchased real estate in Los Angeles, and he had made good money from his various movie ventures. There are two interesting articles about Kosloff in the *Los Angeles Times*. One, although undated, is grouped among the February notices in a scrapbook from 1929 in the Los Angeles Public Library. The unnamed reporter noted that Theodore Kosloff had just returned to Los Angeles after a six-month tour of France, Italy, and Germany "oberving the different activities in regard to the motion pictures, dancing schools and stage." Another article, probably from March 1929, also undated and with no byline, reported that "Theodore Kosloff, Russian ballet master, has ordered an airplane to transport him to his Western and Eastern studios." At that time Kosloff was doing some teaching in Chicago.

By the 1940s Kosloff was devoting most of his time to teaching and was permanently settled in Los Angeles. The biographical entry on Kosloff in Chujoy and Manchester's *Dance Encyclopedia* says that "he taught until the day of his death." By the 1950s Kosloff's prime involvement in dance was his teaching, and until the very end he remained a strict but loving disciplinarian and a charismatic teacher. His obituary in *Dance News* reinforced his involvement in teaching. "He had taught class the day of the attack . . . but complained that he was not feeling well. The attack came as he was being driven to his ranch in nearby Sunland."[26]

Theodore Kosloff left a rich legacy of dance in Los Angeles, the place where he seemed to feel he had a home base in the United States and where he finally settled. It was in Los Angeles that he did his most consistent teaching, and it was where he staged most of his work from the 1920s on. Kosloff, as the first Russian to appear at the Hollywood Bowl, brought to thousands a new ballet experience. His ballets combined the technical and artistic traditions of the past with the early modernism of Michel Fokine.

Kosloff had an ambiguous attitude toward his ballets and the Russian tradition. He was uncomfortable with change but felt things needed to be more "spicy" for the average American audience. It seemed to be somewhat of a patchwork attitude. In a 12 July 1932 *Los Angeles Times* interview he claimed: "The dance of yesterday would seem as odd as the dress of yesterday. It lacked the dash that the modern age demands—it lacked the element of the spectacular, the daring feats, the mass effects." He seemed to sense a need for change but did not really understand how to accomplish it. The "dance of yesterday" may best be kept close to the form that made it vital in its day. Americans probably were moving beyond the point where they needed their dances "spiced up," whereas Kosloff continued to translate his experiences from movies, vaudeville, and extended touring. He was most successful when he was able to remain as close to the original impulse of the Russian ballet as possible. When he tampered too much, adding what he thought was audience appeal, he only succeeded in creating ballets that were overdone and superficial.

In *Ballet, The Emergence of an American Art* George Amberg's remarks about the early ballets that Fokine created are also applicable to Kosloff's work.

> It is unfortunate that Fokine himself did not control the fate of these works; since he left them to Diaghilev, numerous revivals have been staged over the years, though few of them by himself. This practice is of doubtful merit, for Fokine's works are no longer revolutionary and it is absurd to pretend that they are the supreme balletic achievement of all time. . . . These lovely revivals of Fokine's ballets are an offense to Fokine's memory and an insult to the audience . . . no longer revolutionary but rather the starting point of contemporary ballet.[27]

Theodore Kosloff was perpetuating a great tradition, but he was also living artistically in the past. Even if he did not use Fokine's choreography for the ballets that carried Fokine's titles, he was choreographing with the style and substance of another era. Kosloff, however, made a great contribution to the dance in Los Angeles through his teaching, his professionalism, and his heritage of the early Diaghilev repertory. It is unfortunate that artistically he did not challenge himself to bring new ideas to his ballets and that he did not trust the American audiences to meet him at least half way. Kosloff brought the past to Los Angeles, but he did not bring the present to his work.

4

Serge Oukrainsky (1885–1972): Spectacle, Sensualism, and Plastique

Serge Oukrainsky, born Leonidas Orlay de Carva in Odessa,[1] came to dance relatively late. His parents were separated, and he lived mainly in Paris with his father, who entertained a great deal. It was at a dinner in his father's house in 1911 that Oukrainsky began his career in dance. Present that evening was Nathalie Trouhanowa. She had been a dramatic actress in Moscow but had decided to become a dancer and studied with Ivan Clustine in Paris. She was interested in having a gala musical festival made up only of French composers and wanted to stage an evening of ballets created to their music. It was at this dinner that she announced the lack of a partner for her ballet evening. Oukrainsky recorded this incident in his book, *My Two Years with Pavlowa*: "Then addressing me in the most direct manner she said, 'What a pity that you are not a dancer. You are the perfect type for a premier danseur, the only one who could expect to be compared to Nijinsky.'"[2]

Oukrainsky was interested but felt that his father would never agree to his going into the theater. As it turned out, his father was a frustrated singer and did agree to his son studying dance. Oukrainsky started his studies with Ivan Clustine, who had been a premier danseur at the Imperial Theatre in Moscow and boasted at having been the instructor of Mordkin, who afterward succeeded him. Oukrainsky worked with Clustine for two years. During this period of study he made his debut in the theater playing the role of a lover opposite Trouhanowa in *Istar* by Vincent d'Indy. On the same program he was St. John the Baptist in *La Tragédie de Salomé* by Florent Schmitt.

Oukrainsky was beginning to form aesthetic perspectives related to dance during this period, 1911 to 1913. He was impressed with the Diaghilev season. He recalled seeing *Le Carnaval*, *Les Sylphides*, *Le Spectre de la Rose*, *Schéhérazade*, and *Firebird*. He was very taken with the ballets he saw, especially the ones that seemed to forge ahead in new directions.

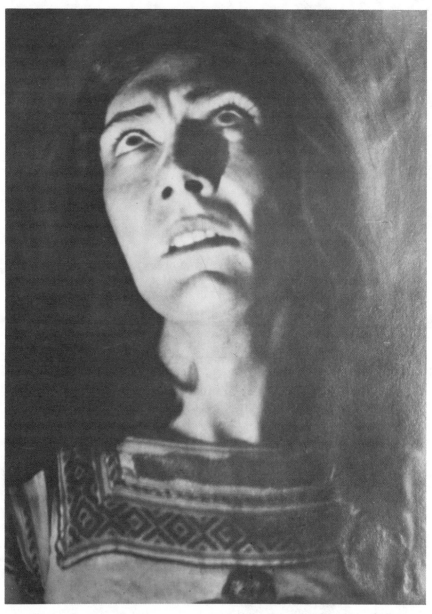

Serge Oukrainsky in Scene from *A Crucifixion*, 1920s
(*Courtesy Archives for Performing Arts, San Francisco*)

On coming out of the opera, I thought of the very beautiful spectacles I had seen. I was filled with admiration for Bakst, recognizing in him the originator of an entirely new mode of theatrical decoration. Michel Fokine, too, I saw had broken away from the "already done" coming out of rigidity of the old ballet and extending its conventional limits. He, by his new conceptions, was creating a new horizon.[3]

Oukrainsky felt that this was the "great epoch" of Diaghilev. He created a new repertory, rightly abandoning the old demoded ones of the Maryinsky Theatre. Oukrainsky saw later seasons of the Ballets Russes and was extremely dissatisfied. He had for himself determined during this period what constituted a ballet that was both modern and pleasing. He would not accept "modern ballet" that did not fit his requirements of beautiful plastique, recognizable techniques, and acceptable use of story and music to create a strong mood. Modern did not mean distorted, angular, contemporary, or violent: "*Le Sacre du Printemps* (exception made to the music) was the commencement to the end of Diaghilev. There he began to be compelled, regardless of the production, to make novelties using much ballyhoo with the aim of attracting the populace if not the admirers, at least the curious who would pay the same price for their seats. The results of these tactics is the ballet *Parade*."[4]

His conception of what was modern in the dance began to develop as an emphasis on visualization of the music in a spectacle that portrayed feeling and emotion using "plastique"—i.e., expressive posing of the body. He saw "modern" as a rejection of dances that used only steps and techniques. His comments on Isadora Duncan's performance during the years in Paris studying ballet emphasized what he valued in her dancing but also what he disliked.

Isadora Duncan also had a season at the Châtelet Theatre and I went to see her. At that period she was still more the dancer than the plastique tragedian. So I did not see her at her best. . . . She had certainly made enormous progress in the dance, by realizing the possibilities of the "symphonic poem," interpreting them, instead of utilizing only the waltzes, gallops and polkas of the old school.[5]

Oukrainsky's conception of dance required that there be a strong element of spectacle and a heavy emphasis on costuming, color, and style. He appreciated the fact that Duncan eliminated scenery and used a velvet curtain that showed the beauty of gesture and the plastique of the body. He was not happy with her artistic simplicity and her rejection of variety in mood, color, and visualization. He rejected anything that seemed to him primitive and ugly.

She freed the feet of conventional foot gear, toe slipper, ridiculous for the Greek, Oriental and other dances. . . . But a foot a little bent can be beautiful on a bas-relief. In action, a foot flat, is ugly. It is too primitive, too inartistic, too near the Zulu. The same type of costume is monotonous for all the dances and in the Greek dances her coiffure seems to me also to be entirely lacking in style.[6]

While he was studying with Ivan Clustine, Oukrainsky created solos for himself: a musical sketch representing the biblical serpent tempting Eve with the forbidden fruit, an Oriental dance, and a Persian dance. It was this last dance with which he auditioned for Anna Pavlova's company and was accepted in 1913. Oukrainsky was engaged for Pavlova's company "principally for my specialties—dancing the genre nouveau and not the routine of the old ballet."[7] The *Persian Dance* remained a favorite of both Oukrainsky and his audiences over the years. In the book on his two years with Pavlova he has two pictures of himself in this dance. In one he is posed supporting himself on the floor on the points of one leg and with two arms behind his torso. He is wearing a brief, beaded and tassled costume, a sultry look, and a tight cap on his head to match the costume. The other picture shows him in another, slightly different version of the first costume, this time standing on the toes of both feet with arms uplifted and elbows bent.

It was in Pavlova's company that Oukrainsky met the man he was to work with closely as cochoreographer and coperformer for almost two decades. The man was Andreas Pavley, who was to have a good deal of artistic impact on Oukrainsky's work over the years. Born Andres Von Dorph de Wever in 1892 in Batavia, the capital of Java, Pavley began dancing at age 13. He studied with Emile Jaques Dalcroze for a year and a half in Geneva and at 17 staged a dance spectacle in Amsterdam to Beethoven's *Prometheus*, using over 100 performers. In 1912 he collaborated with the painter Arild Rosenkrantz to stage a ballet at the Savoy Theatre in London with music arranged from Beethoven's piano sonatas.[8] When Pavley joined Pavlova's company in 1913 he studied ballet under Ivan Clustine and Enrico Cecchetti, who gave class regularly before rehearsal.

Pavley and Oukrainsky toured for two years with Pavlova and in 1915 performed with her company in Chicago at the Midway Gardens. It was at this time that they went on their own, starting to perform and teach in Chicago. Their stay in that city was to be a rich and fruitful one; it was there that they began to develop their teaching and choreographic abilities. Selma Jeanne Cohen, the dance historian, wrote about Oukrainsky and Pavley: "Both men played extremely important roles in the development of ballet in America."[9] Their influence was through both choreography and teaching, and Chicago was home base until 1927. They taught from the minute they left Pavlova's company. Their first big assignment was the preparation of dancers for a program at the Murat Theatre in Indianapolis on 7 October 1916, in which Ruth Page had her first public performance. That same year they received a contract to work with the Chicago Grand Opera and began teaching a group that would perform with them.

They also taught private lessons whenever possible, and Doris Humphrey was one of their pupils in 1916. In her autobiography she wrote of classes with Pavley and Oukrainsky in the grand ballroom of the Congress Hotel in Chicago.

> To me, these lessons were the most exciting of occasions. The furniture of the huge ballroom was covered with ghostly sheets, and a place had been cleared of spindly gold chairs in the center of the room. Pavley and Oukrainsky didn't bother with music, but hummed some little tunes from Glinka, or made clicking noises on the beat when this seemed called for. . . . I learned quickly, so soon I was flying around the ballroom, clicking my heels and turning in what I imagined was a very Russian manner. It was more fun with Pavley than Oukrainsky. When the former danced with me, a little pink would begin to show in the pale face, and the black curls would bounce. Oukrainsky was full of Slavic melancholy, and would lean heavily on the piano while he said, "Do ziz one; now do zat one." At the end of an hour, they would bow from the waist, surreptitiously accept some money from my mother, and disappear into their mysterious lives.[10]

Late in 1916 Pavley and Oukrainsky formed a company of their students and took them on tour. In 1917 they appeared in Carnegie Hall with Walter Damrosch and presented to the public as a soloist one of their first pupils, Anna Ludmilla. In that same year they gave their company the name Ballet Intime and toured with George Barrère's Little Symphony. In 1919 Pavley and Oukrainsky gave a special gala performance at the Metropolitan Opera with six of their students. The evening was in honor of Marshall Foch, General of France, and consisted of original choreography for Février's *Gismonda* and Debussy's *Afternoon of a Faun*.

It was in 1919 that Pavley and Oukrainsky were hired to become the ballet masters and choreographers of the Chicago Opera, and they were to work in this capacity, off and on, until 1926. They created opera ballets as well as ballets that were independent of any opera productions. They hired male dancers for the corps de ballet, an innovation at that time. In 1922–23 they took a company of 32 that they had trained to Mexico City, Cuba, and various cities in the United States. Among those in the company were Edward Caton, Edris Milar, Lydia Arlove, John Patri, and Leon Varkas. During the years 1923 through 1926 they had a summer dance camp in South Haven, Michigan, and toured with their company in Brazil, Uruguay, Argentina and throughout the United States.

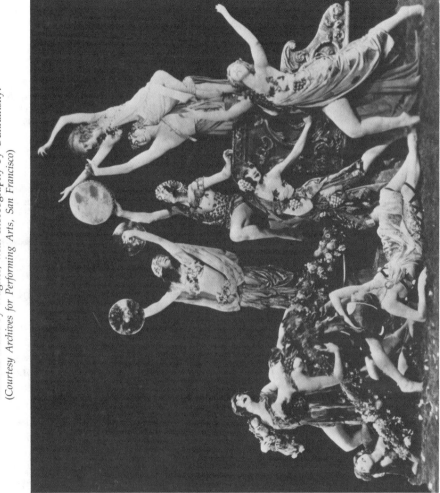

Scene from "The Venusberg" in *Tannhäuser*, ca. 1927
Ballet to music by Wagner, with choreography by Oukrainsky.
(*Courtesy Archives for Performing Arts, San Francisco*)

Scene from *Orpheus*, ca. 1927
Ballet to music by Gluck, with choreography by Oukrainsky.
(*Courtesy Archives for Performing Arts, San Francisco*)

Ann Barzel in "European Dance Teachers in the United States" wrote about Pavley and Oukrainsky and their influence in Chicago.

They taught there for over a decade and almost every teacher now teaching in Chicago had at one time or another studied with them. . . . Pavley and Oukrainsky taught a combination of "plastique" and ballet. Both teachers believed in "free movement" and emphasis was on lyric movement rather than on technique. There was a great deal of barefoot work; Oukrainsky even taught toe dancing on the bare toes. The influence of the school was wider than generally credited. A Denishawn ad in 1924 carried a picture of one of its own teachers with the caption, "Pavley backbend as taught by the Denishawn School." The Pavley-Oukrainsky School was conducted very formally. The atmosphere was almost devout, but was relieved by the fact that there were always productions to be arranged and both teachers were excellent showmen.[11]

Serge Oukrainsky first came to Los Angeles to teach a summer course from 7 June to 27 June in 1927. In the fall of 1927 he was the choreographer for the fall season of the Los Angeles Grand Opera Association at the Shrine Civic Auditorium from 3 October through 17 October. The ballets that season were listed in the opera announcement as: *Romeo and Juliet, Falstaff, Carmen, Tristan and Isolde, Cavalleria Rusticana, Aida, La Bohème, La Tosca, Manon Lescaut, Turandot, Il Trovatore,* and *Pagliacci.*

Pavley and Oukrainsky had not given up their activities in Chicago or elsewhere, and Los Angeles was not yet a permanent base of operation. In 1926–27 Oukrainsky stayed in Chicago while Pavley toured with the Pavley-Oukrainsky Ballet, which appeared on a double-bill with the Manhattan Opera Company. Presented by L. E. Behymer by arrangement with Frank T. Kintzing, this double-bill played the Philharmonic Auditorium in Los Angeles from 28 December to 1 January.[12]

The Pavley-Oukrainsky group presented two ballets and a series of divertissements on these 1926–27 programs. *The Temple of the Sun,* with music by Hypolite Ivanoff, according to the program notes, was about "the rise of the cult in Syria, 200 years B.C. On certain occasions a youth and two virgins were chosen to be sacrificed to the Sun after having their bodies whitened and anointed with sacred oils. . . . At daybreak the sacrificers . . . led them toward the altar . . . their bodies were burned in honor of the Sun God." The dancers were listed as Andreas Pavley, Mlles. Milar, Compton, Allen, Edgcumbe, Metzger, O'Brien, Winnie, Gibbard, Gumm, Rayya, Kitchel, Raymond, and MM. Bublitz, Luttman, Pause, Gregg, Lennep, Winsor, Grenvil, and Spear. *In Knighthood Days* was subtitled a "Fantastic Doll Ballet in Two Scenes" and featured music by Halévy and Sokolow. The *Divertisse-*

ments on the programs covered a wide range—from "Holland Dance" to "Blue Danube" to "Cubist Dance."

In 1927 Oukrainsky had announced the opening of a branch school in Los Angeles. Pavley would be in charge of the Chicago school, and Oukrainsky would be in charge of the West coast division. The *Los Angeles Times* of 1 May 1927 carried the following announcement in its "Terpsichore" section: "Pavley and Oukrainsky have come to Los Angeles to create a ballet for the Los Angeles Civic Opera Company and will locate permanently making important affiliations with the motion picture studios. Mr. Oukrainsky is recruiting raw material for the Opera Ballet." Another announcement in the *Los Angeles Times* "Terpsichore" section, this time on 29 May 1927, noted that "Pavley-Oukrainsky were to open a permanent branch of their Chicago school."

In 1928 Oukrainsky was active in Los Angeles on his own and was joined by Pavley for the summer performance at the Hollywood Bowl. Oukrainsky functioned, in that year, as ballet master for both the Los Angeles Grand Opera Association and the San Francisco Opera. He taught in Los Angeles at 4157 West Fifth Street and created dance sequences for a movie. Working with Fox Studios and Dolores Del Rio, he created an elaborate Oriental ballet for the film *The Red Dancer.*

The 30 August 1928 program at the Hollywood Bowl was composed of divertissements performed by Andreas Pavley, Serge Oukrainsky and a company of fifteen. The divertissements were grouped in two sections. *Ballet Divertissements I* had five dances: "Siamese Dance" ("Hymn to the Sun")—danced by Serge Oukrainsky (Rimsky-Korsakoff); "Gavotte" ("Petits Riens")—the ensemble (Mozart); "Fire Dance"—Andreas Pavley (de Falla); "Adagio Classique" ("Nocturne")—Mlle. Flaige and Mr. Ewing (Chopin); "Marionette" ("Tarantelle")—Serge Oukrainsky (Halévy). The next section of *Ballets Divertissements* also had five dances: "Gypsy Dance"—Mlle. Flaige (Sarasate); "Persian Dance"—Serge Oukrainsky (Mussorgsky); "Pastorale" ("Caprice Viennois")—Andreas Pavley and Mlle. Flohre (Kreisler).

The program note for this Hollywood Bowl presentation emphasized the modern aspect of these ballet divertissements: "These international favorites are known and beloved the world over. In the modern ballet we have one of the most poignant of our cultural inheritances. With the accompaniment of a 100 piece orchestra, in the magical setting of the Bowl, the divertissements presented by Messieures Pavley and Oukrainsky and their corps of assistants will offer the acme of aesthetic enjoyment for both eye and ear." The 1928 program featured many of the dances that the two men had been associated with during their careers. Oukrainsky's *Persian Dance* had been in his repertory since his Pavlova audition. The "Gavotte" with music by Mozart may well have been a close relative of the famous *Pavlova Gavotte* created for her during the tours of 1913 through 1915 and for which Oukrainsky designed the costume. The "Marionette" had precedents in Oukrainsky's appearance in *Dances of Animated Dolls* performed by the Pavlova company. The Metropolitan Opera House Program of 1914–15 lists his role as "Automaton Louis 14th."

The *Los Angeles Times* of 31 August 1928 gave the evening a good review. The reviewer, Isabel Morse Jones, was particularly pleased with performance and costuming.

> It was ballet night at the Hollywood Bowl last evening and the moon hung high in the heavens. The hills of Hollywood held fully 20,000 and the crowd was the largest since Schumann-Heink sang. Eugene Goosens conducted an interesting program. . . . One of Goosens' most attractive characteristics is his graciousness. He conducted the music for the ballet divertissements of Serge Oukrainsky and Andreas Pavley with the utmost interest and abandon. In a Mozart number he stepped down to the piano and played a Gavotte with the same ease and grace. One realizes that he likes ballet and aids it in every way. Messrs. Oukrainsky and Pavley arranged two series of divertissements of contrasting moods. The dancing was finished, the company was well trained and each divertissement completely and beautifully costumed. In the costuming, which contributed so largely to the success of this ballet in the vast space across the Bowl stage, was seen the masterhand of Mr. Oukrainsky. His weird Siamese image of Vishnu in the first ballet, the fantastic structures used by the company in the "Mozart Gavotte," which made the dancers look like a picture by Goya and the modern designing in the costume of Pavley's "Fire-dance," displayed great gifts of color and line, as well as rare imagination. The Pavley-Oukrainsky Ballet would do well to regard the music with more attention. Perhaps it was due to distance, but usually the dancers, not excepting the principals, were not sensitive to the nuance and change of the very fine orchestral inspiration which Mr. Goosens was directing. Too often the mood of the dances changes several beats or even measures after the new musical idea had been announced in the orchestra. A course in musical appreciation would not be wasted on this company.

It is interesting that Isabel Morse Jones singled out the relationship of the dance to the music. Jones's comments help focus on the choreographic perspective that was consistently important to both Pavley and Oukrainsky—emotion and mood. Music was conceived as an important but canvaslike background to the lines and shapes of the spectacle. In a June 1927 article in *The American Dancer*, "The Dance, What It Is, Was and Should Be," Oukrainsky wrote that music should give atmosphere to dance. All the pictures of both Pavley and Oukrainsky give the feeling of two dancers whose movements were created in broad strokes, moving from picture to picture. The transitions were of less importance than the final plastiques. Their programs were characterized by beautiful and varied costumes. Movements created a mood rather than intricate combinations of steps and patterns. The music was most likely used in large phrases. Nuances of change and smaller phrasing could well have been ignored so that the group or individual visualization could come to completion or make the necessary statement.

In the August 1928 *Los Angeles Times* review Isabel Morse Jones had nothing but praise for the various performances on Pavley-Oukrainsky's first Bowl program.

> Marvelous technique was exhibited by Mr. Oukrainsky in his Siamese dance. Toe dancing in bare feet seems to require no unusual effort on his part but his uncanny skill in the muscular action of his feet and limbs spoke eloquently of his artistry. Eleanore Flaige has the ethereal grace of a fairy. She is lovely to look at with her dark hair and her spiritual contour. Her ballet dancing grows ever lighter and she conveys her refined and winning charm over the footlights in a manner that would be becoming in Pavlowa. Andreas Pavley has a warmth of emotion in his dancing and he has a fascinating gift of pantomime. In the concluding Pastorale with Mlle. Flohre the effect of delicate enticement and fleeting charm created a lovely finale.

Oukrainsky and Pavley utilized their time in Los Angeles and their association with the movies in 1928 to create *The Videoballeton*.[13] In Oukrainsky's unpublished autobiography he explained *The Videoballeton* as a "combination of five live dancers and corps de ballet on film enlarged to human size, all synchronized together."[14] He wrote that he presented *The Videoballeton* on concert tours in 1928. In his manuscript he listed five sections: "Grecian Bacchanal" (Gounod); "Snow Bird Toe Dance" (Braga); "Futuristic Town" (Gershwin); "East Indian Dance" (Glazunov) and "Intermezzo, Ay-Ay-Ay" (Mexican song); and "Caprice Espagñol" (Rimsky-Korsakoff). An undated program gives the name of the cameraman who worked with the dancers as Mr. Physioc, and the dances have slightly different names on that program: "Bacchanal" (Gounod); "Plume Dance" (song); "Futuristic Dance" (Gershwin); "Oriental Dance" (Glazunov); and "Gypsy Scene" (Rimsky-Korsakoff).[15]

The Videoballeton, while being a most interesting experiment, also provides valuable insight into the choreographic ideas of Pavley and Oukrainsky. Oukrainsky stated in the book on his experience with Pavlova that he met Pavley and "we were in accord in our approval of the new movements of the dance."[16] An illuminating program note in *The Videoballeton* program helps explain what Oukrainsky did, and did not, mean by "new movements." The use of music by Gershwin and the title "Futuristic Dance" seem at first very strange in the context of the rest of the Pavley-Oukrainsky repertory. They only used the work of American composers on two occasions. One was a commission for an Oriental ballet *Bondour*, written by the Chicago-based American composer Felix Borowsky and premiered in 1919 with costumes by Norman Bel Geddes. The other was a piece composed by John Alden Carpenter, *The Birthday of the Infanta*. Adolph Bolm did a version of this in 1921, and Oukrainsky and Pavley did another version in 1922 with scenery and costumes by Robert Edmond Jones. Behind their use of the Gershwin music and the unusual (for them) title is the fact that this piece in *The Videoballeton* carried an artistic message. Underneath the title, "Futuristic Dance," the two choreographers had placed the following program note: "A characterization of the strife between the classics and fad and fashion in which fad and fashion ridicule the classics. Fad and fashion envelope the representation of the classics, but fad and fashion slowly fade into oblivion while the classics go on forever." This dance was a trio. "Classics" was danced by Mlle. Flohre, "Fad" was danced by Andreas Pavley, and "Fashion" was danced by Mlle. Arlova.

Oukrainsky and Pavley felt that much of what was being called "modern" was simply fad and would soon go away. Their concept of modern was based on a vision of early twentieth-century romanticism—a lush and sensual expressiveness that rejected anything that could be considered ugly or depressing. While they rejected the traditional ballet, they also rejected anything overly contemporary or seemingly primitive. Jazz fell into this category: "Jazz . . . is nothing less than an incorrect and angular ballet with atrophied arms, as in all inferior and primitive dances."[17]

A look at the music and titles for the various dances Pavley and Oukrainsky did in Chicago and at the Hollywood Bowl is instructive. At the Hollywood Bowl in 1934 *La Fête à Robinson*, with music by a French composer, Gabriel Grovlez, was performed. In 1935 and 1936 Oukrainsky staged evenings using the music of Rimsky-Korsakoff, Mussorgsky, Halévy, and Bizet. A list of the music used for original choreography by the Pavley-Oukrainsky Company showed that they used pieces by Debussy, Saint-Saëns, Liszt, Halévy, Schubert, Ippolitov-Ivanov, Wagner, and Mozart. Various titles of dances created before the Hollywood Bowl performances were: *Prelude à l'Après-Midi d'un Faune, Danse Macabre, The Gate of Redemption, The Captive Princess, Dance Poem, Gypsy Camp, The Temple of the Sun, The Temple of Dagon,* and *Japanese Ballet.*

In his foreword to *My Two Years with Anna Pavlowa* Oukrainsky said dance could be divided into four categories.

> First, the group of ballet dancers who believe that to be a better performer one must remain on toe longer, jump higher than the others, those who disregard beauty of

line to give only an exhibition of boring gymnastic exercises, and have no real conception of the character or feeling of the dance. The "Hoofer" whose principal advantage is to become a dancer within a short period of time. The only purpose
being a rhythmical monotonous sound effect made by the feet, but without the
beauty of movement, musical conception and interpretation of style existing in classical Spanish work. The third group consists of Fans, Balloons, etc. For this dance
the necessary requirements are merely to be a beautiful girl. This type should be
rather called academic models in motion.[18]

Having dismissed the first three categories of dance for little interest or
value, he proceeded to deliver what he probably considered a death-
blow to "Modern Dance." This passage on what he calls the "fourth"
category of dance not only delivers a strong blast at what he did not
like but also helps clarify what he did like and why his choreography
remained consistent over the years. He had formed his artistic visions
during the first two decades of the twentieth century in Paris, and they
were to remain the same throughout his life. His four categories are all
equally distasteful, but perhaps the fourth bothers him the most.

The fourth is what they call Modern Dance which these addicts have substituted for
the natural school created by Isadora Duncan. This natural school was a comical
paradox because if it is natural they do not need to study and if you have something to learn it ceases to be natural. In this school each one can be a dancer without exertion. The necessary requirement was to obtain a piece of chiffon or a flute
and skip around to classical music and you were a dancer. But this natural dance
had the purpose to express mostly happiness and attempting to loveliness in accord
with the epoch. The modern dance is a continuation of that school but living in the
time of depression, war and revolution. Their aim is to portray morbid prosaic conception and make ugly, grotesque, disconnected gestures without meaning. Pavlowa's style of dance has scientific and mathematic principles when studied cor-
rectly, but with the modern dance so many teachers, so many rules.[19]

It is interesting that Oukrainsky dated the beginning of "Modern
Dance" from Nijinsky's choreography for *Le Sacre du Printemps*. He
wrote a long diatribe against Nijinsky, that particular ballet, and modern dance. He then stated that "these facts that I mention do not apply
to Martha Graham or the Jooss Ballet Company." He did not mention
why he excluded Martha Graham or what he had seen and liked of her
work. He did mention that he excluded the Jooss Ballet from his diatribe because they showed ballet training. He did not mention Jooss's
masterpiece *The Green Table* but said he particularly liked their ballet
Old Vienna. When he talked about the beginnings of the ugly and
grotesque movements that he so disliked, the discussion was particularly angry at what Nijinsky tried to do.

The first performance of an exhibition of that sort was in 1913 the *Sacre du Printemps* [sic]. This ballet meant to represent savage races and for that interpretation

Nijinsky tried to reproduce the primitive movements that the human can conceive. In this A-B-C of ballet schools four steps are the principal foundation. One is to *plier* in elementary ballet second position, the second is to raise the leg like a beginner with bent ankle; third, to lie on your back, and fourth, to jump with both feet in Kangaroo-like fashion. If you can accomplish these four principal steps as in the natural dance, you are quite an artist in modern dance which is twenty-six years old.[20]

On 25 June 1931 Andreas Pavley died, the day that Oukrainsky was able to finalize a contract for performances at the Paris Opéra that summer. When the Pavley-Oukrainsky Ballet had their second performance at the Hollywood Bowl on 17 August 1934, Oukrainsky had moved to Los Angeles permanently, to teach and choreograph. The 17 August performance was a repeat of a 1922 Chicago premiere, *La Fête à Robinson*. It was called a "comedy ballet in one act" and was set to music that had been composed specially for the dance by the French composer Gabriel Grovlez. *La Fête à Robinson* was a light period piece with a complicated fin de siècle plot. Oukrainsky had wanted to have music composed by Maurice Ravel, but that was not possible because of time limitations. Instead, he asked Gabriel Grovlez, whose ballet music for *Maimouna* had interested him. Oukrainsky wrote in his unpublished "My Life in Ballet" about the genesis of *La Fête à Robinson.*

In this ballet we wanted to give the story of lovers trying to overcome the opposition of a severe tutor. The scene would be Robinson, a charming hamlet near Paris where picturesque aspects had not as yet been used on stage. We also wished to introduce a special aspect of Robinson. A stylish spot of the 1850's, it had tables built in the branches of the flowering chestnut trees, which were part of the nearby woods. In order to show the great days of Robinson we would feature crinolines, flirtations in a swing, a country wedding, songs by Béranger—all this in our choreography.[21]

The cast of characters for *La Fête à Robinson* was extensive: a waiter, a painter, a coachman, a maiden aunt, a mother, an enfant terrible, a good child, the snobs, the shop girls, demimondaines, a *fleuriste*, a bride, a bridegroom, a mother, a father, a drunkard, a sentimental girl, relatives, guests of the restaurant, and others. The plot evolved as the story of a rural restaurant in the treetops of a Paris suburb of the Second Empire. It was the story of young lovers—a painter and his sweetheart—and a forbidding aunt who opposed their romance. The aunt was put to sleep by a potion in her wine and fell into a basket used to pull food into the treetop restaurant. "All's well that ends well"—the aunt arrived in the treetop and inevitably forgave the young lovers and gave her approval to romance (and most clearly their forthcoming marriage!).

On 29 August 1935 Oukrainsky created a ballet specially for the Hollywood Bowl, *Les Eléments*. It had music by Rimsky-Korsakoff and Mussorgsky. In his own chronology he listed this dance as an "Abstract Ballet," and on his manuscript synopsis he listed it as being 45 minutes, 26 seconds long. The program for the Bowl evening listed the ballet as being "in One Act and Four Moods": first mood—"Earth"; second mood—"Air"; third mood—"Water"; and fourth mood—"Fire." This ballet gives the impression that Oukrainsky might have been trying to develop a new artistic direction. The ballet had no intermission, the music of Rimsky-Korsakoff continued during the change of scenes, and there was no scenery. In his program notes Oukrainsky said that he wanted "to create an atmosphere with the least theatrical illusion and bringing purposely simplification." In 1927 he had also created a ballet called *Les Eléments*, but his comments in the 1935 program notes indicate a different direction: "The symbolic designs of the four elements will be done by the theme of the music, the action of the dancers and the appropriate lighting effects. There are no conventional costumes, but the dancers for each scene will carry the design of the symbol of the element which they portray. There is no story, but it is a ballet of moods and abstract."

While the ballet is abstract, it still carries the romanticism of Oukrainsky's other work. This is not a ballet about elements that fight with one another, or that ultimately destroy, or that man has to fight and conquer. This is a ballet about a world in which harmony is rather easily achieved, expected, and inevitable. Its harmony is warm, sensual, and beautiful. Oukrainsky described the first scene in the program notes: "The first scene represents "Earth," the awakening of the Earth under the warm rays of the Sun, the flowers the product of the Earth, the different colors of the natural, the line, the attraction of the masculine for the feminine element, the entire scene is portrayed like a pastoral spring day, a mystic marriage of a shepherd to a beautiful maid." Having established the mood of "a pastoral spring day" in the first scene, the second scene brings slightly more violent action. It is choreographed "to suggest the 'Air.'" The "Spring of the Air" breaks branches of trees and uproots a beautiful rose, which is finally "broken and carried away." The third scene is gentle and playful, portraying "Water": swimming, waves on the shore, "the legend of the mermaids vamping an imaginary vessel," and fountain sprays. The fourth scene, although it starts with destruction, ends in harmony. The notes for the dance explained this: "The fourth scene is symbolized by the "Fire," the starting of a small fire, gradually spreading, the beginning of the flame and the enjoyment of the spirit of the fire and its destruction, the lost control of the fire, and finally the decline and the dying out of the last flame."

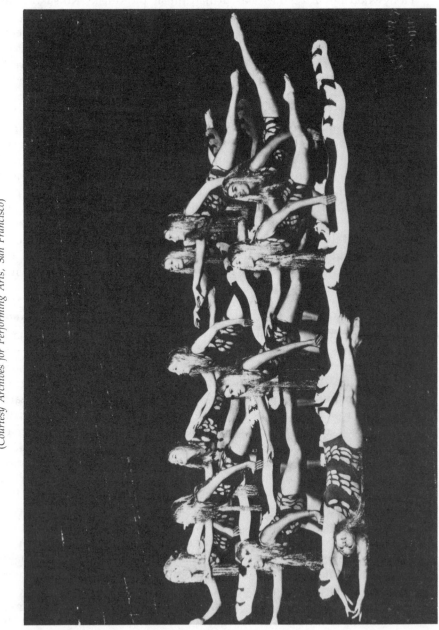

"The Water" Scene from Ballet *Les Eléments*, 1935
Hollywood Bowl ballet choreographed by Oukrainsky.
(*Courtesy Archives for Performing Arts, San Francisco*)

On 16 July 1936 at the Hollywood Bowl Oukrainsky repeated two dances he had created earlier in his career: *The Captive Princess*, with music by Halévy, first created in Chicago in 1926, and *Gypsy Suite*, which he said in the program notes was created for Mary Garden and the Chicago Grand Opera's *Carmen* (ca. 1919). The program notes explained that *The Captive Princess* was "done in the Russian medieval style, arranged as a puppet show done by a group of court jesters. Of the principal characters, only the jesters represent mortals. They present their dolls in a fairy tale romance of love's great victory over great obstacles." The characters listed on the program were: jesters, a knight, soldiers, a princess, a giant, ladies in waiting, a horse, small jesters, country girls, and buffoons.

In 1936, 1937, and 1938 Oukrainsky was involved in several productions at the Hollywood Bowl. On 27 August 1936 he created the incidental dances for the opera *Pagliacci*; on 29 July 1937 he was the choreographer for *Il Trovatore*. On 12 August of the same year he created the dances for *The Bartered Bride*. On 26 July 1938 he presented the "Dance of the Hours" ballet from *La Gioconda*; on 30 August he arranged the incidental dances for the opera *Martha*. In 1937 he worked as ballet master for the San Francisco Opera Association and presented his company at the Wilshire Ebell Theatre.

Serge Oukrainsky wrote his unpublished autobiography around 1940, and he closed it with: "The way things turned out, I had no regrets to have chosen to give much of my time to Hollywood."[22] In Los Angeles he was active as a teacher and choreographer through the 1950s, although the period of his greatest success in the city was probably from 1927 through the mid-1940s. The list of accomplishments garnered by Serge Oukrainsky during his active career warrants a more complete study. This chapter is meant to record and analyze his activities during an important and fruitful part of his life, when he established his home base in Los Angeles. It is difficult to assess only a portion of such a long career, and in conclusion there must be an attempt to look at his accomplishments as a totality, although there has not been a complete analysis of the period prior to his Los Angeles arrival in 1927.

Ann Barzel, in a *Dance Magazine* of 1979, wrote an article called "Chicago's 'Two Russians': Andreas Pavley and Serge Oukrainsky." She noted that these two Russians were looked upon by many as "mere upstarts. They had not been chosen to be trained on Theatre Street nor had they danced in the Maryinsky."[23] The article, which does not discuss Oukrainsky's work in Los Angeles, details Barzel's realization of Oukrainsky and Pavley's importance. She called the 1922 Pavley-Oukrainsky Ballet performances in Chicago, New York, Sioux

Serge Oukrainsky in *Gypsy Camp*, Hollywood Bowl, 1936
(Courtesy Archives for Performing Arts, San Francisco)

Falls, Philadelphia, St. Louis, Mexico City, and other places the performances of "the first American ballet company." She also wrote in her
article: "Scores of dancers and hundreds of dance teachers worked and
studied with the two artists, and, if one searched the lineage of today's
dance explosion, dancers of the Pavley-Oukrainsky influence can still
be discovered."[24] Barzel recalled "memories of the opulent Pavley-
Oukrainsky opera ballets . . . and I was not willing to credit these
memories to a childhood case of discrimination."[25]

There is a list in Oukrainsky's unpublished autobiography of
people who studied with him in Chicago and Los Angeles. It is a long,
impressive one and includes Muriel Abbott, Edward Caton, Florence
Chappel, Eleanore Flaige,[26] Paul Godkin, Barbara Perry, James Starbuck, Iva Kitchell, Lisan Kay, Edris Milar, and Edna L. McRae. Oukrainsky lists 20 dances in the repertory of his company and 47 operatic
ballets.

Serge Oukrainsky was a major force in the early development of
American dance. When he came to Los Angeles he embarked on a
period of important activity, drawing on his experience in Chicago as
teacher and choreographer. He made some attempts at developing
new ideas and spent a good deal of time restaging older works, bringing them to a new generation of eager young artists. His teaching, with
its combination of formal discipline in ballet and free movement in
plastique work, was a new combination for young and sometimes
older dancers in Los Angeles.

It is unfortunate that Oukrainsky's work remained rooted in a
turn-of-the-century approach, and he blatantly rejected disturbing aspects of contemporary society. By the early 1950s his choreography
was dated, and he no longer had the same energy in his teaching. His
last years in Los Angeles were sad, as he could no longer capture the
imagination of young dancers and he could not hold a company together. Yet during the time of his greatest strength in Los Angeles, he
brought sensitivity and theatrical genius to audiences and students,
and the city provided him with a supportive environment.

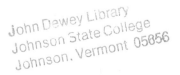

5

Adolph Bolm (1885–1951): Diaghilev and After

Adolph Bolm[1] was the third dancer of Russian Imperial heritage to come to Los Angeles and eventually settle there. Born in St. Petersburg, he grew up in a family devoted to the arts. His father was first violinist of the Imperial Theatre, and many dancers, musicians, and writers came to his home. At the age of nine, Bolm entered the Imperial School of the Maryinsky Theatre and graduated in 1904. As the recipient of first honors, along with Alexandra Baldina (Kosloff's wife), the two were chosen to dance at the Maryinsky Theatre between the acts of a company ballet program.

From a very early age Bolm was exposed to the world of literature, music, and art through discussions that took place in his home. At the Maryinsky School he pursued these interests winning first honors in music, painting, and literature. Following graduation and acceptance into the ballet company, Bolm requested and received permission to go on a study tour of Europe, to visit museums, and attend performances at various theaters. Noting the lack of strong ballet in the various countries he visited after graduation, the seed was planted for the idea of taking a group of Russian dancers on tour, a most unusual project at that time.

In 1908 Bolm was given permission to take a troupe to Helsingfors, Stockholm, Copenhagen, and Prague during summer vacation. Anna Pavlova was the star of this group. Bolm was her partner, and there were six other young artists, including Vera Karalli from the Bolshoi Theatre. The tour was a great success, and Bolm was beginning to make a name for himself. As a result, in August 1908 he was asked to partner Lydia Kyasht at London's Empire Theatre. They both received rave reviews and were offered three-year contracts, which Kyasht accepted and Bolm rejected. He decided to return to the Maryinsky Theatre.

Adolph Bolm, ca. 1930
(*Courtesy Hollywood Bowl Museum Archives*)

In 1909 Bolm once again went with Pavlova and a small group of dancers to perform in Europe. While fulfilling an engagement in Berlin, they received a request from Serge Diaghilev. He wanted Bolm and the group back in Russia, as he was planning the first performance of a large Russian company outside their own country. And so, on 19 May 1909 Bolm and Pavlova were among the great Russian dancers to launch the activities of the Ballets Russes in Paris. When Diaghilev was planning the second season in 1910, he asked Bolm to become maître de ballet as well as principal dancer. Bolm accepted and resigned from the Imperial Ballet of the Maryinsky Theatre.

Adolph Bolm was to become a very significant member of the Ballets Russes—as premier danseur, maître de ballet, and choreographer. He stayed with the company until 1917, at which point he left to initiate an independent career in America. He first made a mark in the Ballets Russes as a performer, and in 1909 audiences were stunned by his performance in the "Polovtsian Dances" from *Prince Igor* (music by Alexander Borodin, choreography by Michel Fokine). Tamara Karsavina in the July 1951 *Dancing Times* reminisced about Adolph Bolm after his death. Of his first appearance in Paris she commented: "His brilliant dancing as the Chief Warrior in *Prince Igor*, a role he created, electrified Western Europe and did much to rehabilitate the male dancer with the general public." Karsavina also noted that his performance in this dance "created a real furor in Paris. That is the only word to describe something that was more than a mere success, something that was in the nature of a prodigy of vigour, temperament and barbaric grandeur."

Bolm developed great strengths as a character dancer and mime and became identified with several important roles in the Ballets Russes repertory: Pierrot in *Carnaval*, the Prince in *Thamar*, the Moor in *Petrouchka*, the slave lover of Zobeide in *Schéhérazade*, the Egyptian youth Amoun in *Cléopâtre*, and Prince Ivan in *The Firebird*. But Bolm was never satisfied with performance as his only creative outlet. His entire career was marked by the need to produce and choreograph as well as perform. He began small choreographic ventures after his debut at the Imperial Theatre in St. Petersburg, staging small ballets for various members of the aristocracy when they had entertainments. In 1912 he began creating works with members of the Ballets Russes and in that year did the dances for Rameau's opera *Les Fêtes d'Hebe*. In 1913 he created the Persian dances for Mussorgsky's *Khovantchina*, in 1914 dances for Rimsky-Korsakoff's *Une Nuit de Mai*. In 1915 he created choreography for Rimsky-Korsakoff's *Sadko*, which he was to develop and expand in 1916.

The Ballets Russes presented a gala performance in London five days before World War I broke out, in the summer of 1914. Diaghilev gave the company a summer vacation with the intention of bringing them together in Berlin during October for performances. The circumstances of the war changed the situation of the company, and Adolph Bolm was to play a major role in bringing the Ballets Russes back to life. After the London season, Fokine, Karsavina, and Grigoriev returned to Russia. Fokine and Grigoriev could not get permission to leave the Imperial Theatre, and Karsavina became pregnant. Nijinsky by that time was no longer part of the company, as he had resigned when he married Romola. Nijinsky and his wife had traveled to Budapest, where they missed the diplomatic train for Russia. They found themselves interned as enemy aliens, confined under house arrest in her mother's home.

By 1915 Diaghilev had been lent the Villa Belle Rive near Lausanne, Switzerland. He was trying to bring the company back together, but many were unable to join him in Switzerland because of the war. There was no money, there were no engagements in Europe, and Diaghilev was anxious to have a North American tour. When this tour was offered to the company in 1915 under the leadership of Otto Kahn, chairman of the Metropolitan Opera House, the company was in shambles. Diaghilev, along with Leon Bakst and Igor Stravinsky, decided that Adolph Bolm was the only one who could remember the repertory, bring in new people and train them, and also command the respect of the older members of the group.

Bolm had spent the early months of the war helping the Red Cross in Biarritz, carrying the wounded from the railroad station to the hospital. He became ill and was sent to Switzerland to recuperate, and it was there that he was convinced to put the Ballets Russes in shape for an American tour. Merle Armitage, who at that time was on the staff of the Metropolitan Opera, and who later became a great impresario, wrote about Bolm's role in his book *Dance Memoranda*. "The fact that America saw the Diaghilev Ballet with its character unimpaired, is largely due to the prodigious efforts of Bolm."[2] The writer Hamilton Easter Field in *Arts and Decoration* wrote: "Adolph Bolm made it possible for us to have the new Russian ballet in America, much as it had been produced in Europe, although the dancers were not always the same."[3]

Adolph Bolm revived, cast, and rehearsed the complete repertory of the Ballets Russes during an intensive three-month period in Lausanne. R. C. Brownell, in Europe and reporting for *Musical America*, wrote of the enormous task Bolm had in bringing together artists who had been apart for almost a year and a half.

The work is enormous, as not only the traditions of the Classical (Italian) School are required, but also the intense expression of the entire corps de ballet in pantomime, characteristic of the Russian School. To obtain this end each dancer has to be encouraged and imbued with an individual temperament, followed by plastic grouping, moulding the whole into one mass of palpitating beauty. Bolm's is a master mind. His memory, patience and physical endurance are without limit. I have seen him repeat a step or gesture time and again for a weary dancer always with the same enthusiasm and gentleness causing him to be idolized by all his troops. . . . We have to pay homage to such energy and congratulate Bolm this artist; so remarkably talented, who directed with knowledge, tact and kindness, thus obtaining perfect authority over his entire troops.[4]

The Ballets Russes was seen for the first time in the United States during an engagement at the Century Theatre in New York from 17 to 29 January 1916. This was followed by a tour of 16 cities from 31 January to 29 March and an engagement at the Metropolitan Opera House from 3 to 29 April. The public was not aware of Bolm's role as producer, director, and organizer; they saw him mainly as a performer. He was often singled out for the vibrancy and strength of his dancing. Typical of the reviews was one dated 2 March in the *Minneapolis Journal* that called Bolm a "pantomimic marvel as well as a dancer of extraordinary rhythm. . . . 'Le Prince Igor' gave Adolf Bolm an opportunity for virile dancing of a type that seems to need the steppes for its frenzy."[5]

In its second American tour the Ballets Russes featured Adolph Bolm as a choreographer, in a season that ran from 16 to 28 October 1916 at the Metropolitan and from 30 October 1916 to 24 February 1917 throughout the United States. Bolm's ballet *Sadko* was featured as an American premiere along with Nijinsky's *Til Eulenspiegel*. Nijinsky rejoined the company in April 1916 and had created this ballet for the America tour.

Frederick H. Martens, writing for *Musical America*, felt that Bolm's ballet *Sadko* was "an extremely poetic and musical ballet."[6] Based on a Russian fairy tale, it was the story of a wandering singer from earthly regions. He wins Volkhowa, the daughter of the Czar of the Seas, and holds the Czar and the entire submarine court in spell by virtue of the power of his music. On 25 November 1916 an unnamed writer for the *Philadelphia Public Ledger* headlined a review "Russian Ballet Seen in 'Sadko': New Submarine Dance-Story Is a Rare Delight to the Eye." The reviewer went on: "The picture offered was one of rare beauty, with personified goldfish, seaherbes, currents, seahorses and seaflowers all gorgeously arrayed and attuned in their motions to the aquatic sinuosity of the lovely accompanying music by Rimsky-Korsakow."[7]

American reviewers and audiences were beginning to place Bolm in a broader context, as a choreographer as well as performer. Frederick H. Martens concluded his comments in *Musical America* with these thoughts: "In all that he says it is evident that Adolf Bolm is the artist by conviction, that his art is more than a mere professional issue with him, that he believes in it and its artistic ideas. And this no doubt explains his great and abiding success in his chosen field. His terpsichorean technique is informed with intelligence, his pantomime on true dramatic values, music and poetry are to him real and living elements of his art life."[8] In an unsigned article on 13 November 1916 *Musical America* reported on Bolm as performer and choreographer: "At present Boston likes Bolm better than it likes Nijinsky . . . he is as Egyptian as Verdi's "Aida"; he burns with Puccini passion; his feet are robust tenor. His *Sadko* equisitely conceived and exquisitely mimed, was one of the notable ballets of the week."[9]

It was during the second Ballets Russes tour that Bolm was injured. While recuperating he decided not to rejoin the company but instead to seek his own artistic pathways in America. From 1917 through his death in Los Angeles in 1951, he became known as entrepreneur, choreographer, performer, and teacher. He created his own company, for which he functioned as producer, manager, and ballet master. He also became known for his restagings of Fokine's ballets as well as for his role as first ballet master for American Ballet Theatre.

Adolph Bolm played a role in the development of ballet in New York, Chicago, San Francisco, and Los Angeles. His work in Chicago is probably the most completely documented. This is because Ruth Page, who studied and worked with him during the 1920s, has written extensively of her experiences as student and ballerina with Bolm. John Martin in his biography of Ruth Page has also written of Bolm's work in Chicago. There has been some documentation in various articles of his work in the other cities, but there has been very little about his career in Los Angeles. John Dougherty, in the January, February , and March 1963 issues of *Dance Magazine*, gives a good overview of Bolm's varied career.

This chapter's main focus is on Bolm's work in Los Angeles, but it is necessary to review highlights of his career to place the West coast work in perspective. It is also necessary to pose some questions regarding Bolm's work and career from 1917 through 1951. What was his greatest influence—as teacher, choreographer, performer, or as some combination of both? Did each city that he worked in influence his development in a particular way? Was his influence mainly as the bearer of some of the best of the new and old in the Russian ballet traditions? Did he integrate the American experience into his work? How important is his career in Los Angeles in the broad context of his work in America?

Adolph Bolm's first two years in America show him trying many things—from starting a company, to starring in a Broadway spectacle, to restaging a Fokine ballet, to producing a live spectacle in a movie house prior to the film showing (what came to be known as a movie prologue). His very first venture was the establishment of a small company, Adolph Bolm's Ballets-Intime. Reports in the newspapers indicated that he planned this group as the core for a permanent organization in America that would be in the nature of a "Petit Ballet Russe."

The first Ballets-Intime (the spelling later changed) was somewhat short-lived, and it is the one that is least documented. Bolm realized he needed important patrons to support him. His first performance on 5 August 1917 took place at the New Nixon Theatre in Atlantic City under the auspices of "The American Ambulance in Russia." The list of those involved as sponsors was impressive. Hamilton Fish, Jr. was the chairman and among those on the executive committee were: Nicholas Murray Butler, Otto H. Kahn, Adolph Lewisohn, William Forbes Morgan, Jr., Theodore Roosevelt, Jr., and Oscar S. Straus. Patronesses for the event included: Madames Perry Belmont, Benjamin Guiness, W. K. Vanderbilt, Harry Payne Whitney. The Atlantic City performance was followed by another in Washington, D.C., and a two-week engagement at the Booth Theatre in New York started 20 August. The company then disbanded, regrouping with different personnel in 1919. It is unclear whether Bolm disbanded the company because of other job offers, because of mixed reviews, or because the anticipated society backing for further performances did not materialize. The organization, personnel, and programs for Bolm's first company are important for the information they provide about directions he was attempting to pursue.

Adolf Bolm's Ballets-Intime in 1917 was a collection of individual artists performing their own work. The major artists were: Roshanara performing East Indian dances; Ratan Devi singing Indian melodies; Michio Itow (he later dropped the "w") described on the program as interpreting "historic, poetic and legendary Japanese dances familiar in the art centres of three continents." Three other featured artists were a young ballet dancer, Mary Eaton; Tulle Lindahl (then Ito's wife and described in different publicity as Danish or Dutch); and Rita Zalmani, who had been with Pavlova. A 23 August 1917 review (Bolm Clipping File, Dance Collection) listed additional dancers for a Booth Theatre performance: Mary Palay, Janka Mieczkowska, Marshall Hall, and Alexander Umansky. Designs for costumes and sets were by Willy Pogany, Livingston Platt, and John Wenger, and a small orchestra was directed by Marcel Hansotte.

The program was mixed. Either Bolm felt he had to put something together quickly to establish himself as soon as possible, or the mixture was representative of his own search for identity. The question will be, in terms of Bolm as a choreographer and teacher, whether he successfully did define his own identity during his work in America. Bolm created one new piece for Ballets-Intime: *Danse Macabre* to the music of Camille Saint-Saëns. The dance was in contrast to the other solo he performed, *Assyrian Dance,* and the short piece he created for Mary Eaton, *Butterfly* (to Mussorgsky's music).

On 4 August 1917 Harry Birnbaum, the reporter for *Musical America,* watched a rehearsal and reported that *Assyrian Dance* was "one of the wildest, most savage dances that we have ever seen."[10] This same reporter was very impressed with *Danse Macabre,* which was highlighted by all the other reviewers. One reviewer commented that "it has the uncanny quality of a Poe fantasy and likewise the fascination."[11] The story was relatively simple: Death interrupts the romantic idyll of two lovers and finally conquers the young woman of the pair. *Danse Macabre* had none of the Oriental background and flavor that had characterized much of the work of the Ballets Russes and of Bolm, and it had a far simpler story, with a new ambiance. In 1922 Bolm made a film using the choreography for *Danse Macabre,* with Ruth Page as female lead, Dudley Murphy, director, lighting by Francis Bruguiere, and scenery and costumes by Nat Eastman. The movie was shown in March 1922 at the Rialto in New York, along with a German Paramount feature, *The Mysteries of India.*

In the various programs given by Ballets-Intime in 1917, Bolm was doing some experimenting. Programs always included: Roshanara's *Hindu Fantasy, Snake Dance,* and *Ceylon Harvest* as well as Ito's *Wine Dance* and *Fox Dance.* Bolm introduced on several of the programs condensed versions of *Carnaval* and *Prince Igor.* Harry Birnbaum's article in *Musical America* quoted Bolm as saying:

> Americans have a remarkable sense of rhythm and they are good dancers. But the ballet is not encouraged in America. In Russia the schools are supported by the government. The Americans are in a hurry to earn money. They have no time to spend in serious study, or they cannot afford the time. The trouble with art in America is that the artists permit themselves to be led by the people. That is wrong. The artist must educate his public, not cater to its desires.[12]

Perhaps Bolm was trying to decide which path he personally should take. In September 1917 he signed a lucrative contract with Dillingham and Ziegfeld. His job was to stage dances for *Miss 1917* at the Century Theatre. The cast included Lew Fields, Irene Castle, George White, Marion Davies, Ann Pennington, Bessie McCoy Davis, Van and

Schenck, and others. The rehearsal pianist was George Gershwin, then 19. Bolm's contributions were a ballet called *Falling Leaves* (music by Victor Herbert), which included young dancer Ruth Page, and a series of tableaux on a revolving stage designed by Josef Urban.

In 1918 Bolm was hired by the Metropolitan to stage Rimsky-Korsakoff's *Le Coq d'Or*, after the original by Fokine. The years 1919 to 1922 were busy for Bolm. In 1919 he was hired by the Rivoli Theatre to stage a live dance sequence prior to the showing of the movie. Called *Spanish Choreographic Episode*, with music by Albeniz, one newspaper article reported it to be a "dance pantomime of poetic conception."[13] In that year he also staged *Petrouchka* for the Metropolitan and was involved in the first of a series of associations with the Chicago Opera—the choreography for John Alden Carpenter's *The Birthday of the Infanta*, with costumes and designs by Robert Edmond Jones. In 1920 Bolm reactivated Ballet Intime, although by this time it was a different company with a new spelling and repertory. They performed in London (1920), Los Angeles (1920–21), New York, Philadelphia, Indianapolis, and many other cities. The 1920–21 tour was made with George Barrère, a flutist with the New York Symphony Orchestra who had organized his own Little Symphony. In February and March there were two concerts in Carnegie Hall: one part of the Young People Series and the other for a regular concert audience.

The 1920 reviews of Ballet Intime showed Bolm trying to venture into new territory. One solo for Bolm, where he appeared as a Roman warrior to Rachmaninoff's *G-Minor Prelude*, was a holdover from his previous work. Otherwise, he seemed to be trying different music and ideas. New dances on the program were: *Chopin Etude, Mazurka, Humoresque* (music by Tchaikovsky), *Dream of Love, The White Peacock* (music by Charles Griffes), and *Pavane* (music by Fauré). Performers as listed in reviews were Ruth Page, Marshall Hall, Margit Leeras, Alexander Oumansky, Caird Leslie, Francis Veath, and Bolm.

In 1923 Bolm moved his base of operations to Chicago when he was appointed ballet master of the newly reorganized Chicago Civic Opera. He began teaching and established a studio at 624 South Michigan Boulevard. Bolm had done some teaching in New York, and in 1921, from 11 July through 6 August, in a special summer session at the Cornish School in Seattle, he had done his first teaching outside New York. In Chicago in 1923 Bolm opened his studio with two summer sessions—18 June to 14 July, and 16 July to 11 August. The syllabus and faculty provided a wide range of courses. Bolm taught ballet and toe technique, dance composition and dances, pantomime, and character and was assisted in these by Konstantin Kobeleff and Alexandre Maximowa. Margaret Heaton taught Dalcroze eurythmics,

Anna Neacy taught stage costuming, and Charlotte Foss taught folk dancing. The summer courses were designed mostly for teachers, and in the fall Bolm expanded the program to include classes for children and adults in ballet, character dancing and pantomime, and classes in hygienic and aesthetic body culture (Mensendieck System).

Chicago was Bolm's primary home base until he came to Los Angeles in 1930. In 1924 he was appointed artistic director and choreographer of a new organization, Chicago Allied Arts, Inc. Devoted to the contemporary arts, it had the backing of Frederick Stock, Mrs. Rockefeller McCormick, George Peabody, John Alden Carpenter, the composer, and other well-placed individuals in Chicago. Eric DeLamarter was musical director; Nicolas Remisoff was designer. The Chicago Allied Arts sponsored three series a year of three performances each. The organization was seen as one that supported activity that was somewhat ahead of its time.

During the years of his association with Chicago Allied Arts, from 1924 to 1927, Bolm trained and developed a high-quality, small ballet company and created many new ballets. Among these were: *Elopement* (Mozart), *Le Foyer de la Danse* (Chabrier), *The Rivals* (Eichhaim), *El Amor Brujo* (de Falla), *Little Circus* (Offenbach), *Parnassus au Montmarte* (Satie), *Pierrot Lunaire* (Schoenberg), and *Tragedy of the Cello* (Tansman). John Martin in his biography of Ruth Page had mixed feelings about Bolm's choreography, although he later liked his work in Los Angeles. He said of the Chicago period: "The truth was . . . that though Bolm himself produced some unconventional things, sponsored some unusual artists and used a great deal of modern music, he was far from being avant-garde; if he was even 'modern,' it was in the well established 'standard' sense of Fokine with the Imperial Ballet rather than in the radical kick-over-the-traces style of the contemporary Diaghileff."[14] Martin in another section of his book on Page said about Bolm: "He never proved to be an outstanding choreographer on his own, but he was excellent at reproducing Fokine's and other people's ballets."[15] It seems as if Martin was judging Bolm in a way that had nothing to do with the artist's training and background. The question is not whether Bolm was an avant-garde choreographer, but whether he was a good choreographer within the goals he set for himself. There are many other issues: How did he utilize his background and training? Was he capable of musicality, visual imagery, and inventiveness within his training and knowledge? Given the state of American ballet in the 1920s and 1930s, what contribution did he make? What role did he play in training American audiences and dancers and in developing standards?

On 27 March 1921 the New York League of Composers sponsored the Adolph Bolm Ballet in their New York debut at the Jolson Theatre. Olin Downes wrote a review in which he recognized the valuable heritage that Bolm brought to his work: "Bolm and his associates showed their admirable and enterprising art, and their cultivation of a form bequeathed to this country by the original Ballet Russe, which merits wiser and more intensive cultivation than it has received hereabouts."[16] He noted that Bolm's choreography was "well-devised" and that "there was an excellent ensemble, nor was Mr. Bolm the only dancer who merited the enthusiastic applause." A preperformance article about the New York debut in the 13 February 1921 issue of the *New York Telegraph* gave some background on Bolm.

> For several years he has been devoting himself to the organization of a ballet corps of American dancers, training them in a school, and giving brilliant performances of new works. He has been constantly on the search in Europe and America for music by contemporary musicians which would lend itself to choreographic treatment, and in Chicago has produced with amazing success the results of his co-operation with these living musicians and painters.

In 1928 Bolm was given a great honor with a commission by art patron Elizabeth Sprague Coolidge to choreograph a Stravinsky premiere. *Apollon Musagète,* performed 27 April 1928, was the first performance of ballet at the Library of Congress in Washington, D.C., and predates the Balanchine-Stravinsky collaboration. Shortly after the Library of Congress venture Bolm arrived in Los Angeles. It is quite likely that Bolm was looking for new vistas to explore, and he felt Hollywood, the movies, and Los Angeles held great promise for the arts. He taught at Norma Gould's studio from 3 March through 29 March 1930; in the school's brochure this was announced as his "first teaching engagement in Los Angeles." In May 1931 *Theatre Arts Monthly* reported that he was at work on a movie, *The Mad Genius.*

> Adolph Bolm is at work in the First National Studios in Hollywood as technical director, advisor and ballet master of a film for John Barrymore dealing with the life of a Russian ballet impresario. Since the film calls for four ballet scenes and a dress rehearsal, Mr. Bolm will have full opportunity to test his skills as a choreographer for the screen. Grot has designed the settings and Mosolow, one of the most modern of Russian composers, has created the score. So while Hollywood producers and public are still, as one feature writer says, "singing dirges over dancing" as far as the talking picture is concerned, a new opportunity to test the art of the dance in this new field is progressing towards completion.[17]

The ballet that Bolm conceived for the movie was never used in its entirety. A few fragments, set to an unrelated score, were included in

Costume Design for Ballet *The Spirit of the Factory*, 1931
Choreography by Bolm, costumes by Robert Lee Eskridge.
(*Courtesy Archives for Performing Arts, San Francisco*)

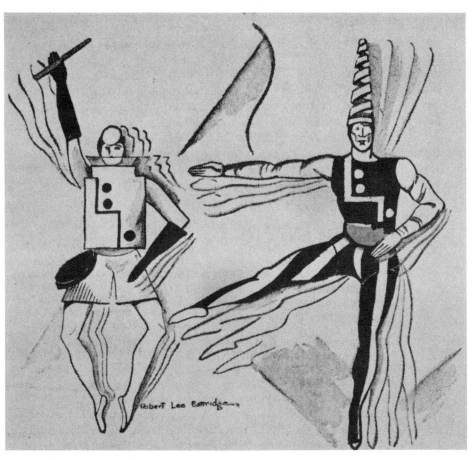

Costume Designs for Ballet *The Spirit of the Factory*, 1931
(*Courtesy Archives for Performing Arts, San Francisco*)

the film, but Warner Brothers did not want to negotiate for the rights to the Mosolov music that Bolm had chosen. The management of the Hollywood Bowl announced in April 1931 that they had secured Adolph Bolm's services for an evening of dance to be presented that summer. The performance was scheduled for 28 July, and due to the international prestige of the choreographer, there were preperformance reports and articles in the newspapers. Bolm was sought after for interviews, and great excitement was generated. Possibly in response to the recognition he was getting, possibly in response to the challenge of the large open-air theater, and possibly in response to a feeling of freedom and creative potential he associated with Los Angeles, Bolm produced a ballet, *The Spirit of the Factory*, that marked a coalescing of his creative energies. To this work he brought the technical skill and craft he had learned, combined with a new sense of invention.

The *Los Angeles Times* of 26 July published a preperformance article that gave the reader information about Bolm's intentions. The article was written as if it were based on an interview with Bolm but never actually stated that an interview had been conducted. The writer sought to understand Bolm's work in greater depth and to prepare the audience.

> The dance molded upon an architectural basis, its foundation and fundamentals set firmly upon music—the finished product dancing, if you will, but in all events a composition in unified movement. This is the manner in which the ballets, to be presented Thursday evening, are described by their creator, Adolph Bolm. They are to be patterns in movement, definite designs molded about the threads of melody woven by such composers as Debussy, Mosoloff, Rimsky-Korsakoff, and Chopin. . . . In *Clouds* and *The Factory* . . . Bolm has sought a uniqueness in presentation. He has made a definite study of the Hollywood Bowl from the audience standpoint. He has worked out his patterns to appear at advantage from every angle.

The first ballet to be presented on the evening of 28 July was *Les Nuages*, which Bolm had created to music by Claude Debussy. The program lists the cast as follows: "Celestial Stars"—Elise Reiman, Edith Jane, Evelyn Wenger, Helen Doty, and Philip Hilber; "Group of Clouds"—60 dancers; and "Last Cloud"—Dorothy Wagner. Although Arthur Rodzinski was announced as the conductor for the evening, the program listed Henry Svedrofsky as the conductor for the ballets. A *Los Angeles Times* article of 26 July had a description of this ballet.

> Suited particularly to this out-of-doors theatre, and offering an atmospheric bit which will in all probability be remembered, is the ballet, *Clouds*, danced to the music of Debussy . . . 6 will appear as individual figures, the others are completely covered by more than 1,000 yards of veiling, shading in color from foggy grays to

brilliant orange. Representing the clouds at sunset, the dancers drift in their rhythmic patterns about the stage, finally disappearing, leaving but one tragic little cloud who has strayed away from the rest, but who scurries away when she discovers she has been left alone. Hiding behind the clouds, but emerging in full brilliance when the last bit of chiffon has drifted away, are five stars and as a final climax, the moon.

The other ballet that Adolph Bolm created for the Bowl evening on 28 July was to become one of his most famous works, repeated by popular request twice more at the Bowl. It was chosen for the first performance of the San Francisco Operatic and Ballet School on 2 June 1933 at the War Memorial Opera House and was repeated for the 1940 season of Ballet Theatre. This often-repeated ballet has undergone an "identity crisis" in the dance literature. On the original program the dance was titled *The Spirit of the Factory*. The program notes gave the title of the music by Alexandre Mosolov as *Factory* and explained that the music had been called *Steel Foundry* when it was premiered in Liège in the summer of 1930. When the dance was repeated on 7 August 1931, it was also called *The Spirit of the Factory* on the program.

Confusion has probably set in due to the different titles used when the ballet was presented for the third time on 12 August 1932. The announcement of the forthcoming ballet in the previous week's program read: "The Hollywood Bowl Association, Inc., presents Adolph Bolm's spectacular ballet, 'The Spirit of the Factory.'" The program note for the 12 August evening read somewhat differently: "Tone Pictures: 'The Iron Foundry' (The Spirit of the Factory). Music of the Machines." The part of the program that listed the cast read as follows: "Adolph Bolm presents for the third time by popular request the Ballet, 'Iron Foundry,' music by A. Mosolov." To further compound the confusion, Cyril W. Beaumont's *Complete Book of Ballets*, published in 1941, listed the ballet as *Iron Foundry*, with the first production given as "Hollywood Bowl, California, August, 1932." *The Dance Encyclopedia* by Anatole Chujoy and P. W. Manchester listed the title as *Ballet Mécanique* to music of Mosolov, with a date of 1932 for the choreography. Merle Armitage in *Dance Memoranda* listed the ballet as *Le Ballet Mécanique*. John Dougherty in his three-part article on Bolm in *Dance Magazine* also called the work *Le Ballet Mécanique* and said that it was given three performances in 1931.[18]

The title Bolm gave the dance for the premiere, *The Spirit of the Factory*, will be used in this discussion. The first performance of this ballet made the reviewers sit up and take note. The ballet occasioned a very positive response and was commented on in great depth in reviews the next day. Jan Murrill in the *Los Angeles California Record* felt that it was "one of the most spectacular dances I have ever seen. . . . No ballet number ever given in the Bowl has excited so much comment." The *B'nai B'rith Messenger* called the ballet "spectacular," and Richard Drake Saunders in the *Hollywood Citizen News* said that the performance was "the outstanding choreographic number that has yet been presented in the Hollywood Bowl."[19]

The title, *The Spirit of the Factory*, was very descriptive of Bolm's choreography. He was interested in capturing the spirit of mechanization that he felt was becoming a dominant feature of our era. When Bolm developed the idea for his presentation at the Bowl he used 60 dancers. The dancers were in formations that would enable them to execute machinelike movements and to simulate gears, pistons, and so on. Cyril W. Beaumont in *The Complete Book of Ballets* describes the action.

> The ballet opens with a blast on a steam siren which is the signal for the dancers representing various units of machinery to begin to move. The immense stage reflects a red furnace-like glare into which the dancers, clad in close-fitting metallized fabrics, make their way in various groups, their movements exactly synchronized with the music. Enter the Dynamo, a danseuse in gleaming silver and cellophane, whose whirling causes her pleated silver skirt to spread out and form a wheel. Her dance, which is rapid and graceful, and full of spinning motions, represents the magic of electricity. She is followed by another Dynamo, a male dancer dressed in black, scored with silver spirals and bound at the waist with a red sash. His dance is expressive of the might of electricity. The groups continually change in accordance with the pounding rhythm of the music, each group a complete unit in itself, yet all contributing to present a tremendous spectacle of concerted rhythm.[20]

Pictures of *The Spirit of the Factory* clearly show various aspects of Bolm's inventive ballet—the bold groupings, the expressive torsos, the striking costuming, the use of poles as props, the defined angular movement, the use of head and arms to amplify the concept of a mechanized society. The work provokes thoughts about several of the European movements in art from 1909 to 1924 that were concerned with mechanization and machines in their theater work—the Italian and Russian futurists, the Bauhaus State Workshop, and the Russian constructivists. It is speculative at this point to say there are direct influences on Bolm from some of the European experiments, but with his background in the creative ferment of the Ballets Russes and his experience living and performing in France, Italy, Germany, and England, he was probably in touch with many of the ideas of the European avant-garde.

The Spirit of the Factory was a new experience for the Hollywood Bowl audience, and from the accounts of the performance they loved it. The music was harsh and jarring, the movements were unusual and angular, the message was strong and contemporary. The dances that

Rehearsal of Scene from *The Spirit of the Factory*, Hollywood Bowl, 1931
(*Courtesy Hollywood Bowl Museum Archives*)

had been given previously on the Hollywood Bowl stage were also in their own way seeking to make dance a contemporary expressive art form. Belcher, Oukrainsky, Kosloff, and Gould, along with the others who had given solo performances, such as Ruth St. Denis, Ted Shawn, and Maud Allan, were in their own eyes trying to forge a pathway for American dance. They were often doing this with a good deal of romantic borrowing either from non-Western cultures or from the past. Their dances had a theatricality that rejected the twentieth century with its cacophonies and rapid change. Bolm in *The Spirit of the Factory* sought to come to terms with modern man in a society increasingly dominated by new technology.

The critics were delighted that dance was coming of age, and they applauded Bolm's ballet as an exciting move forward for this art form. Bertha McCord Knisely, *Los Angeles Saturday Night*, 31 July, saw Bolm's venture as a definite step forward for ballet at the Hollywood Bowl.

> Faith in the ballet possibilities at the Bowl was renewed by Adolph Bolm's production. If we are to have ballet, it must be significant. No one wants to see an exhibition of aimless posing in elaborate costumes or "sans drapes." . . . No question that the dance will find its place in modern expression. As in the case of other art forms failure to find acceptance is due to wrong presentations. Humanity is quick to sense truth in art, I believe, given the proper opportunity. In this Bolm creation, the tragedy of modern factory existence is portrayed in vivid symbolism.

John Martin, in a 6 September 1931 article in the *New York Times*, called Bolm's presentation "an important premiere." Martin noted that the dance consisted of "all modern pattern, nowhere the set movements of tradition." He felt that the ballet had managed to make a statement and present an integrated, liberating aesthetic experience: "Such ballet liberates the mind, for it reveals the dance as an art capable of innumerable new combinations of form, colors, movements and an inexhaustible mine of aesthetic pleasure." Bruno David Ussher, 29 July, *Los Angeles Evening Express*, found the ballet a telling picture of our age: "Before the evening was over, another picture of this era, which some are fond of naming the robot age, had been unfolded to the mechanistic pounding, clanging, scraping and hissing of Mosolov's music some 60-odd dancers went through the motions of dehumanized beings which would have elated the . . . makers of Golems." Richard Drake Saunders, 29 July, *Hollywood Citizen News*, did not feel that the harshness of the music or, perhaps, the harshness of the message were any deterrent to the appreciation of the audience, for "they stood and applauded for many moments, in desire for an encore." And John Dougherty, writing in *Dance Magazine*, quoted Rozelle Frey, a dancer and teacher who had come to Hollywood in 1929. She remembered

Bolm's ballet as "terrific" and said "we considered it then to be Bolm's best work."[21]

After creating the 28 July evening for the Hollywood Bowl, Bolm did most of his work on the West coast. He was successfully involved with three other movies, *Affairs of Cellini, Men in Her Life,* and *The Corsican Brothers.* He taught in Los Angeles and worked extensively with the San Francisco Ballet from 1932 through 1937. In 1932 he accepted an invitation from Gaetano Merola to become ballet master of the San Francisco Opera, but he insisted that he be given the opportunity to establish a school and train the dancers. This resulted in the first all-ballet evening given by the San Francisco Opera Association, on 2 June 1933, an event that is credited as the beginning of the San Francisco Ballet as a separate entity. The program consisted of 11 solo and group dances; among the performers were Elise Reiman, Irene Isham, Nico Charisse, Evelyn Wenger, Robert Bell, and Bolm himself.

On 15 August 1936 Bolm staged another concert evening at the Hollywood Bowl. On this program were three dances to the music of Johann Sebastian Bach and a recreation of *Schéhérazade* based on the scenario and ballet of Bakst and Fokine. The three pieces of Bach music were *G-Minor Fugue, Prelude No. 8,* and *Toccata and Fugue in D Minor;* the three respective dance titles were "Danse Noble," "Lament," and "Consecration." The picture in the program of "Lament" shows a grouping of three women, close together, in shapes that go beyond pose. Heads, torsos, and bodies are expressive of an inner feeling of grief, and the costuming is black and stark. John Dougherty in *Dance Magazine* quoted dance photographer Maurice Goldberg's comments to dance critic Irving Deakin after seeing Bolm's works to the music of Bach: "I don't remember when I have had such a thrill at any performance. I was deeply and profoundly moved. I experienced an intense moment of real happiness, which nothing but true art can give."[22]

Adolph Bolm taught for many years in the Los Angeles area, influencing hundreds of students in the development of a fine classical technique and in an appreciation of the poetic and spiritual nature of ballet. Many of his students received a deeper understanding of this art form, and he had a long-lasting effect on the work of those who were to become artists in their own right: James Starbuck, Jocelyn Vollmar, Nancy Johnson, Nana Gollner, Ruth Page, Ann Barzel, Cyd Charisse, Sono Osato, and Thalia Mara, among others.

Irving Deakin in his book *Ballet Profile* wrote that Bolm had been one of the most influential individuals in the development of the American dancer and American dance.[23] John Dougherty quoted a letter he received from Martha Graham in 1962, in which she wrote that

Bolm was "a kind of catalytic agent . . . he had a great dream which far surpassed the traditional in dance . . . he was fearless in experiment and did not protect himself. . . . He was ruthless where mediocrity was concerned . . . an artist who never received the honor that he earned, and should have had."[24]

There needs to be a full-length biography of Adolph Bolm, completely analyzing his work and contributions to the development of American dance. Los Angeles played an important part in his career, and he reciprocated by helping to develop dance and dancers in this city. His movie work provided money. The Hollywood Bowl and the San Francisco Ballet provided creative opportunities. He may not have been able or willing to compete with the young people initiating new ventures in New York, such as George Balanchine and Lucia Chase. But Los Angeles provided an atmosphere with less competition where he could still be involved or that could be a base for other ventures.

In all of his teaching, choreography, and directing Adolph Bolm was not intent on keeping for himself the image of an Imperial Russian, nor was he intent on only reproducing the Diaghilev repertory. For Bolm, the tradition of Imperial Russia and the early reforms within that tradition were a point of departure, not a resting place.

Part Three

New Forms and Experiments:
Michio Ito and Benjamin Zemach

Introduction to Part Three

Michio Ito and Benjamin Zemach both arrived in Los Angeles in 1929. Ito stayed in the city until he was deported in 1941. Zemach taught briefly, leaving in 1930 for Israel and later New York. In 1932 Zemach came back to Los Angeles and was active in dance until returning to New York in 1937, at the request of the director/producer Max Reinhardt. Both Zemach and Ito came to Los Angeles after they had begun their careers as independent concert artists. They initiated many creative ideas in the city and found an environment that afforded them the opportunity to establish studios and develop their choreography.

The work of Michio Ito has been documented in a biography by Helen Caldwell, but she does not focus on the very special contribution he made to American dance during the 1930s. Benjamin Zemach has been neglected in the dance literature, and yet his contributions to American dance are very important. When Ito and Zemach came to Los Angeles, they developed performing groups and taught extensively. They were both commissioned to do major work for the Hollywood Bowl. They received great acclaim and attracted enormous audiences. There is no attempt here to provide complete documentation of the entire life of each of these artists. Caldwell's biography provides complete listings of Ito's solo and group work and an overview of his career. In the case of Zemach, it is hoped that there will be a biography one day and that the analysis to follow will provide a future researcher with substantial material.

There are many interesting commonalities shared by Ito and Zemach. Both drew from their own indigenous traditions not in the mainstream of Western theater and dance in the 1920s and 1930s. Ito had knowledge and experience with the Japanese forms of Noh and Kabuki and was well versed in their vocabulary, style, and spiritual content. Zemach was deeply grounded in Judaic history and ritual and was intent on drawing from the universal spiritual message that he saw in his traditions. In drawing from their indigenous backgrounds,

Ito and Zemach brought to their choreography movements that drew from a vocabulary and language of dance that was new and different for that time. Oriental "interpretations" were common in the teens and twenties, but these were not grounded with the spiritual content and meaning of a specific Eastern culture. The ballets created by Michel Fokine for the Ballets Russes, and the works of Theodore Kosloff and Serge Oukrainsky, when they had Oriental motifs, were usually exotic treatments of somewhat unknown cultures. Ruth St. Denis and Ted Shawn utilized the material of non-Western dance as a way of reaching for alternatives to what they saw as the Western tradition of ballet spectacle. They did not have at their command in-depth knowledge or experience with any particular Eastern culture. They created generalized interpretations that were important explorations in an attempt to reach for a dance expression that was rooted in the universal spirit of ritual and the essential nature of movement in all cultures.

Many of Michio Ito's dances were drawn from Japanese culture and tradition, and he often talked about the inner content of his work. The vocabulary and formal structures utilized in Noh and Kabuki were reflective for Ito of a way of life that was neither exotic nor spectacular but, rather, had a particular sense of quiet balance with the environment. Benjamin Zemach also talked about the inner content of his choreography. He utilized the Judaic traditions of secular folk dance and religious ritual to make a statement about the ecstasy of the human spirit. People survive in spite of oppression and change through a relationship with the supreme forces of the universe and community with others. Both of these artists derived their strength from concentrating on the particular tradition they knew best—and they drew intimately from a form and content that gave them a distinctive vocabulary and method. Neither Ito nor Zemach was interested in developing choreography that was authentically Japanese or Judaic. They integrated a knowledge of Western dance and music with their own special heritage and in the process emerged with new forms.

One of the elements that became an important part of the integration process for both artists was firsthand knowledge and experience with the European experiments in theater, music, dance, and lighting during the first two decades of the twentieth century. Michio Ito studied at the Dalcroze School from 1912 through 1914. It was there that he encountered the work of Adolph Appia and Gordon Craig, both of whom were developing new ideas of music, theater, and movement. Primary to their experiments were the integration of all aspects of a work and the creation of a nonrepresentational, symbolic experience that would develop the inner content of any piece. Benjamin Zemach's work was influenced by his experience with the advanced ideas of the artistic revolutionaries in Russia during the years 1917 through 1924—Constantin Stanislavsky, Yevgeny Vakhtangov, and Vsevelod Meyerhold. Gesture, movement, music, set, and speech were all symbolic expressions of character and inner conflict that developed from the internal elements of any work.

When Ito and Zemach first came to the United States, they concertized in New York and on the East coast and came into contact with such artists as Adolph Bolm, Ruth St. Denis, Ted Shawn, Martha Graham, Doris Humphrey, and Charles Weidman. Ito performed with Bolm and Graham; Zemach performed with Graham, Weidman, and Humphrey. At various times they both performed at the Neighborhood Playhouse on the lower east side. They were well known among the new concert artists in New York and were more intent on performing than on teaching.

When they came to Los Angeles, teaching became an important aspect of their creative life, and it was in this city that they fully developed their teaching ideas and had a chance to work with large groups. Their work at the Hollywood Bowl is well documented and provides insight into their ideas, methods, and impact. Ito never returned to Los Angeles from Japan after his deportation in 1941. Zemach did come back in 1942 and stayed until he moved to Israel in 1971. The later portion of Zemach's career in Los Angeles forms a separate chapter in his life and will not be discussed.

6

Michio Ito (1892–1961):
The Eye of the Mind

Michio Ito grew up in a household with a rich sense of Japanese tradition and an openness to Western ideas. Ito's paternal grandfather was a samurai. His father, Tamekichi, the first Japanese to graduate from the University of California, was an architect and a friend of Frank Lloyd Wright. His mother, Kimiye Iimima, was the daughter of a well-known zoologist. As a youth in Japan Ito had a close association with Noh drama and received training in Kabuki.

In 1911, at the age of 18,[1] he went from Tokyo to Paris in order to study singing and to be absorbed in the artistic activity of that city. He was in Paris during performances of the Ballets Russes and became interested in studying dance. From Paris he went to Berlin, also a center of artistic activity and a place that provided a young, curious man from Japan with new horizons. A performance by Isadora Duncan reinforced his interest in dance, and in 1912 he enrolled at the Dalcroze School in Hellerau. There he could combine his interests in music and movement. The experiences at the Dalcroze School were to have a lifelong impact on his work.

Emile Jaques Dalcroze (born in Switzerland in 1865) started as a music teacher and composer in Geneva. In the 1880s and 1890s he developed a way of working with music and movement that became known as "eurythmics." In this method the students were led to understand various facets of music such as rhythm, dynamics, and tempo not just by listening and playing the piano but also by moving their bodies. The purpose was to develop an aesthetic perception and awareness of the musical structure and intent through kinesthetic, indeed physical, response. Dalcroze became well known for his methods and attracted students and teachers from all over the world to his classes. In 1906 he began working with Adolph Appia (born in Switzerland in 1862). Appia, also initially a music student, became concerned with the relationships of the moving actor to the stage space, design, and lights. Appia became involved with experiments in total theater that provided an overall symbolic illusion and a three-dimensional experience that emphasized space, volume, mass, and light as opposed to any naturalistic statement. In working with Appia, Dalcroze developed his exercises to include emotional values and began to experiment with mass groupings.

In 1909 Appia made a series of drawings, "Rhythmic Spaces," and although never used for that purpose, they were meant for Dalcroze's exercises. In 1910 two wealthy German manufacturers built Dalcroze a school in Hellerau, a suburb of Dresden, and Appia, in collaboration with Alexander von Salzmann and Heinrich Tessenow, designed the auditorium, stage, and lighting. Oscar Brockett, the theater historian, noted that this was "the first theatre build in modern times without a proscenium arch—that is the first completely open stage."[2] It was on this stage that Appia and Dalcroze created in 1913 their highly unusual and experimental production of Gluck's *Orpheus and Eurydice*. The production consisted of symphonic movement choirs—music responded to by means of large groups of bodies symbolically organized to move to the inner meaning of the rhythmics and qualities of Gluck's opera. The sets consisted of formal arrangements of steps, platforms, and draperies. The lighting provided a rhythmic element, adding another component of atmosphere and composition.

If Ito was a student at the Dalcroze School in 1913, it is highly probable that he was involved in this production of Gluck's *Orpheus and Eurydice*. He certainly took part in this atmosphere, highly charged with questions about the meaning of music, movement, and theater. Any experience he had with the symbolic use of gesture and the emphasis in Noh and Kabuki on illusion rather than on realistic representation, were certainly reinforced at the Dalcroze School.

In 1914, because of the outbreak of World War I, Ito left Germany and after escaping to Holland arrived in England. His two-year stay in England was an important experience for the young artist. Here he met and worked with William Butler Yeats and Ezra Pound, both interested in Oriental theater. Their interest in the forms of Noh and Kabuki stemmed from their questioning of the realistic theater and their search for a theater of illusion and absolute beauty. Ito met these artists through his performances at the home of Lady Ottoline Morrell, the wealthy art patron. Lady Morrell and her husband, Philip, had regular Thursday evening get-togethers, and Ito performed at many of these between 1914 and 1915. During this period he also performed at the homes of other wealthy patrons and at the Coliseum Theatre in London.

Ito sustained an injury after the Coliseum engagement in 1915 and turned down offers to appear as a dancer in theaters outside of London. It was during the period 1915 through 1916 that Ito became involved with Ezra Pound and William Butler Yeats in a project based on Noh drama. This project, the development and production of the play *At the Hawk's Well*, was to be a cornerstone in Ito's work and, along with what he learned at the Dalcroze School, formed the aesthetic basis for all future endeavors. In 1913 Pound had been given translations of Noh plays as well as related historic notes, both written by the scholar Ernest Fenollosa. Pound shared these with Yeats, who became fascinated with this form of theater and the potential of symbolic illusion created by an integration of music, movement, words, costumes, lights, and sets. In 1915 Ito shared his knowledge of Noh and Kabuki drama with Yeats and Pound and studied the Fenollosa translations and notes with them. The result was Yeats's completion of *At the Hawk's Well* and Ito's partnership in its production.

Ito had immersed himself in the study of Western art forms since the age of 18 when he left Japan for his travels in the West. The joint venture with Pound and Yeats meant he had to reevaluate an important part of his heritage and investigate the Noh texts and commentary with a new perspective. Could he use the Noh and Kabuki in their pure state, or would he be able to integrate these forms with the knowledge and experience he had absorbed in his studies over the last four years?

The production of *At the Hawk's Well* provided a process of artistic clarification for all the artists involved. The study of Noh drama created an important and long-range focus for Pound and Yeats. Ito began to clarify which aspects of the traditions he brought from the East would be meaningful for him as a twentieth-century artist living in the West. It is interesting that Ito created productions of *At the Hawk's Well* each time he found himself in a new place—at turning points in his life. The play proved to be a constant affirmation of his conviction about the nature of art, theater, and dance. Thus, he was to stage this play shortly after he moved to New York in 1918, when he moved to Los Angeles in 1929, and on a 1939 visit to Japan for the celebration of his parent's fiftieth anniversary.

The play consisted of three main characters—an old man, a young man, and the guardian of the well. The old man, who has passed his life at a dry well, sleeps at the rare moments when the waters of immortality gush into it. The young man comes in search of the waters and is bewitched by the hawk's dance at the time of the well's overflowing with water. Ito attempted to capture an inner quality of search and longing in this symbolic movement drama or "play for dancers" as Yeats called it. His archetypal characters were involved in the search for immortality and reconciliation between life and death, hope and despair, acceptance and understanding of life's forces. For Ito it was important to capture the inner essence of man's struggle with himself—a struggle for wisdom and beauty.

On 2 and 4 April 1916 the play was performed in London in the homes of two art patronesses: first in Lady Emerald Cunard's home and then in Lady Islington's. Ito played the hawklike guardian of the well. The movements were symbolic abstractions of a bird's gliding flight in the air, and arms and upper torso were designed to create an image of large, spread wings and airborn passage of the imaginary creature. The movements established a close relationship with the music, characteristic of the interpretive methods taught by Dalcroze and used by Ito throughout his choreographic career. Gestures were occasionally drawn from the Noh vocabulary, and although conflict was portrayed, the choreography was characterized by an underplayed subtle, simple demeanor and an inner silence.

The use of masks and a screen in the 1916 productions were also important aspects of Ito's aesthetic ideas. The old man and the young man wore masks. Ito had a headdress that covered the sides of his face, and what was uncovered was painted in exaggerated style to resemble a mask. Members of the chorus had their faces painted in similar style. A screen and a platform provided the only scenery. The use of the mask, screen, and platform derived from Ito's synthesis of traditional Japanese theater forms and the new ideas to which he had been exposed at the Dalcroze School, in his own readings, and during his sojourns in Paris and London.

Ito was interested in the ideas of Gordon Craig (1872–1966). Craig felt the mask could portray the soul of the character in a play. The actor's face, in Craig's perspective, was too naturalistic and immediate, while the mask provided an abstraction of the inner state. In Noh theater the mask also represented a simple, symbolic statement about the character portrayed. In Kabuki makeup replaced the mask to give a similar effect. In *At the Hawk's Well* Ito wore a partial mask and Kabuki-style makeup; the two actors wore full masks. The screen and platform in the play were also ideas that came from Ito's background, Craig's writings and theatrical ventures, and Appia's work. Craig created screens of different sizes for various productions. He wanted to create an abstract, mobile setting that would move with the lighting and the actor and help create a dynamic illusion. Ito may have based the use of a platform in *At the Hawk's Well* on those used by Adolph Appia in the production of *Orpheus and Eurydice* at the Dalcroze School in 1913.

Michio Ito left London for New York a few months after the two presentations of *At the Hawk's Well.* He was offered a contract to appear in a New York theater and arrived in the fall of 1916. The contract was not to Ito's liking and was cancelled, but he soon became active in the dance and theater life of his new home. Ito stayed in New York until 1929, at which time he went to Los Angeles, attracted by a movie contract. During his 13 years in New York he did many things. He created and performed solo and small group works and taught extensively. He also was the director and choreographer of many plays, both in the Japanese and Western traditions, and he directed and choreographed operas, operettas, musical reviews, and pantomimes.

The nature and extent of Ito's influence on American dance in New York during a crucial period of its development remains to be examined and is not the focus here. Many of his pupils during 1916 through 1929 became leading figures in dance and theater: Nimura, Pauline Koner, Angna Enters, and Felicia Sorel, among others. His choreographic and performance activities were very extensive, and he worked with many artists who were in the process of formulating their own aesthetic vision. A summary of Ito's ventures in New York shows his varied activities. In 1917 he created two works for Adolph Bolm's Ballets-Intime and toured with the company. In 1918 he produced *At the Hawk's Well.* In 1917 and 1921 he created two productions of *Tamura* (Noh translation by Fenollosa-Pound). In 1928 he choreographed for the Neighborhood Playhouse group using Martha Graham and Benjamin Zemach. The group performed at both the Manhattan Opera House and the Neighborhood Playhouse.

Ito's emphases on distillation of emotion, inner concentration, and symbolic use of gesture and space were influential directions for others to explore in the artistic ferment and search during the years 1916 through 1929 in New York. Martha Graham, Charles Weidman, and Doris Humphrey after leaving Denishawn were in the process of forging their own artistic pathways. Adolph Bolm had left the Ballets Russes and was experiencing the new energies in America. John Martin in *America Dancing,* published in 1936, had this to say about Michio Ito:

> Of all the foreign artists who have been active here in recent times, none has had so direct an effect upon dance as Michio Ito. With a winning personal quality, a racial beauty of movement, a sensitive artistic nature, and a fine background, he came to New York by way of Dalcroze at Hellerau and Yeats's "plays for dancers" in London, and put his mark strongly upon the local dance world. His dancing was largely pictorial in quality and charming rather than profound. It was very much simpler and more contained than the previously prevailing type of scarf-and-

garland dancing. Its movement was more clean cut, and besides being exotic, it had that mysterious thing known as quality. A great many young dancers found it an excellent form of training.[3]

Martin had some concerns about the profundity of the choreography, but his overall comments would indicate that there was indeed substance to Ito's work. It is likely that many of Ito's dances were more pretty than probing, but there must have been a substantial number of pieces that made Martin and others sit up and take notice because of their craftsmanship, originality of statement, and strength of image.

Ito created a Japanese sequence for the movie *No, No Nanette*, a film released in Los Angeles sometime in February 1930. His arrival in Los Angeles probably coincided with a movie contract for this undertaking. On 28 April 1929 at the Figueroa Playhouse Ito presented his first concert in Los Angeles and in July repeated much of the material in a concert at Barnsdall Park. It is interesting that on these programs Georgia Graham presented choreography by her sister Martha and also danced in Ito's work. Also performing were Estelle Reed (teacher of May O'Donnell) and Dorothy Wagner.

During the summer Ito started teaching and presented his students in concerts at Argus Bowl. No longer in existence now, at that time this was an outdoor theater on the Argus estate in Eagle Rock, outside the city of Los Angeles. Students listed on the programs that summer, which took place on Monday evenings, 5 August through 2 September 1929 were: Lester Horton, Beatriz Baird, Dolores Lopez, Dorothy Wagner, Edith Jane, Hazel Wright, Xenia Zarina, Anne Douglas, Lillian Powell, and Arnold Tamon.

It was at Eagle Rock during those Monday evening series in 1929 that Ito presented once again *At the Hawk's Well*, this time with Lester Horton in the role of the hawk/guardian. The production was very well received and seemed to signal a new direction for both audience and critics. An unnamed critic in the 29 August *Los Angeles Times* noted that it was perhaps not easily accessible to a wide audience. He felt that dance/drama presented ideas that had not been explored by other dance artists in Los Angeles. He called it a "fantastic drama" and went on to say: "It is for the few, perhaps, straying as it does so vagrantly from the beaten path."

Helen Caldwell provided a description of the performance in her biography of Ito.

Although *At the Hawk's Well* was mounted with a far greater sophistication than that of the chandelier-lit drawing room advocated by Yeats, it still had no theatricality in the usual sense; the effect was poetic simplicity. . . . High above the actors one saw in dim outline the jagged peaks of a sierra. All around were dark trees.

And there was a wizard named Lewis Barrongton behind the lights to give the scene the otherworld reality Yeats had sought. This new setting called upon the spectator's imagination, with its black night, the faint suggestion of hills, and light that seemed a part of the verse. . . . Besides the chorus, there was a harp and an oboe, and Ito played the drums and cymbals. . . . Yeats would have been pleased.[4]

In this production costume, gesture, rhythm, setting, and words were integrated to symbolize a universe in which struggle was abstracted through a harmonious balance of forces. The 29 August *Los Angeles Times* review noted that "Lester Horton, the hawk, surpassed my earlier good impression of his artistic accomplishments. He is rhythmic, poetic, pliable and touched with the spirit of 'make believe.'"

The pictures of the play as performed at Argus Bowl illuminate the quality and style of movement developed by Ito. In a picture with four women—one standing, two on chairs, and one on the floor—the overall impression is one of an attempt to portray the balance between reaching out to powers outside oneself and reaching within to find understanding. The woman stands with feet in parallel position, and her body gives the impression of creating a tight, vertical unit. One arm is tightly at her side while the other is lifted in a contained gesture. She is serene and pleading—both struggling and at peace. We see a figure whose drama is internal, and the smallness and tight feeling of hand, body, torso, and feet give an abstract sense of harmony resulting from an inner search. The three other figures repeat the contained right-hand gesture of the standing woman—with the palm at shoulder level and facing outward and the elbow pulled in tightly at the waist. All four women show containment in their bodies, in opposition to the pleading gesture, and the entire grouping gives the impression of harmony. Ernest Fenollosa's comments about Noh drama corroborate the intent of Ito's production.

The beauty and power of Noh lies in the concentration. All elements—costume, motion, verse and music—unite to produce a single calcified impression. Each drama embodies some primary human relation or emotion; and the poetic sweetness or poignancy of this is carried to its highest degree by carefully excluding all such obtrusive elements as a mimetic realism or vulgar sensationalism might demand. The emotion is always fixed upon idea, not upon personality.[5]

Soon Ito's work in Los Angeles began to take on a new dimension. For the most part his choreography in the city was characterized by large group works accompanied by live orchestra. He called these "symphonic choreographies." In them Ito was able to pull out all the stops, putting together all his ideas and years of experience. The work of a mature artist, these symphonic choreographies built on the Dalcroze background, his experience with the ideas of Craig and Appia, his collaboration with Pound and Yeats, and his continuing effort to integrate his Japanese roots and always expanding immersion in the Noh and Kabuki forms. Three of the symphonic choreographies were created for the Hollywood Bowl, one for an evening at the Pasadena Rose Bowl and one each for the Redlands Bowl and the Greek Theatre.

There may have been several factors contributing to this particular development in Ito's work: the climate, the numerous outdoor facilities, and a large group of dancers, many of whom may have been involved in movie work, who provided a corps of ready and able bodies. The interest in his Japanese background and aesthetic thrust may have been stimulated by the existence of a large and affluent Japanese community. The fact that Ito came to Los Angeles after many years as professional and the salary he received from his movies may have also helped him proceed with these large endeavors. Ito began teaching at the Edith Jane Studio, 1759 North Highland Avenue, immediately after his first concert. According to Helen Caldwell, he had classes for professionals as well as a class he called "Community Dance." She noted the community class was made up of writers, musicians, sculptors, teachers, and simple amateurs of various arts.

On 20 September 1929 Ito presented 180 dancers with symphonic orchestra and a chorus in the Pasadena Rose Bowl. He had been asked to create something for a "Pageant of Lights" to celebrate installation of the largest sun arcs ever used in the Rose Bowl. Choreography was created to Tchaikovsky's *Andante Cantabile,* two Chopin waltzes, Grieg's *Peer Gynt Suite,* and Dvořák's *New World Symphony.* Once again Ito used a screen as a backdrop—this time a gold folding screen 40 feet high and 125 feet long. Five thousand people were in the audience.

On 15 August 1930 at the Hollywood Bowl Ito used 125 dancers in an interpretation of the "Polovtsian Dances" from Borodin's *Prince Igor.* One of Michio Ito's seven brothers came to create the costumes. Kisaku Ito was a stage designer, president of Haiyuza Theater in Japan, and author of several books on the theater. He was best known in the United States for the settings of films such as *Gate of Hell* and for sets of the Azuma Kabuki company. For the *Prince Igor* production he created costumes that would be seen from the last rows of the large amphitheater: cheap cotton cloth in bold patterns of brilliant color and boots of brightly colored oilcloth.

The Hollywood Bowl in 1930 was a performing space with several levels—almost an innocent and coincidental interpretation of Appia's ideas about platforms. First there was a narrow straight space adjoining the orchestra's stage; this was followed by a flight of eight steps leading to a flat, narrow, curved space planted in grass and enclosed by a four-foot hedge; then six more steps led to another curved green separated from the audience by a low wall or curb. Ito used these different levels and spaces for the groups to interpret the musical themes, finally uniting the whole group on the stage itself. Helen Caldwell noted that Ito prepared large charts for his symphonic interpretations. Beneath the musical notation he would make sketches for particular gestures and for group movement. Everything was worked out in great detail and was ready for the dancers at the first rehearsal.

Patterson Greene in the *Los Angeles Examiner* on 16 August wrote about this Hollywood Bowl presentation. "The whole spectacle was a triumph of gorgeousness that inspires the hope for others of its kind. Such an artist as Ito is an asset to the community." Richard Drake Saunders in the *Hollywood Citizen News* (reporting on 16 August) was enthusiastic: "Michio Ito and his ballet were given a veritable ovation by a crowd that overflowed the Bowl and filled every available standing space on the hillsides last night. The ensemble was particularly fine, and parti-colored costumes that enabled instantaneous change of colored patterns according to the angle presented by the dancers were exceptionally effective." Charles Daggett in the *Los Angeles Record* (16 August) was perhaps the most enthusiastic of all the critics.

> There have been many ballets at the Bowl, but never such a beautiful one as that presented and staged by the Japanese artist. Instead of running foot races, or forming pretty pictures, Ito and his dancers threw themselves headlong into a strict interpretation of Borodin's ballet music from *Prince Igor*. The dancers clad in gorgeous oriental dress—costumes that were partly Russian, Chinese, Persian, and Arabian—presented a fascinating ensemble against the gauze drapes drawn in front of the orchestra shell. These drapes, black at the far end, white and painted with a striking tree design in the center, served both as background and a means to shut off sight of the black-coated orchestra which would have been wholly out of keeping with the dance and the colorful dress of the dancers. Ito is a splendid asset to the community. May he and his dancers be called upon often to perform at the Bowl.

On 26 June 1936 Ito presented a smaller version of a symphonic choreography at the Redlands Bowl—35 dancers in movement designed for a production of Gluck's opera *Orpheus*. This was a smaller venture, for the dances were part of a larger production. The most important of Michio Ito's large-scale presentations was commissioned for the Hollywood Bowl and took place on 19 August 1937. Two vastly different compositions were given that night: one based on Japanese forms and the other on Strauss's *Blue Danube Waltz*.

Etenraku, the dance based on Japanese forms, represented a culmination of Ito's ideas. Based on a sixteenth-century text, the name came from the accompanying musical score, which translated means "Music

Ballet *Etenraku*, Hollywood Bowl, 1937
Choreography by Michio Ito.
(*Courtesy Toyo Miyatake*)

Coming through the Heavens." The form of the music was Gagaku—
which is identified with the Imperial court of Japan between the eighth
and ninth centuries. Viscount Hidemaro Konoye, a major conductor of
Japan at that time, was responsible for leading the musicians that evening and for creating the contemporary orchestration of the traditional
music.

Helen Caldwell in her biography of Michio Ito talked about the differences in approach between Japanese and Western dancing for Ito.

> The background of Japanese dancing, in Ito's words, is literature; that of Western
> dancing is music. In both instances dance is used as a medium of expressing
> human thought and emotion. But Western dancing produces a more abstract effect,
> for in the accompanying music the spectator is left free to imagine what the dance
> is saying, while in dance accompanied by poetry (or prose) the effect is concrete
> and definite since the description is given in words.[6]

When Ito created the dance for the musical score *Etenraku* he used elements of both Japanese and Western dance. Ito's dance was based on
the contemporary orchestration of the Gagaku music, while he used
the images and symbols in the Noh text as a reference point. His text
was a stanza from a poem in the sixteenth-century Noh play *Hagoromo*
and was printed in the Hollywood Bowl program.

> Spring mist everywhere. Sunlight on the flowers,
> This earth is your heaven for even here comes the
>   heavenly
> Wonderful wind. . . . Oh Blow. . . .
>
> There is a magic song from the East, the voice of
>   many and many; a sound of music filling the sky.
> Dance, filling and filling. . . .
>
> Mountains of dyed red in the sunset . . .
>   Green waves . . .
> A rain of flowers . . . Clouds . . . snow white . . .
> Oh Beautiful world
>
> The kingdom—the power—the glory—
> For ever and ever this dance . . .
> Shall be a dance of praise . . .

Etenraku was performed by 22 men and women against a stage
background of a long gold folding screen. A rehearsal picture of *Etenraku* at the Hollywood Bowl shows the dancers placed on the stage in
clear symmetrical groups. There is a group of two dancers on each side
of the stage, a group of four downstage right, and six downstage left.
These form a symmetrical picture from the centerstage sight line. There
are also six dancers across the back of the stage, evenly spaced in a bal-

anced formation. The quality of the picture formed by the dancers is one of formal elegance. There is the same sense of containment and verticality present as in the pictures of Ito's production of *At the Hawk's Well*. The dancers in *Etenraku* have backs that are upright and elbows that are close to the body. Their feet are parallel and close together, and their heads are quiet on top of restrained torsos and limbs.

The costumes for *Etenraku* are Japanese in their heritage but abstractly and playfully so. One of the most striking elements of the costumes are the headdresses—a clear giveaway that Ito is not trying to duplicate a Japanese costume but wanted to use the idea of the costume as a takeoff point for an interpretation. One of the pictures of *Etenraku* shows three women and two men dancing. The three women have different combinations of shapes and forms resting on their heads. One woman wears a horizontal cylinder with flowerlike objects on top, another wears a series of abstract shapes going in several different directions, and the third wears a conelike structure. These headdresses are not literal duplications of either Noh or Kabuki headdresses.

One picture of *Etenraku* shows a couple. The man is holding the woman at the elbows and they are both facing in the same direction. The woman's knees are bent, and her torso is leaning ever so slightly forward to accommodate the body of the man. The man is gently looking at the woman, and she is looking to the side—as if gazing in the distance. There is a delicacy and understatement in the stance of this couple and an air of mystery. They are close together, but they are also apart in their looks. The man is hovering over the woman. She presents a strong image. Her feet are planted firmly on the ground, her elbow is at her waist, and her fan is held low and close to her thighs— almost ready to use as a striking force if necessary.

Michio Ito's technique was based on 10 arm gestures that he used with numerous variations of context, rhythm, space, and energy and that he combined in many ways. He felt the upper body and the movements of arms and head were the important communicating mechanisms. Movements of the lower body were auxiliary and would follow the direction and intent established by the upper body gestures. This was certainly in great contrast to the Western tradition of classical ballet, in which the legs and feet carry so much emphasis. For Ito the important aspects of dance were the symbolic gestural ones—never gesture in the sense of pantomime, indicating a literal or realistic idea.

Critic Isabel Morse Jones in the 20 August *Los Angeles Times* called *Etenraku* "subtle" and noted that "its ritualistic form seemed as ageless as truth." For the first time since the Hollywood Bowl opened in 1922, the audience was invited to share in a dance that was based on authen-

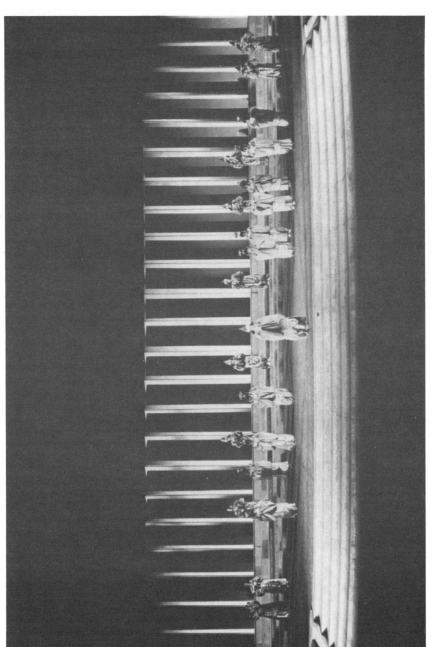

Scene from *Etenraku*, Hollywood Bowl, 1937
(Courtesy Toyo Miyatake)

tic Japanese forms. Michio Ito's choreography for *Etenraku* presented an ancient tradition of movement and music that became the basic structure for a more open-ended, abstracted form of expression. The gestures of Noh and Kabuki embodied symbolic movement that taught lessons and told stories to the Japanese. Most often the dance in these traditions was related to a poem written to celebrate an event, a happening, a feeling, and was performed with appropriate symbolic gestures.

In *Etenraku* the use of gesture and movement was no longer literal but, rather, was tied in with the general feeling of both the Noh poem Ito used and the Gagaku music. Much about the dance that Ito composed was Western—the groupings on stage, the freedom from event and specific context, and the use of the expressive power of the music. But much in Ito's *Etenraku* was different from the Western traditional ballet or the reforms of Duncan and Diaghilev. Ito's dance was characterized by economy of movement, conciseness of statement, mystery of mood, and abstracted symbolic gesture.

Ito emphasized that gesture, movement, and form all should combine to create a central idea. "Is dancing art? As long as it expresses an idea—yes. Nothing, however, is art without an idea behind it."[7] Michio Ito's central idea in *Etenraku* was contained in the subtitle "Music Coming through the Heavens." Ito in this dance was concerned with abstractly portraying a heaven on earth—a world of balance and spirit, of beauty contained in the formal poetry of motion. The pictures of this dance suggest movement that has a continuous flow, an inner peace, and outward balance. Spirit and beauty were suggested rather than spelled out. Helen Caldwell commented on Ito's art.

> Ito avoided spectacle . . . relied upon suggestion rather than elaboration, believing that an idea, including emotion, exerts more power on the imagination when not completely revealed. Even in his use of metaphor there is no fixed or rigid symbolism, but rather a fine network of subtle associations that link the spectator's thoughts with those of other human beings and draw him out of himself into the life of dance. . . . Our minds are not tabulae rasae; we all have memories, of artistic as well as of actual experiences. It is this common culture and experience that Ito drew upon for ideas and for its visible embodiment. Hence the excellence of his style will strike responsive chords in almost all spectators. Outstanding among these excellences are: the strong, incisive gesture; the symmetry of continuous movement and its melding with music; the strength and beauty of line for which Japanese art is noted; the power of suggesting space, atmosphere, and distance by swift, forcible strokes; the economy and simplicity by which he attains emotional effect; the subtle allusion; the satisfying dignity and formality; the buoyancy, lyricism, feeling of joy and freedom; and the tenderness betokening brotherhood.[8]

On that same evening at the Hollywood Bowl 54 dancers performed in Ito's choreography for Strauss's *The Blue Danube*. There is a feeling in examining this program that there was some concern about the audience's reaction to a piece as exotic as *Etenraku;* perhaps there was also uneasiness about the critics' response. *The Blue Danube* was not Ito at his most original, but the large audience may have been more at ease with the contrast in the programming. Isabel Morse Jones, again in her 20 August *Los Angeles Times* review, was favorably impressed with the Strauss interpretation. "Ito's admirable restraint in the important matters of line and movement made the simple waltz utterly charming. The romantic period of 1830 was portrayed with fidelity and the dance won its audience completely." On 24 September *The Blue Danube* was repeated at the Bowl; 32 dancers also performed in Ito's choreography for two Mozart minuets.

Michio Ito's contribution to the dance was an important statement in a direction that was new for many in Los Angeles. In a program note for the production of *Etenraku* at the Hollywood Bowl, Michio Ito made some comments that clarify the influences of his work on two decades of American dancers: "When the technique of any art form is mastered, it is possible to express the inner life. Everyone has his own individual feeling and mode of expression, therefore the dance should be a creation, not an imitation."

In the late 1970s and the 1980s there has been renewed interest in the work of Michio Ito that has included several concerts of his solos by Satory Shimazaki. Ito was considered an important artist during the period he worked in New York (1916 through 1929). John Martin and Elizabeth Selden wrote about him in a way that heralded a new presence in the dance world, one that should be watched and valued. The critics seem to have lost sight of Ito when he came to California, and after Martin's *American Dance* (1936) and Selden's *The Dancer's Quest* (1935) there was no mention of him in the major dance histories.

An analysis of Ito's work in Los Angeles, however points to his continuing influence as well as his own development as an artist. It was in California that he created his large symphonic works as well as a major work in dance form, *Etenraku*, which fully integrated his ideas on East and West. Ito perhaps is even more contemporary today than he was in his own time. Many artists are trying to bring together their background in indigenous forms with their lives as Western artists, and Ito's work deserves study in that regard. His dances were evocative meditations, utilizing gesture, rhythm, space, and sound to provide an understated abstraction of feelings and ideas.

Rehearsal of *The Blue Danube Waltz*, Hollywood Bowl, 1937
Music by Johann Strauss, choreography by Michio Ito.
(*Courtesy Toyo Miyatake*)

The Japanese forms that were a rich source of influence for Ito were the Noh drama, the Kyogen (comic interlude), and the Kabuki play. Noh and Kyogen arose in the fourteenth century. The Noh developed from the song and dance representations that originated in the pantomimic dance performed at ancient Shinto and Buddhist festivals. Noh is characterized by a formal presentation. A chorus sits at the right and musicians sit at the back of the stage, which has only the barest essentials of scenery. The tone of the performance is restrained and suggestive. Wooden masks are used to help minimize any realistic effect, and the symbolism of the play is usually quite complex. The Kyogen, or comic interlude, also developed from the dances and songs at Shinto and Buddhist festivals. Its humor is broad, its composition mostly dialogue and monologue. Kabuki developed in the seventeenth century as a broader form of drama. It allows greater freedom to deviate from set rules, and the highly stylized acting is exaggerated. Strong makeup in symbolic color is used instead of masks. In both Noh and Kabuki the tableau is used as a climactic point, when the actors strike and hold an elaborate pose.

Michio Ito drew from his background in Noh the notion that art and beauty are greatest when they are simple and restrained. Noh is precise and restrained, and yet because of its symbolism, it is nonrealistic and indirect. An event is often used to evoke a mood or an emotional state and often to define a moral point of view. Ito frequently developed his dances as gentle parables, symbolic expressions of life's larger conflicts. Western forms and rhythms also became interpreted in Ito's work. He explored the music and dance forms of Western tradition—the waltz, the minuet, the music of Mozart and Strauss. In his symphonic choreographies he composed a broad Western scale that maintains the subtle, restrained, and suggestive tradition of the Noh.

Benjamin Zemach (b. 1901): From Darkness to Light

Benjamin Zemach was immersed in the world of theater as a young child growing up in his native Russia. When Benjamin was four his father died and Nachum, his older brother, was put in charge of him. Nachum Zemach was already interested in becoming an actor and director, and this early pathway of Nachum eventually led to Benjamin's dedication to theater and dance. Benjamin's older brother was an ardent Zionist who believed Jewish survival involved settlement of Palestine and revival of Hebrew as a spoken language. In their hometown of Bialistock Benjamin watched as Nachum brought his interests in theater and Zionism together when he staged his first Hebrew play.

In 1980 Benjamin recalled Nachum's realization that Bialistock represented artistic isolation. Nachum left his hometown in around 1916 with the promise that he would care for Benjamin, his mother, and his sister when he found another place to live and work. Nachum's goal was to work in conjunction with others who were exploring new ideas in theater. After spending some time in Warsaw, he came to Moscow in 1917. Moscow was the logical choice for a young Russian artist/director intent on his own development and an encounter with new ways of thinking. Although the Russian theater had been bound by old traditions, significant changes took place between 1900 and 1917. As Oscar Brockett noted in *Century of Innovation:* "No longer backward, it was now one of the most experimental and fruitful theatres in the world. Its enormous range probably exceeded that of any nation at the time."[1]

After living for a brief time by himself in Moscow, Nachum Zemach brought his whole family to join him there following the winter of 1917. This was to be a crucial decision for the future careers of both Nachum and Benjamin, who also quickly became immersed in theater. Their training with Constantin Stanislavsky, Yevgeny Vakh-

Benjamin Zemach, ca. 1930
(*Courtesy Amielle Zemach*)

tangov, and Vsevelod Meyerhold from 1917 to 1924 established for them lifelong perspectives and technical foundations. For Benjamin it also meant the opportunity to explore fully his interest in dance with a variety of great teachers.

Stanislavsky, cofounder of the Moscow Art Theatre in 1897, was interested in theater that would explore illusion, spirit, and feelings as opposed to spectacle and mannered traditions. A significant contribution made by Stanislavsky was his method of training actors. He emphasized emotional memory and inner justification regarding character portrayal, along with rigorous physical training of voice and body. Stanislavsky was also interested in integration of sets and actors—eliminating the conflict between the two- and three-dimensional facets of the stage. In 1908 he asked Gordon Craig to design a production of *Hamlet,* which was not staged at the Moscow Art Theatre until 1912. Craig's three-dimensional screens were movable and meant to indicate different scenes, but they proved too abstract an experiment for the Moscow Art Theatre.

Benjamin and Nachum worked most closely with Vakhtangov, who labeled his approach to theater "fantastic realism." He wanted the stage to reshape inner realities. One of his methods with actors was improvisation, whereby a desired audience response was achieved through a creative adventure between director and actor. This was an approach that was characteristic of Benjamin Zemach's work throughout his career, whether he was directing a play or creating a dance. The experience the brothers had with Meyerhold was briefer but also long-lasting. Oscar Brockett called Meyerhold "the most dedicated experimenter in the Russian theatre between 1900 and 1917. . . . His creative urge led him both to seek new means and to explore the limits of old ones."[2] After 1917 Meyerhold's experiments covered a wide range of ideas in the theater, reaching into new methods of presentation and suggesting a variety of approaches into meaning, staging techniques, and training methods.

The year 1917 was the time of the Russian Revolution, and the Zemach family made the trip from Bialistock to Moscow at a time fraught with the remainders of the civil war. It was an ambitious and dangerous journey. Benjamin Zemach was 15 and in 1980 still remembered the trip vividly.

The journey took two weeks from Bialistock to Moscow. We changed from one freight train to another, and there were thousands of other refugees. Here some were cooking over a fire they made, in another place were some moaning over a member of the family who had died. When we finally got to Moscow there were many refugees everywhere, and fighting was all over. Bullets shattered our windows. Everyone became a proletarian, and the rich hid their diamonds.[3]

This trip imprinted images of displacement on Benjamin Zemach's sensitive mind. He always remembered the feelings of chaos created by the war. In later years, particularly when he created *The Victory Ball* at the Hollywood Bowl (1935), all of these feelings and images served as raw material for his antiwar ballet.

The family settled in Moscow, and Nachum Zemach soon was able to realize his dream of a Hebrew theater, a dream he had always shared with young Benjamin. Nachum Zemach rented a buiding and gathered a group of Jewish actors and actresses with whom he could work and share in the creative process. Over the door of the building, in blue letters on white, they placed a sign that read "Habima"—from the Hebrew word for stage. Benjamin was considered too young and inexperienced to be in any productions, but he was party to much of the planning, the intellectual discussions, and the vibrant hopes of the young group.

During the period 1917 through about 1924 the Russians allowed the Jews to worship and did not close the synagogues. In the excitement and dream of the Revolution there was a sense of creating an atmosphere of freedom and brotherhood for everyone and a tolerance of divergent beliefs within the Communist framework. The young artists who were struggling to give expression to new forms in painting, theater, dance, and music were seen as part of the total ferment in the creation of a new society.

As soon as he could Nachum Zemach began to utilize the resources available to him in Moscow. He turned to Constantin Stanislavsky for help, and Benjamin remarked about this in later years: "Stanislavsky was not afraid and did not think it would lower his prestige to work with the Habima. He was obsessed with continuity. He also felt that the people in the arts owed something to the Jewish people since they had contributed so much to culture in the past."[4] Stanislavsky himself could not take the time to work with the Habima group on a regular basis, but he sent his top pupil—Yevgeny Vakhtangov. The 12 men and women of Habima studied with Vakhtangov for a year without producing any plays. In 1918 they had a public showing of one-act plays and gradually began to rehearse and produce evening-long productions.

Soon Benjamin was allowed to participate, and when Vakhtangov started working on Habima's production of *The Dybbuk*, Benjamin was a full-fledged member of the group. He had close contact not only with Vakhtangov but also with Stanislavsky, who came to give classes and lecture. During the rehearsals for *The Dybbuk* Vakhtangov became seriously ill with stomach cancer. He saw a general rehearsal of the production but, according to Zemach, never saw a performance and died

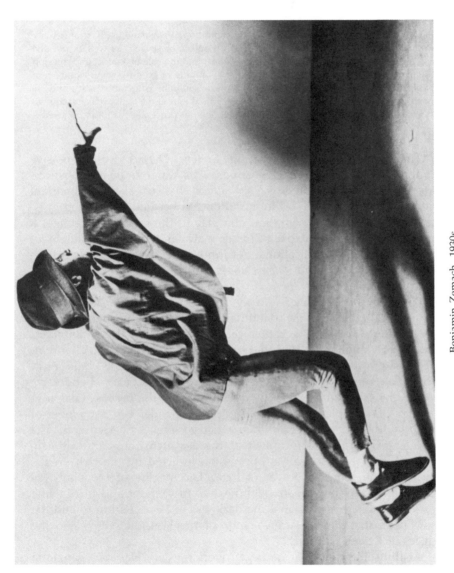

Benjamin Zemach, 1930s
(*Courtesy Amielle Zemach*)

in 1922 just before the premiere. Vsevelod Meyerhold volunteered to help out and worked with Habima after Vakhtangov died. In 1983, looking back at his youth in the theater, Zemach summarized the influences of Stanislavsky, Vakhtangov, and Meyerhold.

> From Stanislavsky I learned about concentration, imagination, physical activity, purposefulness, relaxation, rhythm and the music of speech, as well as the divisions of parts into larger and smaller sections, and the role of conflict and development. From Vakhtangov I learned "inner continuity of gesture, composition, combination of content and form, as well as a sense of contemporaneity and the abstraction of flights of imagination." Meyerhold taught me to approach each work with freshness of mind and an attempt to look at process at hand as opposed to past ventures.[5]

The influence of participating in *The Dybbuk* was pervasive throughout Benjamin Zemach's career. This was one of the most important productions created by Vakhtangov. It also was the hallmark of the Habima Theatre both on tour and once it became established in Israel. The first major presentation of a play in the Hebrew language, it proved a guideline in the use of Judaic material to develop a statement that had universal implications. As innovative theater utilizing symbolic characterization and stage sets, it was a formative experience for young Benjamin.

Based on the work by S. Ansky, the story of *The Dybbuk* was about two young lovers: Leah, daughter of the wealthy businessman, Sender, and Channon, a rabbinical student of less than abundant means. Leah's father insisted that she marry a wealthy man. Channon, when not allowed to marry Leah, became lovesick and died. His spirit, a dybbuk, entered Leah's body and gave her no peace. Sender requested the sages to exorcise the dybbuk, but in the process Leah also died. Specifically placed in a Jewish setting, Sender was a member of the Hassidic sect, known for their strict adherence to tradition. The messages of the play were universal: the destructiveness and ultimate defeat of rigid traditions, the oppression inflicted by the rich on the poor, and the timeless power of love. The staging of the play was stylized and symbolic. Leah's lightness of movement and pure white dress were juxtaposed against the darkness of Sender's house and the heavy, almost grotesque, movements of the Hassidic elders and the beggars at Leah's wedding.

At the same time that he began working with Habima, Benjamin Zemach started his dance studies in Russia. He had three major teachers, all of whom were responsible for developing different facets of his imagination and dance vocabulary. Inna Tchernezkaia, a pupil of Alexander Sacharov, was his first teacher. She had her own modern dance studio in Moscow, and from her he learned "a dramatic approach to movement." Vera Moslova, formerly a ballerina of the Bolshoi Theatre, was responsible for his solid background in ballet. Alexandrova, the director of the Dalcroze Eurythmics Institute, gave him "a firm appreciation of the relationship of music and dance, and a sense of freedom and exploration in movement."[6]

In 1925 the artistic freedom that had characterized the early years of the Russian Revolution began to disappear. The tolerance of various religious and nationalist affiliations and beliefs also vanished. The Jewish Communists began to take the position that Hebrew was a counterrevolutionary language, and they succeeded in cutting off financial help and other support to Habima. The group left Russia ostensibly to tour but clearly seeking a way to establish themselves in a more tolerant and hospitable environment. In 1927 the Habima members came to New York, where they went through a period of internal dissension about permanent place of residence and artistic philosophy. Half the group left for Israel, where they established what has become a permanent Habima Theatre. The other half stayed in the United States, including Nachum and Benjamin Zemach. Benjamin found in New York an active dance community, and it was there that he began to develop his choreographic interests.

One of the first performances Benjamin gave in New York was an evening shared with Jacob Ben Ami and Michio Ito on 25 September 1928 at the Yiddish Folks Theatre. During this time Benjamin also became active in the group that worked and performed at the Neighborhood Playhouse. It was there that he performed with Martha Graham, Charles Weidman, Doris Humphrey, and Michio Ito and created several solo concert pieces. One of the dances Zemach still remembers is one choreographed by Michio Ito to music by Claude Debussy, *Fête et Nuages*. In 1983 he recalled: "I was a dark cloud who stole Martha Graham from Michio Ito."[7] Other concert pieces created during this time included *The Beggars Dance, Roumanian Rhapsody* (music by Enesco), and *Tocatta and Fugue* (music by Bach).

Benjamin utilized New York as home base from 1928 through early 1932. During those years he had additional teaching and performing tours of Palestine, the West coast and several other eastern American cities. His performances in New York marked him as a figure to be watched and heralded. Critic Elizabeth Selden wrote of his impact in *The Dancers Quest* (1935).

> Benjamin Zemach goes even further back than does Doris Humphrey toward that ancient oneness in which the dance embraced all media of expression, serving as a repository for the epic memories of the race and as its confession of faith. He represents in America a unique type of ritual dancing, not only because it has the un-

mistakable ring of true conviction, being neither an imitation nor an adaption of some cult foreign to the dancer, but also because it represents a synthesis of all the "isms" that we have carefully been taught to separate into the desirable and the un- desirable. Benjamin Zemach seems blissfully unaware of this distinction and emerges in the end with a composition fascinating for its exoticism, yet essentially right in every way. The transplanting from his native Moscow seems not to have impaired his creative talent: somehow America is a crucible in which all metals mingle and melt and undergo chemicalizations that leave the right ones none the worse for their purging as well as for use in new combinations.[8]

Two works were created by Benjamin Zemach during the period 1928 through 1932 that became signature pieces, *Ruth* and *Farewell to Queen Sabbath.* Characterized by lyric flow, sequential movement, dra- matic conflict and resolution, Zemach's choreography in these two pieces (and later as well) was a personal synthesis of his work in eurythmics, ballet, and modern dance. In addition, he emphasized inner characterization, emotional gesture, and dramatic rhythm, all of which were part of his theatrical training in Russia.

The program note for *Ruth* had this quotation from the Bible: "And they went back from the land of the Moabites to Judea; and Naomi said to them, 'Do not come with me, my daughters, for God has embittered my life'; and Orpah kissed her and went away while Ruth remained bound to her." Although the dance was based in part on the Judaic heritage, Zemach was concerned with making a universal statement. The dance was not a realistic telling of the story. It was an abstraction, with the emotional relationships and motivation of three women as the predominant characteristics. The dance had something to say about women that would speak to everyone. Zemach abstracted the essential inner quality of these three relationships and the strength that carries women through their various roles and accompanying hardships. Sel- den remarked that in *Ruth* "there are no poses; one is conscious only of beauty lifted into space and vanishing again as new movement emerges." She found Zemach's work a model that others could follow. "It is what Paul Valéry calls 'l'acte pur des metamorphoses'—the es- sence of the dance. . . . The extraordinary inner and outer dynamics of this unaggressive composition depends in the last analysis on its re- markable tempo. The entire . . . process is conducted at a pace which lifts it out of the realm of ordinary experience into that of pure vision."[9]

Farewell to Queen Sabbath, also created during Zemach's early years in New York, was based on the Jewish ritual of welcoming the Sabbath as a Queen. On Friday night she came bringing peace, harmony, and rest, and after sunset on Saturday there was a ceremony in which Queen Sabbath was bid farewell. Zemach took this age-old ritual and transformed it into an ecstatic experience wherein the individual and the group commune with each other and with the universal forces of change and recurrence. The dance was accompanied by a mixture of traditional chants and Hassidic songs. It was not necessary for the audience to comprehend the words or the specific religious source. The choreography succeeded in creating a mood that moved the audience from a physical to a spiritual plane. Each person could identify with his own particular ritual of special times in which emotions transform daily lives.

The choreography for *Farewell to Queen Sabbath* consisted of a soloist and a group functioning as chorus. Zemach, as the soloist, faced the chorus, who were meant to represent the congregation. Dressed in the traditional long black kaftans of the orthodox Jews, the group began a slow rhythmic motion from side to side. This swaying gradually increased in tempo and intensity and then began to slow down, until the stage was as quiet at the end as it was when the curtain opened. In this rhythmic rendering of joy and sorrow Zemach captured the growing anticipation and joy at the coming of the Sabbath: the promised release from the mundane activities of the week and the joining with higher forces of the Sabbath, followed by the sadness but inevitability and acceptance of Queen Sabbath's departure. Selden felt this dance was characterized by "immediacy of abandon and strength of inner concentration."

On 23 May 1932, at the Pasadena Community Playhouse, Benjamin Zemach gave his first concert in the Los Angeles area. He was to stay in Los Angeles until invited in 1936 back to New York by director Max Reinhardt to stage a Broadway play. These four years in Los Angeles were filled with activity and growth for Benjamin. He was able to develop a concert group and taught extensively. During this time he directed *The Golem* and other plays for the Pasadena Playhouse; he also created a movie short as well as the dances for *She* (1935) and *Days of Pompeii* (1935). Along with his own work, he was influential in the development of several young artists. Many dancers studied and performed with Zemach in Los Angeles, among them: Arnold Tamon, Robert Bell, Waldeen Falkenstein, Ella Serruier, Teru Izumida, Karoun Toutikian, Ruth Sharp, Lisa and Miriam Levitsky, Margaret Mayo, Charles Ewing, Thelma Babitz, Adela Cutler, and Frieda Flier.

Babitz and Flier went with Zemach to New York in 1936 and in 1937 became members of the Graham Company. Flier in 1986 spoke of the lifelong impact Zemach had on her as an artist and dancer.

> Benjamin made you participate in the creative process; he made you feel you had something in you, that you had ideas. It was fascinating. He opened up a whole world of expression and possibilities to me. He gave meaning to dance. It was not

Benjamin Zemach in Dance for Olympic Festival, 1932
As part of the ongoing celebrations of the Olympic Games, which
were held in Los Angeles in the summer of 1932, the Los Angeles
Philharmonic hosted a week-long festival of music and dance, in
which Zemach was a featured dancer.
(*Courtesy Amielle Zemach*)

Benjamin Zemach in Dance for Olympic Festival, 1932
(*Courtesy Amielle Zemach*)

just technique. Each class was based on a theme, and you learned to improvise and look into yourself. Performance was also a creative, shared experience. Benjamin made sure that dance for us was not superficial, but it was a deeper, inner process.[10]

Zemach's first Los Angeles program in May 1932 was long and varied, with 14 pieces listed: *Jacob's Dream, The Worker on the Soil, Toccata in D Minor, The Menorah, Three Palestinian Folk Songs, Beggar, The Cheder, The Study of the Talmud, Eccentric, Destiny, Ruth, A Chapter from "Psalms," Farewell to Queen Sabbath.* Fourteen dancers and Benjamin performed, accompanied by pianist Verna Arvey and singer Arcady Kaufman. The next involvement for Zemach was the week-long Olympic Dance Festival, Philharmonic Auditorium, 8 through 13 August 1932. He was listed as a guest artist for all performances, and his contribution consisted of: *The Beggar* (solo), *Ruth* (trio), and *Farewell to Queen Sabbath* (quintet, five men). Zemach began to attract notice, and soon he and his group were touring and performing in Los Angeles, Carmel, San Francisco, and in Seattle at the Cornish School.

Recognition by community leaders took the form of an invitation to create a ballet for the prestigious Hollywood Bowl. On 5 August 1933 Zemach's *Fragments of Israel* was presented at the Bowl and utilized 49 performers and a chorus of 23 men. The orchestra was conducted by Bakaleinikoff; costumes were designed by Willis Knighton. This commission signified major public acceptance for the choreographer and gave him the opportunity to utilize a live orchestra, a substantial vocal chorus, and a large group of dancers.

Fragments of Israel comprised two sections. The first section was a reshaping of *Farewell to Queen Sabbath;* the second was a new work— "Ora." In this ballet Zemach was developing all his ideas on a larger scale. The two sections allowed him to make a broader statement about the need for recognition of the Jewish people—the rich heritage and the necessity to survive. The dance was intended to convey a universal plea for all people to maintain their identity against oppression. Zemach was continuing in the vein of ecstatic, symbolic dance and was also making a social statement about the need for all to live and fight against oppression. By creating the second section Zemach celebrated not only the contribution of the Jews to the religious and cultural heritage of Western civilization but also the rebirth of the Jewish people as a nation. He created a dance about the right of the Jews to worship in their own way and about their right to rebuild a nation in Palestine. He celebrated the beauty of worship and of work and used authentic folk material for inspiration in creating a contemporary statement in expressive movement.

Isabel Morse Jones, music critic, was impressed with the work. She noted that Zemach was "as worthy a representative of the Jewish race as Ernest Bloch and his music."

His *Fragments of Israel* at the Bowl, was a profound and beautiful ritual, with choral chants of ancient Hebrew origin, and orchestral interludes conducted by Bakaleinikoff from manuscript. Jacob Weinstock directed the folk song. The scenes were of Bible times, the very sources of culture—humanly fundamental and powerful. It was great dance drama for the Bowl, and the young dancers felt privileged to work under Zemach in two numbers, "Farewell to Queen Sabbath" with its Chassidic rites from meditation to ecstasy, and "Ora" a vigorous Palestinian theme in which the old pioneers sing, "God will rebuild Palestine!" and the young ones shout, "The peasants will rebuild Palestine."[11]

The Hollywood Bowl had never presented any ballets based on Jewish content or Jewish folk material, and the press did not ignore the opportunity to highlight this unusual offering. There were pictures and articles in several newspapers, and both the message and the form of the dance occasioned considerable comment. The *Hollywood Citizen News* on 4 August 1933 featured a large picture of the ballet with the heading "Zemach Ballet Distinctive . . . Unusual Bowl Offering . . . Hebrew Folk Dance Basis." The picture in the *Hollywood Citizen News* shows the performers grouped not as a single unit but arranged in a dramatic sculptural interplay of mass and shape. Except for a unison group of women on stage right, every dancer is arranged in a different shape: sitting, lying, standing, and leaning. Each individual dancer contributes a particular shape to the total vision of three major sculptural groupings. Six dancers closest to the back of the stage hold large columns—symbols of the tablets of the ten commandments. The three tablets on stage right and the three tablets on stage left are held so that they lean toward the center of the stage. This gives the feeling that the tablets meet in the center, forming a triangle whose apex reaches toward God and the heavens. The three multishaped groupings of dancers also create a sense of focus toward the apex of a triangle.

The *Los Angeles Times* published a picture in its 30 July edition with the comment: "This production is based on Jewish folk dances, and in the words of the producer, is 'serious but not heavy.'" This picture shows a trio, in which once again the sense of sculptural shape and mass are emphasized. Each of the three dancers is in a different position. The trio creates a sense of a three-level unit, all leaning and yearning toward a central focus. There is a strong feeling of the weight of the bodies as well as a fluidity created by the leaning torsos and the interconnected, molded use of shaped arms.

Benjamin Zemach's comments on *Fragments of Israel* were quoted in the program notes for the performance.

> The Jewish race has been crowded out of its natural surroundings. The Jews are naturally a people of the soil, of the vineyards. They have been crowded together in large cities. Today their movements are nervous and unbalanced; sharp jerks in syncopated rhythms. Looking for a typical Jewish style not only in the past, but going back to the very source of our life and culture—to the Bible and Biblical times . . . we find there not only scenes which are humanly fundamental and powerful, but a style richer and older than those we know already. This style is, and always will be, ancient and modern at the same time. Just as the modern dance goes back to the primitive for its fundamentals—so does this movement, "back to the soil" started so strongly with the Jewish race all over the world, go back to the Bible.

Zemach wanted his dancers to represent the average mass of humanity. In particular, these people are Jews, with their own traditions and their own songs and movements. In universal terms, these Jews represent all of us who celebrate some relationship with a higher being to give meaning to our lives and whose week is composed not only of the need to work but also the need to seek spiritual reinforcement, solace, and exaltation. The traditions of religion come not only from the rules and rituals of formal worship but also from within the moods and traditions of all the people.

In the second sequence of *Fragments of Israel*, "Ora" (a Hebrew word for light), a strong statement was made about the dreams of the Jewish people for the rebirth of their heritage in Palestine. It also clearly relayed the message of the joy and necessity for people to come together and work to achieve their goals. Zemach was not unaware of the conflict in the rebuilding of Palestine—the conflict between those who would wait for a Messiah and those who would take tractor and plow to reclaim the land in an active attempt to shape their own destinies. Without negating the necessity for spiritual guidance portrayed in the first sequence, the second sequence of Zemach's dance portrayed the need for a life of action to make dreams come true.

In 1935 Benjamin Zemach had his second major commission for the Hollywood Bowl, creating *The Victory Ball* (music by Ernest Schelling). This ballet, presented 1 August, marked a major development in his choreography, for it was a work that made a solid statement on a broad scale. It was an impressive, compelling, mature work with complex movements for soloist and group. The critics were unanimous in their praise, and due to such interest it was repeated at the Mason Opera House. It was because of this dance that Max Reinhardt invited Zemach to be choreographer for the New York premiere of *The Eternal Road* in 1936.

Rehearsal of *The Victory Ball*, Hollywood Bowl, 1935
(*Courtesy Hollywood Bowl Museum Archives*)

The Alfred Noyes poem, "The Victory Ball," was the inspiration for Zemach's ballet. It was printed in its entirety on the program as follows:

The cymbals crash,
And the dancers walk,
With long silk stockings
And arms of chalk,
Butterfly skirts,
And white breasts bare,
And shadows of dead men
Watching them there.

Shadows of dead men
Stand by the wall,
Watching the fun
Of the Victory Ball.
They do not reproach,
Because they know,
If they're forgotten,
It's better so.

Fat wet bodies
Go waddling by
Girdled with satin,
Though God knows why;
Gripped by satyrs
In white and black,
With a fat white hand
On a fat wet back.

"What did you think
We should find?" said a shade
"When the last shot echoed
And peace was made?"
"Christ," laughed the fleshless
Jaws of his friend,
"I thought they'd be praying
For worlds to mend.

"Making earth better,
Or something silly
Like white—washing Hell
or Pecca-dam-dilly.
They've a sense of humour,
Those women of ours,
These exquisite lilies,
These fresh young flowers!"

"Pish," said a statesman
Standing near,
"I'm glad they can busy
Their thoughts elsewhere!
We mustn't reproach 'em,
They're young, you see."
"Ah," said the dead men,
"So were we!"

"Victory! Victory!
On with the dance!
Back to the jungle
The new beast's prance!
God how the dead men
Grin by the wall,
Watching the fun
Of the Victory Ball.

The *Hollywood Citizen News* in an article on 1 August carried the headline: "Victory Ball Symphony Due at Bowl Written as Protest on Indifference to War Cost."

Ernest Schelling's symphonic work *The Victory Ball* . . . with Benjamin Zemach presenting his ballet to this great work, was composed as "a tonal protest to those who seemed so indifferent and forgetful of the sacrifice of the war, and who were celebrating with victory balls all over the world" the composer said today. . . . It was composed as a "symphonic tableaux" by Mr. Schelling after his return from the World War as "a tribute to those who gave their all" so that "we might live in peace and happiness" he declared.

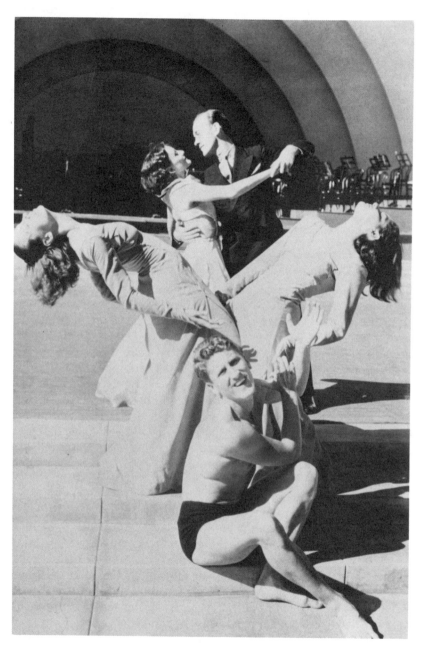

Rehearsal of *The Victory Ball*, Hollywood Bowl, 1935
(*Courtesy Hollywood Bowl Museum Archives*)

The cast of characters for *The Victory Ball* listed on the program included generals, diplomats, profiteers, dowagers, debutantes, soldiers, mothers, crosses, and death. The ballet opened with Irving Pichel reading the poem by Albert Noyes. Blandings Sloan created a projection painted on glass that filled the arch of the Hollywood Bowl with crosses. Viola Hegyi Swisher described the ballet in her 2 August review for the *Hollywood Citizen News*:

> While the dancers whirled about in a gayly colored ballroom scene silent shadows of war played an obbligato across the Bowl shell. Fields fertile with dead men and marked by crosses, soldiers going over the top to infinity—these were silhouetted in the background while sub-debs and statesmen, smartly tailed officers and sleakly gowned women danced and flirted at the Victory Ball. Then came a war scene, leaving some of the dead and bereaved to make a chilling lacy pattern along the front of the stage when the lights flashed again upon the ballroom scene. Thus the Zemach ballet went its way to a crashing climax that left spectators thrilled and silent for a moment before breaking into rounds of applause.

Two rehearsal pictures of *The Victory Ball* taken at the Hollywood Bowl are helpful in understanding the way Zemach used movement to develop his antiwar theme. One picture shows a group of six women. Each of the women is expressing an intense sense of anguish and despair, but each does so in her own way. The bodies are twisted at the torso, and knees and feet press deep into the ground. There is a great deal of tension in their bodies and faces. One standing woman has her arms in front of her, crossed at the wrists with the fists clenched. Her shoulders are pressed forward and raised, and her chest has the feeling of being almost concave with despair. Another woman is standing but with knees more deeply bent. Her torso is twisted stage left and slightly rotated to the back. Her palms are facing each other and cradling her head, as if to protect it from injury. Her elbows are angular; she is in a deep plié, with weight unevenly distributed, leaning more into her right knee. All six bodies are angular, and the overall impression is of six women in pain.

Zemach was interested in using the body to express the deep inner anguish of the soul in this ballet. He was never interested in pretty movement, nor in virtuosity, and each dance required its own expressive vocabulary. He was interested in movement that had meaning, and more often the torso, pelvis, and arms took the brunt of the expressive message. Amielle Zemach once asked her father about being trained so that she could lift her legs in handsome and elegant arabesques and extensions. Zemach replied, "Why would you want to lift your leg. It is pretty only."[12]

Form and content came together in *The Victory Ball*. Zemach was not interested in interpreting the words of the Noyes poem literally.

He used them as a jumping-off point and developed visual and sculptural sequences of movement that would abstract and probe the qualities of brutality, despair, and disaster that come with war. The critics were unanimous in their praise of Zemach. Isabel Morse Jones, in the *Los Angeles Times* of 2 August, called the work "real ballet, original, deeply impressive" and said that it had "the touch of genius." She felt that Zemach had produced "a history making ballet."

> The crowd was enormous, one of the largest, if not actually the largest of the season, and the onlookers could not be restrained from breaking into the performance with spontaneous clapping and cheers. Feeling ran high and the tension was ominous. Impersonalizing war and nationalistic folly, as Zemach did, was a master stroke. The banners were just brilliantly colored symbols, not any country's flag. Even the hordes of doughboys marching by in colossal shadows finally merged into gray motion pictures thrown on the great proscenium. . . . No one would fail to "pray for worlds to mend" after this spectacle. The dancers were as clever as a lot of Kreutzberg or Wigman dancers would have been. This was modern ballet with the German technique and an American bride-of-war idea dominating it. The effect was overpowering. It cast a spell over the Bowl. The ghosts of dead soldiers will haunt it for a long time.

Zemach's statement in *The Victory Ball* had originally castigated not only the destruction of war but also those who wanted war to continue because of the profits they could earn from the activities of war. In the version Zemach rehearsed on the Hollywood Bowl stage, he included a scene in which he correlated the enrichment of the stockbrokers with the destruction of war. With each act of destruction there was a corresponding act of profit, exemplified on the stage by the addition of higher numbers to the riches of the stockbrokers. While the management of the Bowl was agreeable to Zemach's antiwar ballet, they were not pleased with the portrayal of the rich getting richer on the spoils of war. Zemach was told to eliminate this scene in his ballet and had to comply. According to Zemach: "There was quite a hullabaloo about the stockbroker scene . . . a stormy session with Mrs. Irish."[13]

In spite of the fact that he had to eliminate this scene, the ballet was strong enough to get its message across. Viola Hegyi Swisher's review in the *Hollywood Citizen News* of 2 August carried the headline: "Zemach's Tragic 'Victory Ball!' Ballet Thrills Vast Bowl Throng: Horror of War Told in Dance." She felt the ballet was a great success: "Genius swept a fleeting hand across the Hollywood Bowl last night. A figurative tear and satire stirred bitterness there while a deeply impressed audience witnessed Benjamin Zemach's dance poem. . . . Music, movement, color, lights all were fused into one powerful expression of protest against blood lust, bombast, shallowness, hypocrisy, greed—in short—War."

The ballet moved continuously from one scene to the next. According to Amielle Zemach: "His work always had a sense of connection, of one thing moving to the next. He never created independent vignettes. There was always a wholeness in his work, with one thing leading organically to the next."[14] In *The Victory Ball* the main action began on the battlefield and then moved to the ballroom, where the soldiers watched from the side. As the ballroom scene faded, with isolated couples repeating the strains of the dances, the battle took center stage again while a group of mothers stage left grieved. During this section the stock market scene was to have taken place stage right.

Amielle Zemach noted that her father's work always went "from darkness to light," with a focus on the plight of the "common man." Although Zemach was making a bitter antiwar statement, he also wanted to say there could be a transition from despair to hope and that there was always the existence of light alongside the actions that constituted the dark side of humanity. Alma Cowdy, in her 2 August review of the ballet in the *Los Angeles Herald Express*, brought out this aspect of the dance.

> The Bowl was thrown into darkness as the Alfred Noyes poem was begun by the speech chorus trained by Bertha Vocha Fiske. This eerie chant, with solo spoken by Irving Pichel, was beautifully done. Conductor Schelling's idea of the slow awakening of the city on the day of the armistice was effected by a small spot of blue-green light enlarged gradually to bring the relief of the brilliantly costumed generals, diplomats, dowagers and debutantes who with mawkish gestures moved down upon the stage and swung into polonaise, foxtrot and exaggerated tango. The most effective of Zemach's drama in movement came in the middle part of the work when the scenario called for sheer terror before the oncoming hordes. . . . A final section to a distorted waltz rhythm was danced hesitantly by a couple here and there and grew to proportions of a bacchanale before they were confronted by the return of the mocking dead and the march of the troops. Simultaneously with the rising and accusing figures of sorrow, the black cross of death disappeared and in its place rose the three white crosses of hope, back center, accompanied in the music by the introduction of the courage raising bagpipes.

The descriptions and pictures of *The Victory Ball* call to mind Kurt Jooss's *Green Table*. Both Zemach and Jooss were creating in a period when artists in dance, music, painting, and literature were concerned with the plight of the individual in face of war, hunger, suffering, and inequality. For Zemach as well as for others the necessity was to find artistic vocabulary that would make a statement about man and his political, social, and economic environment. The choreographer is faced with many problems in dealing with social content, as is any artist. It is easy for political and social art to be less art and more polemic. In dance the social content must be abstracted into movement that is universally meaningful without being literal and pedantic. Kurt Jooss's *Green Table* remains a masterful antiwar statement to this day. From all the available accounts and documentation, Benjamin Zemach was a choreographer who also created a powerful antiwar ballet and whose other work was equally successful in its ability to make artistically meaningful and socially relevant statements.

Zemach brought to Los Angeles new directions in both form and content. The use of words—of spoken and vocal accompaniment—derived from his theater background, provided new elements for many dance audiences. The movements for each dance grew organically from the content. His dances were characterized by expressive use of torso, head, and arms, with a sense of weight in the whole body and flexion in the knees and ankles. Within this he could create a lyric, sequential flow of movement or an angular sculptured pattern.

The concern with the darker side of human experience and the conflict between light and dark may well have been encouraged by his work with Vakhtangov, Stanislavsky, and Meyerhold. In 1980 he spoke of dance as always having been for him an art that would reach "to a consciousness of the world and the human connection and come close to the core of life."[15] It was not a dim view of the world but one in which contrasts existed, and spiritual regeneration could be achieved through understanding. Art was a way of attaining resolution of the human spirit, of resolving the dichotomy of darkness and light.

Zemach was beginning to achieve a strong identity as an independent artist when he came to Los Angeles. In this city he grew and developed, leaving a strong mark on audiences and students. In 1936, as he was beginning to solidify his reputation and his work in Los Angeles, he accepted Max Reinhardt's invitation to stage dances for *The Eternal Road*. During the next decade in New York, where he stayed until 1947, he continued to teach and choreograph but did not develop a permanent company. Los Angeles beckoned again in 1947, and Zemach was active in theater and dance in the city until 1971, when he finally settled in Israel.

Zemach's career needs to be fully documented; only then can his influence and artistry be more completely assessed. In later years he trained Alan Arkin, Adeline Gibbs, Herschel Bernardi, Lee J. Cobb, Sam Jaffe, and Corey Allan, among others. He continued to choreograph and direct plays and attracted large crowds to his productions. Was Zemach one of the crucial figures in shaping American modern dance in the late 1920s and 1930s? Has he been neglected because his work was stronger during the 1930s than it was later? Has he been neglected because he twice left New York at crucial times? Has he been neglected because we are just beginning to evaluate some of the individuals who were not recognized as superstars? How important was the sense of social concern, of the conflict of light and dark, in the totality of modern dance in the 1930s? Did this concern help shape the search for new structure and vocabulary that was so important in the maturing of American dance, and was Zemach influential in this growth? The answer to all these questions is yes.

The value of analyzing Zemach's work in Los Angeles is that it provides both an intensive look at what he did and also an evaluative base. Zemach was noticed as an important artist from 1928 through 1932 in New York. He grew in maturity and developed while in Los Angeles from 1932 through 1936. During this period he was an artist who had something to say and had found an original way to say it. He was a teacher who understood movement and theater and knew how to initiate and share the creative process with students. He was important in shaping dance in Los Angeles in the 1930s, and he shaped the careers and artistic development of many who later went elsewhere and continued on their own. This is a first step in the assessment of Benjamin Zemach's place in the development of American dance and will provide the groundwork for a fuller evaluation.

Part Four

Hollywood and the Emergence of American Concert Dance: Lester Horton

Introduction to Part Four

The purpose of this section is to examine the 1937 ballet *Le Sacre du Printemps* that marked Lester Horton's emergence as a major artist in American concert dance. This focus places Horton in the Southern California context in which he developed and worked.

Lester Horton created his version of *Le Sacre du Printemps* for the Hollywood Bowl in 1937. From the sun-drenched home of movies and mountains, 1937 marked the end of an era in Los Angeles and a new artist emerging to the public at large. Lester Horton, an artist deeply rooted in the multiethnic city and western frontier he called home, arrived in Los Angeles in 1928. Perhaps he could have developed as rapidly elsewhere, but he would not have developed in the same way. From 1928 through the 1937 ballet that brought him great attention, he was like a sponge. All the divergent techniques and aesthetic formulations that coexisted comfortably in what was then the small, intense city of Los Angeles proved to be his shaping influences. But Horton was more than a sponge. His great ability was to incorporate and absorb ideas with great facility until they had acquired the peculiarly original stamp of his personality and emotional framework. The influence of the physical environment of Los Angeles markedly contributed to his artistic development. In Lester Horton Los Angeles finally had its own dance artist.

8

Lester Horton (1906–1953): *Le Sacre du Printemps*

Lester Horton was born in Indianapolis, Indiana, and lived there until coming to California in 1928. While growing up in his native city he developed interests that shaped his work as a mature artist in art, dance, theater, and involvement in the life and culture of the American Indian. According to his biographer, Larry Warren,[1] a visit to Indian mounds in Anderson, near Indianapolis, sparked Horton's curiosity about the natives who had built this archeological site. There was a nearby children's museum with a fine collection of American Indian arts and artifacts, and Horton spent many hours there. An essay written in eighth grade called "The Indian in His Native Art" marked the culmination of these initial browsings. Apparently, the composition was quite good, and the young Lester was asked to read it for the eighth grade commencement exercises.

Horton's interest in the American Indian continued in high school, but during this period he also became fascinated with dance and theater. In 1922 and 1923 Ruth St. Denis and Ted Shawn performed with their company at the Murat Theatre in Indianapolis. Horton's first exposure at 16 and 17 to the Denishawn repertory made him want to learn more about dance.[2] As a result he began formal training with a local woman, Theo Hewes. She was primarily a ballet teacher with what must have been a somewhat eclectic background. She studied with Madame Menzeli in the East as well as with Pavley and Oukrainsky in Chicago.

Horton early exhibited a theatrical flair, a natural talent for teaching, an ability to absorb ideas rapidly, and a facility for invention. Theo Hewes recognized Horton's talents, and after only one year of studying with her he began teaching Saturday morning classes to younger pupils. Karoun Toutikian, a Los Angeles dancer who grew up in Indianapolis, was in several of those Saturday morning classes and remembered her experience vividly in later years. In 1986 she was able to recall an amusing incident that occurred. "We were doing what I know now was a petit battement. When I asked Lester the name of the step, he stopped for a minute to think. After a short period of reflection, he waved his hands in the air and said, 'Just call it a Hortina.'" Toutikian also remembered that the ballet material was often interspersed with other things—steps that Horton seemed to be making up. She recalled that the classes were exciting and his teaching self-assured—characteristics of her later experiences with him in Los Angeles.[3]

Lester Horton was encouraged by his progress and excited by his new adventures in the field of dance. Anxious for more experience he answered a call for an audition in 1925. The audition notice was placed by Forrest Thornburg, a young man who had studied with Denishawn and who was now in charge of a touring company. Toutikian remembered Lester's excitement about becoming a professional performer and also his nervousness at going to the audition. She recalled that he had no need to worry. The only man to show up, he was accepted without a moment's hesitation. It is unclear exactly how long the tour lasted, but Toutikian guessed it was probably several months. She does remember that it was during this time that Thornburg taught Horton everything he had learned at Denishawn in return for Lester's help with the group's rehearsals, costumes, and general production details.

After the experience with Forrest Thornburg, Horton came back to Indianapolis in 1926 and made the acquaintance of Clara Bates. Both Clara and her husband, William, were involved in producing and directing theater. They were also both deeply interested in the American Indian and had a large personal collection of Indian art and artifacts, including clothing, jewelry, and blankets. In addition, they had made a practice over the years of visiting various Indian reservations, where they were able to get a deeper understanding of folklore, songs, dances, and ways of life of various tribes.

The Bateses were founders of the Indianapolis Theatre Guild, an organization that fostered pageants, regional theater, and local dramatic presentations. They were in touch with the activities of the American Pageantry Movement and subscribed wholeheartedly to the tenets of people leading the movement. They wanted to see more theater based on native themes. Clara in particular felt strongly about outdoor presentations as a way to reach large numbers of people in spectacles that included music, dance, drama, and historical material.

In 1926 William Bates passed away and Clara proceeded on her own to develop a pageant based on Longfellow's poem "The Song of Hiawatha." She used a play written by a woman named Olive M. Price

as the foundation but created her own elaborations, adding music and dance. She had heard about Horton's performances at the Hewes School, and she had seen him at a costume ball in a striking outfit he had designed for himself. Clara Bates arranged to meet with Lester, and they agreed to work together on *The Song of Hiawatha*. She wanted him to study firsthand the American Indian and arranged for him to visit several Indian reservations.

The first production of *The Song of Hiawatha* in 1926 was very successful. Horton was involved in arranging the dances, some of the staging, and creation of costumes. The production was repeated again on 4 July 1927 and received even greater acclaim from public and press. A review of that production in an Indianapolis newspaper relayed the viewer's impressions.

> Beneath the glow of the setting sun and with a wooded hill, like the primeval forests, forming the background, the ancient Indian legend *Hiawatha* was presented last evening by the Indianapolis Theater Guild along the old towpath at Fairview park. About two hundred persons witnessed the production. The cast, composed of members of the guild, presented Longfellow's tale of Indian life after a rehearsal of nearly four weeks, and from the opening scene, the rearing of Hiawatha by the venerable Nokomos to the final scene when Minnehaha answers the call to the "happy hunting grounds" the version of life of the Indians was made very real.[4]

Clara Bates spared no effort in making *The Song of Hiawatha* a success. There was a 40-piece orchestra directed by Gale Lorada of New York and Leslie C. Troutman of Indianapolis. The costumes were lavish and based on authentic design. There were wigwams and, according to the program, "backgrounds of leafy branches" and "campfires" to simulate an Indian village. Horton played the role of Hiawatha, and the songs and dances were an important part of the production. The program noted that the pageant would tell the entire story of Hiawatha, from the time Gitche Manitou, the Indian god, promised to send the tribes a leader, through his wooing and winning of Minnehaha, to the tragic death scene.

An Indianapolis newspaper review of the 4 July 1927 production reported: "The execution of the most difficult Indian dances, the weird cries and songs gave even the most unimaginative a vision of Indian life. . . . The steady beating of the drums during the dances and the hair-raising war cries of the chiefs and Indian maidens added to the weirdness of the spectacle."[5] Horton was cited for his performance, particularly for the dance of the invocation to the thunder god, which probably was a show-stopper. This production of *Hiawatha* was an important experience for Horton and helped shape his sense of theatricality, develop his use of indigenous material, and increase his showmanship.

Clara Bates took this production on tours throughout Indiana and Ohio during 1927. In 1928 she accepted an invitation from a California friend, Lysbeth Argus, to bring *Hiawatha* to Los Angeles. Mrs. Argus had a natural amphitheater on her estate, called the Argus Bowl, which was often the site of music, theater, and dance presentations. Clara Bates, Lester Horton, and probably one or two other people from the original production set out for California, along with costumes and assorted homemade and authentic American Indian percussion instruments. The first West coast production of *The Song of Hiawatha* took place at Argus Bowl on 2 July 1928.

The Song of Hiawatha was presented again on six different days in June 1929 at 3:00 and 8:00 each day. The 1929 program described it as a music drama pageant, and the place of presentation was given as "The Argus Garden, 1805 Hill Drive."[6] Sponsored by the Division of Indian Welfare, California Federation of Women's Clubs, the performance involved the support of many prominent Los Angeles women. The advisory committee consisted of Madames Argus, Cheney, Cole, Lane, Mudd, Phillips, Sartori, Smith, Von Kleinsmud, and Wattles. Clara Bates was listed as the chairman of the production committee, and Lester Horton was listed as the director. The music committee consisted of Charles Wakefield Cadman, Homer Grunn, and Sol Cohen— all prominent musician/composers deeply interested in native American Indian music. The music for the 1929 *Hiawatha* was composed by all three men.

Shortly after the 1929 performances at the Argus Garden, Clara Bates went back to Indianapolis, and Lester Horton began his independent career in Los Angeles. One of his first solo ventures was his participation in the ninth annual Desert Play in Palm Springs. The particular play presented in 1929 was *Fire* by a local writer Mary Austin—a romantic story of the giving of the elements to the Indians by the Great Spirit. It was staged in a natural setting in Tahquitz Canyon, near the city limits of Palm Springs. A cast of 60 included prominent citizens of the resort and Cahuilla Indians from the Agua Callente Reservation at Palm Springs. A man named Russell Stimmel was the director; the music was by Homer Grunn. One newspaper article about the performance reported that "weird tribal and ceremonial dances never before presented in public"[7] were included; presumably, this referred to the performance of the Cahuilla Indians. Lester Horton appeared as the Fire God and Homer Grunn's wife, Celeste, appeared as an Indian maiden, Laela.

In July and August of that summer Lester Horton studied and performed with Michio Ito, also at Argus Garden. Ito presented his students on Monday evenings, 5 August through 2 September 1929. It was in these programs that Horton played the guardian/hawk in Ito's production of *At the Hawk's Well*. According to Larry Warren's chronology of Horton's work, the 2 September Argus Bowl program also included a work *Siva-Siva*, performed and choreographed with Katherine Stubergh. Warren also lists a solo *Kootenai War Dance* as a Horton work choreographed and performed on 28 August 1931 at Argus Bowl.

Horton's performance at the Argus Bowl in *The Song of Hiawatha* and in *At the Hawk's Well* brought him to the attention of Jean Abel, a woman who played an important role in his early development in Los Angeles. Abel was a highly respected and innovative art teacher at Glendale High School, which was not far from Eagle Rock, the site of the Argus Estate. Her brother, Rudolph, was a dancer who had studied in Japan in the 1920s. Brother and sister were frequently in the audience at the Argus Bowl events, and Jean Abel was struck with Lester's charisma as a performer and with his dances and costumes for *Hiawatha*. She asked him to come to Glendale High School to work with her young students and create an Indian pageant. Elizabeth Talbot-Martin, part of this original group, remembered the experience of working with Horton as pivotal in her life. "He really knew about the American Indian, and he conveyed an enthusiasm and excitement that were catching. We did everything with and for him, staying after school, working for hours, creating costumes, props, instruments. We danced, acted, sang . . . it was an incredible experience."[8]

The summer of 1932 was a crucial one for Horton. Jean Abel asked him to join her in a teaching venture at the Little Theatre of the Verdugos, northeast of Glendale. She also asked him to direct a play, *The Lady in the Sack* by Conrad Seiler, and to create another pageant. The group that had worked with Horton during the year at Glendale High School came to study with him that summer of 1932, among them Elizabeth Talbot-Martin, William Bowne, Portia Woodbury, Arvin Bowne, Joewilla Blodgett. This group of loyal followers, the first dancers Horton trained, eventually formed the nucleus of his first dance group.

By midsummer this eager group of Glendale High School students and Horton had the opportunity to give their first professional performance during a special Olympic Dance Festival, 8 through 13 August, at the Philharmonic Auditorium. The six evenings of dance were organized by a woman named Wanda Grazer, a former Denishawn dancer, teacher, and impresario. She brought together over 50 choreographers and performers, and there was dancing of all kinds: tap, modern, ballet, interpretive ballroom, ethnic, and folk (listed this way on the program). Not only was it Horton's first chance to present group work, but it also provided him with the opportunity of seeing numerous other choreographers and absorbing their ideas.

The Philharmonic programs featured: Muriel Stuart (an ex-Pavlova dancer), Benjamin Zemach, Michio Ito, Ann Douglas (Denishawn background), Trinidad Goni and Manuel Perez (Spanish dance), Bob Gilbert (acrobatic jazz), Hazel Wright (solo based on *The Cakewalk*), as well as many others. Horton's two contributions to the program were *Kootenai War Dance* and *Voodoo Ceremonial*. William Bowne, who was to be Horton's companion and associate for many years, talked in 1983 about the importance of the Philharmonic Olympic Festival. "It was a confirmation of the possibilities of dance, of ideas that could be realized, and of the strength and potential of movement." Bowne himself was very taken with the work of Zemach. "Zemach was the most sophisticated, with a beautiful use of music and a real understanding of the modern idiom, very personal and yet universal. It was ethnic material with real backing and was deeply rooted."[9]

Horton had experimented with *Kootenai War Dance* in an Argus Bowl performance in 1931, and presented it at the Philharmonic with Bill and Arvin Bowne playing drums. *Voodoo Ceremonial* was a large group work and was to remain in the Horton repertory for some time. Subtitled "Dance to the Forces of Superstition," it was based on a book about Haiti. The dancers were: Doje Arbenz, Brahm Van Den Berg, Jeanne Blodgett, Joewilla Blodgett, Arvin Bowne, William Bowne, Patricia Green, Maxine Heasley, Loys Safier, Elizabeth Talbot-Martin, Portia Woodbury, Karoun Toutikian, and Lavallete Toutikian.

Voodoo Ceremonial allowed Horton to explore concepts of theatricality and ritual that were to be important in his later work. William Bowne remembered that the dance started on a dark stage with pounding rhythms executed by the drummers and the dancers. The dancers wore black costumes. The men wore black pants with no shirts and black headdresses. The women's costumes, made of black Japanese crepe cotton mat, were fashioned by cutting a hole through which the dancers could put their heads, creating a cowl effect. The upper part of their faces, from forehead to just below the eyes, was painted in black and underlined with red lipstick. Both Bowne and Talbot-Martin remembered that the effect was startling, but they could never get the makeup off.

Horton and his enthusiastic group had been launched, and the next two months were filled with important activity. Albert Deano, who had studied with Denishawn, had helped produce the Olympic Dance Festival, but his main job was as a producer for Paramount Theatre. He invited Horton to present *Voodoo Ceremonial* as part of the live show at that theater, and for two weeks they shared the bill with the Gum sisters—Judy Garland and her two sisters. Talbot-Martin reminisced in a 1983 interview about their partners on that Paramount bill. "Judy Garland and her sisters came out and sang 'Dinah,' and then Judy sang 'That's Why Darkies Were Born.' She wore a gold face cap, gold rayon satin palazzo pants, gold lace bolero, black tap shoes with two big bows. . . . It was so ugly even for that day it could not be believed."

The Paramount venture was followed by a performance of Horton's second pageant, *Takwish, The Star Maker,* on 9 and 10 September at the Little Theatre of the Verdugos. The program called this pageant a "California Indian Dance Drama," and the main character was Takwish, God of the Blue Mountain, played by Rudolph Abel. The cast was large: Ralph Neff (story teller); Takwish; Pahalali, daughter of Emecula, promised bride of Chungishnish (Doje Arbenz); Chungishnish, son of Wiyot, chief of the tribe (Toni Masarachia); Tukvachtahat, medicine man (Warren Washburn); Tukwishemish, mad woman (Elizabeth Talbot-Martin); Kunwachmal, lover of Phahalali (Leaster Eaton); Kwikumat, chieftain (Ralph Lloyd); Temecula, mother of Pahalali (Florence Butler Belyear); Chaipakomat, magician (Ernest G. Metcalf). There were eight male singers, seven medicine women, seven children, 11 female dancers, 10 male dancers, and various spirits— coyote, owl, snake, mountain lion. *Takwish* was an important work in Horton's development as artist and choreographer. It was the first long professional work that he had ever done with full responsibility for authorship. (While Horton had been an assistant in the development of *Hiawatha,* he was credited on the program of *Takwish* as sole author.) It included the first group of dancers he had ever trained, and it contained many dances, solos, duets, and various group numbers. The movement was more complex and varied than any he had done before, and the entire production showed a striking cohesiveness and theatricality.

In 1932 two other important events were influential in Horton's development. He saw a performance of Mary Wigman and her group, and he began teaching at Norma Gould's studio. Always receptive to new ideas and blessed with a capacity to absorb everything and make it his own, Horton reacted like a sponge to the numerous activities at Gould's Dance Theatre and to the Wigman concerts. In 1933 he created *Oriental Motifs,* again for the Little Theatre of the Verdugos, and in 1934 he gave the first full evening of his own work at the large Shrine Auditorium in Los Angeles. The announcement for the Shrine concerts read "Lester Horton's California Ballets." The program advertised: "Brilliant Soloists and ensemble in new ballets by Gershwin, Ravel, Stravinsky, Honneger, De Falla, Yamada, Grofe, Antheil, and other modern composers." Horton and his group gave performances on the last Friday of each month: 26 October, 30 November, and 28 December 1934; 25 January, 22 February, and 29 March 1935.

Lester Horton in *Takwish, The Star Maker*, 1932
(*Courtesy Toyo Miyatake*)

Horton's first five years in Los Angeles had exposed him to many influences. Zemach, Ito, Gould, Trinidad Goni, Manuel Perez, Ann Douglas, and Muriel Stuart were artists whose work he saw every night at the Olympic Dance Festival, and Ito had been his teacher on a regular basis. Belcher, Bolm, Michel Fokine, Albertina Rasch, Jose Fernandez, and Theodore Kosloff were choreographers whose works he had seen at the Hollywood Bowl through 1934.

From 1934 through spring 1937 Horton and his company gave concerts at Norma Gould's Dance Theatre, the Figueroa Playhouse, the Tuesday Afternoon Club of Glendale, the Philharmonic Auditorium, the Pasadena Playhouse, and the Hollywood Concert Hall. In the summer of 1937 Lester Horton was given a great honor that marked significant recognition on the part of the Los Angeles community. He was asked to create a ballet for the Hollywood Bowl and on 5 August presented his choreography for *Le Sacre du Printemps* to music by Igor Stravinsky. There, on a large stage for an audience of almost 20,000, Horton emerged into the public eye, creating a work that marked the full emergence of his style, his use of music, his theatricality, and the integration of his varied artistic influences into a long, sustained, mature piece of choreography. Horton's work for the Hollywood Bowl marked the first time the Stravinsky music was used by a choreographer in California, and it was only the fourth time the score had been used for dance. The first choreography to the Stravinsky music was created by Vaslav Nijinsky in 1913 for the Paris season of the Ballets Russes. Léonide Massine had staged two productions of *Le Sacre du Printemps:* 1920 in Paris and 1930 in New York at the Metropolitan Opera House with Martha Graham in the leading role.

In order to understand the nature of Lester Horton's choreography for *Le Sacre du Printemps* it is necessary to have some idea of the productions that preceded his. Nesta MacDonald quotes Eric Walter White from his book *Stravinsky: The Composer and His Work,* in which he describes the inception of Stravinsky's music.

The initial impulse that led to the creation of *The Rite of Spring* was derived from a fleeting vision that Stravinsky had in St. Petersburg during the spring of 1910, when he was finishing the last pages of *Firebird*. This came to him unexpectedly, as his mind was then pre-occupied with different things. In his *Chronicle* (1935) he states: "I saw in imagination a solemn pagan rite: wise elders, seated in a circle, watching a young girl dance herself to death. They were sacrificing her to propitiate the god of spring." At this stage the vision was not accompanied by any concrete musical ideas. Before leaving St. Petersburg he described his dream to his friend, Nicolas Roerich, who he thought would be interested in it from the archaelogical point of view, and on reaching Paris he also mentioned it to Diaghilev, who immediately saw its balletic potentialities. . . . It was not until the following summer, when *Petrouchka* had been successfully launched, that Stravinsky had time to sketch out the new work. Roerich, whom he had chosen as his collaborator, was not only a painter of considerable talent, but also an archaeologist who had travelled extensively, becoming one of the greatest authorities on the ancient Slavs. . . . It was certainly appropriate that he should help Stravinsky with the Scenario of this new work.[10]

In July 1911 Roerich and Stravinsky were both guests of one of Diaghilev's first patrons—Princess Tenisheva. It was at her country house, surrounded by her collection of antique Russian costumes, that Roerich and Stravinsky developed the ballet they had in mind. Roerich at that time also designed a number of costumes for the dancers. They conceived of the ballet in two parts.

Part One: The Adoration of the Earth

Introduction; Auguries of Spring (Dances of the Young Girls); Mock Abduction; Spring Khorovod (Round Dance); Games of the Rival Clans; Procession of the Wise Elder; Adoration of the Earth (The Wise Elder); Dance of the Earth.

Part Two: The Sacrifice

Introduction (originally, Pagan Nights); Mystical Circles of the Young Girls; Glorification of the Chosen Victims; The Summoning of the Ancients; Ritual of the Ancients; Sacrificial Dance (The Chosen Victim).[11]

It was decided that Vaslav Nijinsky would do the choreography and that the production would be part of the 1913 season of the Ballets Russes. Leon Bakst was responsible for the French title *Le Sacre du Printemps*. When the dance was performed in England at the Theatre Royal, Drury Lane, in London in July of 1913 (after the 29 May Paris premiere), the English newspapers contained several different translations of the French title: *The Crowning of Spring, The Spring Ritual,* and *The Spring Rite*. It was not until 1920, when Massine presented the second version, that the English title became *The Rite of Spring*.

It was very clear from the beginning that the impetus for the ballet derived from the history and customs of the ancient Slavs. Roerich wrote to Diaghilev:

In the ballet . . . as conceived by myself and Stravinsky, my object is to present a number of scenes of earthly joy and celestial triumph as understood by the Slavs. . . . My intention is that the first set should transport us to the foot of a sacred hill, in a lush plain, where Slavonic tribes are gathered together to celebrate the spring rites. In this scene there is an old witch, who predicts the future, a marriage by capture, round dances. Then comes the most solemn moment. The wise elder is brought from the village to imprint his sacred kiss on the new flowering earth. During this rite the crowd is seized with mystic terror. After this uprush of terrestial joy, the second scene sets a celestial mystery before us. Young virgins dance in circles on the sacred hill amid enchanted rocks; then they choose the victim they intend to honor. In a moment she will dance her last dance before the ancients clad in bearskins to show that the bear was man's ancestor. Then the graybeards dedicate the victim to the god Yarilo.[12]

The dancers for the 1913 ballet *Le Sacre du Printemps* were dressed in Russian peasant costumes. The pictures show the women wearing embroidered headbands and loose braided hair that fell below the waist. They wore dresses that had embroidery across the shoulders and various embroidered patterns on the skirts. The dresses were simulations of loose, semistraight Russian peasant garments. They were midthigh length for the most part, with a few reaching to the ankles. On their feet the women wore sandals laced to the ankles. The men were bearded and dressed in tunics and laced sandals; they wore Russian peasant hats, and their costumes were embroidered across the shoulders and across the bottom hems. The word "scarlet" is used most often in describing the color of these costumes.

Pictures of the 1913 production show that the dancers' feet were rotated inward, and the arm gestures were close and tight to the body. The use of upper torso produced a look of slight tilting to the side from the waist and head. The group scenes were much like the solo bodies—with a sense of tightness and verticality. The pictures show in both the solo body attitudes and in those of the groups, with their loose embroidered robes, that the dancers were protecting themselves from the cold of the Russian winter and the oncoming of the savage Russian spring.

Massine's choreography both in 1920 and in 1930 attempted to recreate the original Nijinsky movements. The scene was pagan Russia. The 1920 production used Roerich's original sets and costumes, which were still in good condition. Massine made some changes in the original Nijinsky version. According to Richard Buckle in *Diaghilev*: "Massine could find no justification for Nijinsky's bent wrists and ankle movements in old ikons or wood-carvings, so he decided to base his production on simple peasant round dances, with some angular Byzantine poses; and he thought his choreography might also have been influenced by the 'captivating spirit of cubism.'"[13]

Lester Horton's choreography for *Le Sacre du Printemps* in 1937 for the Hollywood Bowl was quite different from either the Nijinsky or Massine versions. Although the basic theme remained the same, a celebration of spring and of the continuity of the life cycles, the movement vocabulary, costuming, and overall quality of Horton's dance gave different visual images and feelings. All of the pictures of the Nijinsky and Massine versions show a ballet that emphasized the darker side of the coming of spring. This is corroborated in a review by Jacques Rivière of November 1913.

This is a biological ballet. It is not only the dance of the most primitive men, it is the dance before man. . . . Stravinsky tells us that he wanted to portray the surge of spring: But this is not the usual spring sung by poets, with its breezes, its bird-song, its pale blue skies and tender greens. Here is nothing but the harsh struggle of growth, the panic terror from the rising of the sap, the fearful regroupings of the cells. Spring comes from inside, with its violence, its spasms and its fissions. We seem to be watching a drama through a microscope.[14]

The feeling created by the pictures and accounts of Horton's ballet were those of ecstasy, largeness, and openness—a welcoming of spring and a welcoming of the universe. Here the dominant motif is not a sense of struggle but a sense of conquest and power over the elements. Man is not conquered or controlled either by nature or by the cycles of life and death—man has a dominant role in molding the cycles to his needs and demands.

The most obvious difference between Horton's production of *Le Sacre du Printemps* and the other versions is the costuming and the visual picture that was created. The costumes for Horton's dance were in vibrant earth colors—red, yellow, sky blue, brown, and touches of white. All of the women's costumes, except for that of the "Chosen One," were in two pieces with the midriff left bare. The tops were tight-fitting, with short, loose sleeves and bold stripes emphasizing the breasts. The women's skirts reached to the thigh, were tight-fitting at the hips, and formed an A-shape from hips downward. They had a bold stripe down the front and center and were split open almost to the waist, so that when the dancers' legs moved freely the thighs were exposed. Some of the men were dressed in leotards with bare legs. Several of the male dancers had bare chests and close-fitting knicker-like pants with bold patterned stripes. Horton used large flowered headdresses for the women and square, conical headdresses for the men.

The movements shown in the pictures of the Horton production of *Le Sacre du Printemps* give an impression that the dance was large and expansive. There are gestures of one leg raised high in the air and extended with bent knees and flexed ankle, reaching out into space. There are pictures of arms raised and extended, reaching beyond the body. A feeling of angularity is achieved in the flexion at the wrist joints and in the occasional flexion at the elbow joints. There are several pictures of dancers with a wide stance in deep second position plié. There are several other pictures which show a wide stance, with one knee bent and one knee straight or with both knees deeply bent but not evenly as in a plié.

There was considerable use of upper back, torso, and hips in Horton's version of *Sacre*. When the dancers are shown leaning to the side in the pictures, the entire torso is stretched and extended, with arms parallel to torso. One picture shows a dancer with her back completely arched, head almost touching the floor. There are also several pictures that show the dancers with their hips thrust forward and torsos leaning backward. The pictures show considerable use of a forward pelvic thrust in Horton's dance. That particular movement as well as the deep second position pliés, the bare torsos, and the bold striping may have occasioned this comment by W. E. Oliver.

> Lester Horton has put the phallic content in this paean to the primitive far enough into the abstract to avoid the censors, although there is still enough plainness left in the theme to make you realize that dancing and music need not be confined to pretty movements and polite moods. . . . Watch for the dance of the adolescents, the tribal war games, the Seer's dances, the ritual of the ancestors and Lewitzky's remarkable work in the immolation scene. They are hot stuff, to take a short cut through the phraseology of the usual dance jargon.[15]

The costumes have a very strong flavor of American Indian dress. There is nothing specified to identify them with a particular Indian tribe, and they are not reproductions of American Indian dress. They are abstractions that derive their lifeblood from a generalized feeling of Indian dress and life as well as life in the West—the strong earth colors, the bare midriffs, the headdresses, the short sleeves, the slit skirts, and the bold stripes. The movements also have the flavor of American Indian dance—flexion in the ankles, knees, and wrists, groupings in straight lines, feet caressing and pounding the floor. In creating *Le Sacre du Printemps* for the Hollywood Bowl, Lester Horton choreographed a dance that celebrated the heritage of America. He also celebrated that part of the American experience that had its roots in the spiritual mythology of the always open, hopeful expanses of the western frontiers.

Lester Horton's choreography for *Le Sacre du Printemps* received enthusiastic reviews from the press and a somewhat hesitant reception from the audience. The music was dissonant and difficult for the audience. The dance was erotic, an extremely contemporary movement vocabulary based on a primitive quality of ritual—with pounding feet, swinging hips and torsos, and flexed elbows, hands, feet, and knees. There was nothing traditionally pretty about this dance, and many in the audience did not know how to react. Frank Eng, a dance and drama critic in Los Angeles and the man who kept Horton's company going after his death in 1953, said: "When *Sacre* was performed the little old ladies from Pasadena were outraged."[16] Johanna Lawrence in a newspaper review noted: "Through the introduction 'The Tribal Response to Spring,' the stylized movements caused titters that travelled

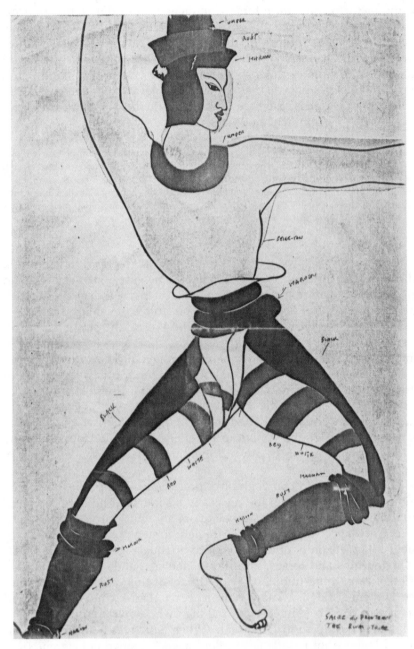

Costume Design for *Le Sacre du Printemps*, 1937
Costume designs attributed to William Bowne and Lester Horton.
(*Courtesy Frank Eng*)

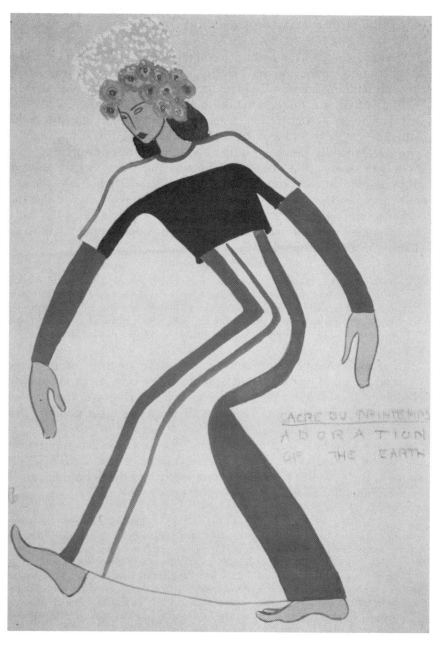

Costume Design for *Le Sacre du Printemps*, 1937
(*Courtesy Frank Eng*)

through the vast audience." And another review of the performance noted that "at first many people in the audience giggled and laughed at the uncommon exhibition of a strange art."[17]

Bella Lewitzky, who had the leading role as the "Chosen One," remembered the performance: "Horton's *Sacre* was way ahead of its times. It had an Americanized feeling, and he emphasized the universality of ritual and the celebration of the seasons. Audience reaction was violent and controversy raged pro and con. I remember the pounding rhythms and a great deal of angularity. The dance opened with the 'Tribal Response to Spring' with the groups beating upon the ground to waken it."[18] The audience was not the only one to have problems with the dance and the score. William Bowne, who danced in the piece and who worked with the costuming, remembered that the orchestra was reluctant to rehearse the score because of its difficulty and strangeness. As a result, there was confusion and there had to be changes in the final product.

> Efrem Kurtz was supposed to conduct, but after rehearsing the orchestra once he considered them inadequate to play the score and walked away, handing the baton over to the concert master. Horton received $1,000 for the performance but turned the money over to the orchestra so that he could have another rehearsal. As it was, the score was still too difficult and the finale was played in modified form.[19]

In spite of the problems with the orchestra, and the initial uncomfortable reception of the audience, critics were very much taken with Horton's ballet. Dorathi Bock Pierre opened her review in the October 1937 issue of *The American Dancer* with words of great praise: "One word describes the ballet Lester Horton created to the music of Stravinsky's *Le Sacre du Printemps,* and that word is: Exciting! It was one of the most exciting dance experiences I have had." W. E. Oliver spoke of the power of both the choreography and the performance and of the originality of the conception.

> Not since the ballet *Machinal* some years ago in the Hollywood Bowl will the good folk who take their music under the stars have seen such a powerful job of dancing as the Horton group are shaping up for the concert Thursday night. No riot should ensue Thursday night, although if the ballet is done with the power I saw in its rehearsal it should cause a tremendous sensation among dance fans and the general public. . . . Following the cue of Stravinsky's music, this new ballet is almost brutal in its strength, and original enough to almost provide a new jumping off place for the modern dance. It should mark the furthest advance this year, and that takes in both coasts dancing and all New York has offered so far.[20]

Everything in Lester Horton's choreography for *Le Sacre du Printemps* spoke to the emergence of an important new choreographer with a personal, original conception of movement and theater. Here was ritual by an American from the perspective of the new western frontier. Everything in the choreography spoke to the large expanses and the freedom of the American West. The movement was broad, the colors were bright, the energy was high. The vocabulary was sensuous, erotic, weighted, and forceful. The theatricality was bold and clean and lent the Russian sonorities and rhythms an American impulse.

This was not the brooding ritual determined by the stark contrasts of Russian winters and springs. This was a ritual of spring that celebrated a California landscape, where flowers bloomed all year and the sun was only intermittently broken with rain and gentle cold. The energy of spring was not a sudden awakening but a continuance of the eternal promise of a utopian environment. This was not a ritual of peasants whose lives were controlled by centuries of embedded religious beliefs and prescribed lives. These were young people who created their own religion of action and adventure, promise and hope. The tight groupings of the Russian *Sacre* (both Massine's and Nijinsky's) were transformed into the large, open spatial patterns of Horton's *Sacre*—symbolizing a land where ritual had to do with daily new discoveries and unfathomed, open-ended landscapes. The intense stepping patterns of the Massine and Nijinsky productions were transformed into thrusting hips, aggressive arms, and thighs reaching out to the landscape. The muted colors and delicately intricate designs of the costumes used by the Russian choreographers were transformed into bright reds and yellows, vibrant browns, whose clarity was disturbed now and again by a strong bold line of contrasting color.

Le Sacre du Printemps marked the period when Horton felt secure in his own development and when his technique became fully his own. When Bella Lewitzky joined Horton in 1934 she felt that he was just beginning to develop his own ideas. In an interview in 1980 she noted: "When I first came to him his technique was totally different. It was rather decorative and closer to what he had learned from Ito and observed in others."[21] She felt that the performance at the Hollywood Bowl marked the time when he had absorbed all types of early influences and integrated them to use in his own choreographic signature. "He developed a technique which tested the capacity of the body to move to its extremes. It would be common for him to say, 'Tip the body to the side—you're standing on one leg and balancing—farther . . . farther than that.'"

Just prior to the Hollywood Bowl performance Horton left Norma Gould's studio and found his own space—a second-floor studio at 7377 Beverly Boulevard. The performance at the Bowl gave him important public acceptance and prestige, and in 1937 he gave a series of lec-

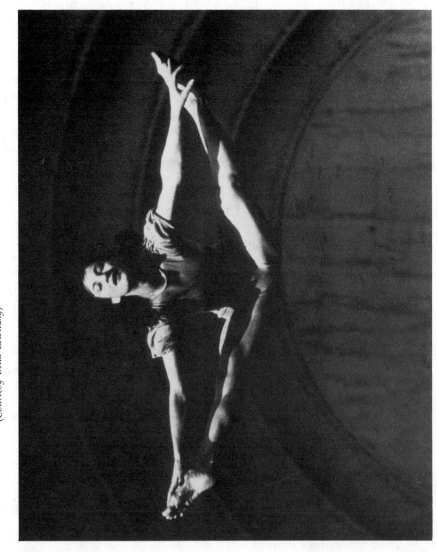

Bella Lewitzky in Rehearsal for *Le Sacre du Printemps*, 1937
(*Courtesy Bella Lewitzky*)

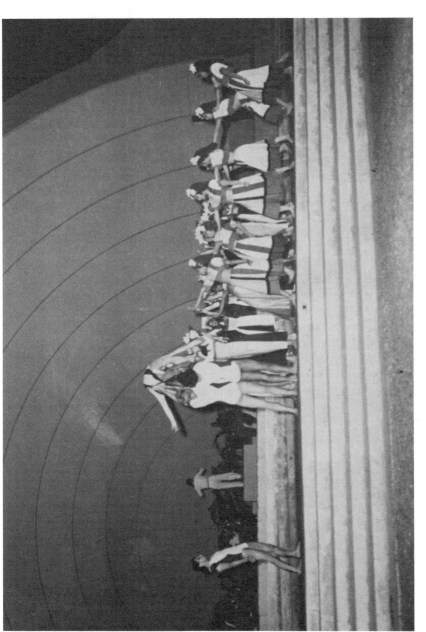

Rehearsal of Scene from *Le Sacre du Printemps*, 1937
Choreography by Lester Horton.
(*Courtesy Toyo Miyatake*)

ture demonstrations. These were considered significant enough to warrant a large article in the *Los Angeles Times* by critic Isabel Morse Jones. In an article on 14 October, "New Dance Explained as Evolution," she quoted Horton, giving official nod to the continued importance of his ideas.

> We all agree that the term modern dance is insufficient. Its name implies that it is ever present and contemporary, which it is. It was born of the desire to create a vital contemporary art form. The classic dance created an elaborate system embellished by masters during several hundred years. It became an art of virtuosity. A performer was noted for his technique. The idea was secondary. The modern dancer as well as the modern painter is cognizant of the past but wishes to go forward. There is much to learn about movement. The modern schools are all concerned with technique but not at the sacrifice of content or something to say. . . . The principal achievement of the new dance is the projection of vital ideas through bodily movement, by distortion, stress and accent, relation to space, change of intensity.

After 1937 Horton and his group were no longer a small modern dance group, unknown and unheralded. In April 1938 they performed at UCLA's Royce Hall, made their San Francisco debut, and in the summer of that year Horton was invited to the prestigious Mills College summer session. Classes at the studio were attracting more students, and Horton was beginning to articulate more clearly his now fully developed ideas. He was creating an approach to dance that was to affect future generations of dancers, an approach that emphasized the development of each individual's potential through movement improvisation, involvement in all aspects of production, and exploration of the multicultural heritage available to him in Los Angeles. A pioneer in offering composition classes and improvisational work in Los Angeles, he explained his ideas in a 1940 article in *Educational Dance.*

> It is essential to define a new point of concentration in teaching choreography. Choreography should be approached in a richer environment. Instruction in choreography should reflect the tendency of current works. It should find the student in a three dimensional environment, rich with sculptural masses, employing color and light in a significant way, utilizing the effectiveness of costume to enrich movement and meaning, and conceiving accompaniment and program note as a fully clarified expression from the beginning. . . . Every teacher . . . is familiar with the utter inadequacy the student feels when he is asked to invent movement. When the problem is to improvise, the reaction is still more general and pronounced. . . . Free fantasy is a priceless attribute which we sell in exchange for a stodgy education during our childhood. Imagination is exchanged for rationality. We need them both to compose. The gift for fantasy, for a free invention of movement, must be regained.[22]

Rehearsal of Scene from *Le Sacre du Printemps*, 1937
(*Courtesy Toyo Miyatake*)

In Lester Horton, Los Angeles finally had its own dance artist—a choreographer who was to become an original and significant force in the American dance. By 1937 the basic components of his choreography and his teaching methods had evolved, and the performance at the Hollywood Bowl was a culmination of the Los Angeles artistic and physical environment that was so important to him. In 1948 he opened his own Dance Theatre. It was there that Bella Lewitzky, Carmen de Lavallade, Joyce Trisler, Alvin Ailey, James Truitte, Norman Cornick, Rudi Gernreich, Carl Ratcliff, and others had their own forum for expression and experimentation, an experience that was to be crucial in their own development as artists. In 1953 Horton passed away, and Frank Eng kept the Dance Theatre going for seven years. By that time, many of Horton's dancers had left to forge their own independent careers and to carry on the work of a genius of American dance, whose life and work lie deeply imbedded in the history of dance in Los Angeles.

Epilogue

Eight Who Danced

The study of the artists who came to Los Angeles and who worked and created in the city during the period 1915 through 1937 is important because it contributes to an understanding of the complex influences in the development of American dance. Los Angeles was probably unique in that the movie industry, the climate, and the utopian notion of the frontier attracted artists in a way that other cities did not. It is likely that a study of dance activity in Chicago during the 1920s and 1930s would also prove fruitful, as that was also a city that held a promise of artistic growth and viability. It is possible that an in-depth study of other cities such as Philadelphia, San Francisco, or Washington, D.C., would also provide valuable insights, but these are distinctly different from Los Angeles, the movie capitol of the United States. Nevertheless, the questions about the development of dance in Los Angeles and why it seemed never to fulfill the richness it seemed to promise are troubling ones.

The dance environment in Los Angeles during the 1930s was a sophisticated one; it attracted highly skilled choreographers and dancers. The fact that it fostered the development of Horton is important, but other questions have to be raised. Why did Los Angeles never produce a major ballet company? The three Russians—Kosloff, Oukrainsky, and Bolm—came to the city, made it their permanent home, and ended up creating a ballet company in San Francisco. Why were there no other young choreographers in the modern dance emerging during the 1940s and 1950s, or did they all leave for New York? Was the period 1915 through 1937 one of the richest in Los Angeles dance and the only one that deserves documentation? Is the increase in professional activity in the city in the 1980s partly a product of the rich heritage that lay dormant for so long? Was it the movies, McCarthyism, red-baiting, geographic sprawl, lack of a dance tradition— what created the time lag in the organization and maintenance of great dance and dancers?

Each of the artists discussed in this book was seminal in the development of dance in California. Los Angeles was never an ordinary city in the United States. As the capital of the film industry and as a city that became from the 1920s on a leader in American commerce and industry, it grew quickly and attracted creative talent from all over the world. The city gave each of these artists an opportunity to develop, providing them with cheap studio space, important performance opportunities, and talented students. The work of these eight artists influenced American dance beyond the confines of Los Angeles. There is need for full-scale biographies of several of these artists, and it is hoped that this book will encourage several such ventures.

What happened to Los Angeles dance after 1937? Lester Horton went on to form his Dance Theatre, create a major body of work, and train dancers who developed into leaders in the field. Zemach went back to New York, and Ito was deported. Bolm did some work with Ballet Theatre and by the 1940s was in Los Angeles most of the time. Kosloff and Oukrainsky kept on teaching and presenting their groups, as did Belcher and Gould. Horton embodied the next wave—and the energy he transmitted in his work was both his own and a product of a dance situation that had provided the fertile environment for his development. But what happened to the rest of the energy that had been generated? What was the effect of the movie industry, which had attracted many in the first place? Did major sponsors appear?

The work of Norma Gould laid the groundwork for the development of dance at UCLA and USC. Martha Deane was to develop an active dance program at UCLA in the Department of Physical Education when she was hired in 1924. In 1962 Alma Hawkins created a dance department in the College of Fine Arts, offering bachelor's and master's degrees. USC maintained its dance program in physical education but also developed a program that was known for the quality of its courses, and students could obtain bachelor's, master's, and Ph.D. degrees.

There was dance activity in Los Angeles for three years from 1937 through 1940, sponsored by the Work Projects Administration through the leadership of the choreographer and performer Myra Kinch and maintained under the aegis of the Federal Music Project. Myra Kinch left Los Angeles in 1940, and by that time, aside from what had been generated by Lester Horton and the two universities, dance was not fulfilling the promise that it had shown in the 1930s.

The reasons are found in a variety of factors. The events that occurred at the Hollywood Bowl after 1937 provide some of the clues. Just as that institution had in the past been a microcosm of dance activity in Los Angeles, it now became the battleground for the continuation of major dance activity. One of the strong points of the Los Angeles dance environment had been its isolation and insulation, the pioneer spirit that allowed for freedom without a history of examples and standards. Local choreographers were not faced with a great deal of competition from visiting groups, and there were only sporadic visits of outside companies. The Jooss Ballet came to Los Angeles in 1936 and 1937, as did Harold Kreutzberg and Yvonne George in 1931 and 1932. Martha Graham brought her company to the city in 1936, and soon other companies began to visit. In 1939 the Littlefield Ballet from Philadelphia was the first imported dance company to appear on the Hollywood Bowl stage. They were followed by the Ballet Russe de Monte Carlo in 1941. After 1941 the Ballet Russe de Monte Carlo and Ballet Theatre became the major dance attractions at the Hollywood Bowl. Gone was the era when a choreographer living and working in Los Angeles was asked to produce a ballet at the Bowl using students and fellow professionals also resident in that city. Gone were the days when a young dancer would perform with a ballet choreographer one week and with a modern choreographer the next.

The dancers in Los Angeles may themselves have been responsible for the move to import companies from outside the community. They had begun to organize and become militant, demanding better conditions and wages for the Hollywood Bowl performances. "In the summer of 1937, a number of Los Angeles dancers convoked a meeting with the purpose of organizing a campaign to remove the appalling abuses which the dancers had been forced to suffer in Hollywood Bowl."[1] An organization was formed, called the Dancers' Federation, with these aims:

> The aims of the Dancers' Federation are to UNIFY THE DANCERS AS A GROUP, to elevate the economic status of the dancers; to provide a meeting place for the dancers to discuss complaints and grievances; to suggest solutions and act as the dancers' representative in presenting such problems to the union in question; to lend the weight of ALL THE DANCERS IN LOS ANGELES to which ever group finds itself in difficulties.[2]

The dancers and choreographers who worked for the Hollywood Bowl received low fees and operated under poor conditions. Lester Horton received $1,000 for choreographing *Le Sacre du Printemps*. This was a dance that required months of preparation and untold hours of rehearsals. Out of the $1,000 he received, he had to pay dancers' fees as well as those for sets and costumes. In the end he gave the money to the orchestra so that he could have more rehearsal with live music.

Benjamin Zemach remembered receiving $2,000 for each of the ballets he created for the Hollywood Bowl.[3] He also had to pay for the dancers, costumes, and sets out of this money. Since the casts for these productions were usually large because of the size of the stage, the expenses could be overwhelming. Karoun Toutikian remembered that in *Fragments of Israel* Zemach, having insufficient money to purchase or order costumes, used parts of an old mop for his beard and an old bathrobe for his costume.[4] He assumed that because the audience was so far away they would not notice the substitutes. The dancers usually rehearsed in the hot sun in the afternoons and ordinarily did not work with the orchestra for more than one rehearsal.

The dancers and choreographers who worked for the Hollywood Bowl did not have formal contracts. This made their situation precarious and indefinite and certainly not very professional. A program could be changed at the last minute, or the choreographer's work could be called into question. Zemach, for example, was told that if he did not drop the stock market scene from his ballet, the performance would be cancelled. After much discussion and without contractual protection, he agreed to the demands.[5]

An article in the 1938 *Dancers' Bulletin*, printed shortly after the new Dancers' Federation had been formed, addressed the issue of contracts. The lead paragraph was succinct and pointed: "There are more sides to a Ballet in the Hollywood Bowl than Bravos. The little matter of contracts for example."[6] The newly formed Dancers' Federation was not a union. It was an umbrella organization designed to identify problems and find solutions in whatever way possible. It was instrumental in having its members resolve the issue of contracts by joining an active musicians union—The American Guild of Musical Artists (AGMA). AGMA housed the dancers in a "ballet division." The first issue AGMA dealt with in relation to its dance members was that of conditions at the Hollywood Bowl. "Most important to us, of course, is that new negotiations are going on with the Hollywood Bowl. What will happen to Bowl dancers next season? One thing is certain: The absurd conditions which have existed in former years are gone. The Bowl Association now agrees in dollars as well as in words that dancers must have better conditions. Now it is up to us!"[7]

Another issue that concerned the Dancers' Federation was that of professionalism. Many of the Hollywood Bowl ballets over the years had been produced using the students of various choreographers. In the first issue of the *Dancers' Bulletin* of September 1938 the lead article read "Unity Keynotes Federation Growth." The Hollywood Bowl was used as an example of lack of professionalism that was being perpetuated and had to be fought. "The Bowl committee was memorialized to the effect that better arrangements should be made to give the public a high level of dance production without sacrificing the dancers to this purpose."[8]

One of the keys to higher standards was a better selection process through open auditions. In the past there had been no auditions for Hollywood Bowl productions. The first open auditions occurred in 1938 and were given under the auspices of the AGMA. This kind of careful selection process, in addition to better wages, good working conditions, and secure contracts, were all positive steps forward for the dancers in Los Angeles. Unfortunately, the greater professionalism desired by the dancers only spelled increased expenses and headaches for the management of the Hollywood Bowl. The demands of the dancers came at a time when the general administrative policies and needs of the Hollywood Bowl itself were changing. Grace Koopal in *Miracle of Music* summarized the overall sense of change: "The entire concept of the Bowl was gradually changing from the original reverent, sensitively conceived community project, with dedicated volunteer workers possessed of an almost religious zeal, into a vast commercial project with cliques and power struggles, and a passion, above all else, to show profit. It is singularly revealing that it was no longer referred to as OUR Hollywood Bowl, but simply as 'The Bowl.'"[9]

Some of the factors that had made the Hollywood Bowl a successful "People's Theatre" were the same ones that were now creating new directions and needs. Dance had become visible and important at the Bowl through the employment of choreographers, students, and dancers who were working and living in Los Angeles. It was an important outlet during many years for creative talent in dance. In the more idealistic days of Los Angeles and the Hollywood Bowl, there was a great deal to be gained by appearing at the Bowl. Now, in the late 1930s, there were large numbers of dancers trained by the various artists who had performed at the Bowl and worked in Los Angeles. There were also increasing numbers of trained dancers who had arrived to work in the movies. It was now not just a matter of interest and prestige to perform at the Bowl. It was important that any performance not just exist, but that it also be sufficiently professional to establish the legitimacy of dance as an art. Standards of training for dance were becoming higher, and American dance was coming into its own.

The Bowl itself was changing because of its own success and because of the enthusiasm of its early leaders. The volunteerism of the first years, together with idealism, energy, and daring, helped create an institution that became world prominent and prestigious beyond anyone's wildest dreams and expectations. With that prominence came great success and more complex managerial problems. The Hollywood Bowl by the late 1930s was becoming increasingly expensive to operate and required more professional personnel. Trained staff was needed to carry out the more complicated facets of publicity and management, and the large number of improvements to the grounds required more hired hands.

In short, by the late 1930s the management of the Hollywood Bowl felt beseiged by increased costs and complexity of operation. It had to raise ticket prices and also felt the need to produce programs that had broad popular appeal. Gone was the idealism that favored programs fostering local talent or evenings that would educate the masses and provide spiritual and moral uplift for the citizens of Los Angeles.

An example of the new trend at the Bowl was the performance of Benny Goodman and his band in 1939. One may imagine the shock his performance occasioned for those who had envisioned an institution that would never produce anything except "great art." Grace Koopal's description of Benny Goodman's performance reflects some of that shock. "A noisier and more 'mod' group had never been heard anywhere, much less the Bowl . . . and Mrs. Carter, in the audience that night no doubt through curiosity, is said to have left at intermission in outraged tears."[10] In view of the move toward attractions that seemed to have broader appeal, and in view of the fact that local dancers (who had been a cheap commodity) began to ask for better wages and conditions, it is perhaps not too surprising that the Hollywood Bowl management began to turn toward dance attractions they felt would bring larger audiences and would be easier for them to produce.

The needs of the Bowl coincided with the popularity of a company that was touring the United States with great acclaim—the Ballet Russe de Monte Carlo. They had already appeared in Los Angeles at the Philharmonic and Shrine Auditoriums during the winter seasons of 1935 through 1941. The Ballet Russe was far easier for the Bowl management to produce than a single evening of a local choreographer who created an original ballet that was perhaps difficult in concept and hard to execute. The Ballet Russe de Monte Carlo came with a well-rehearsed and "sure fire" repertory, their own public relations and business staff, and their own costumes and sets. They also came not just with one famous name but with several stars of world renown—Leonid Massine, Alexandra Danilova, Alicia Markova, Igor Youskevitch, Serge Lifar, and Tamara Toumanova.

The only move that might have stemmed the tide of imported companies would have been the establishment of a permanent ballet company in Los Angeles. Dance is an expensive art. It needs patrons and established financial support as well as organization. Dancers need to function within a secure format that affords them continuity, training, and exposure to varied repertory and performance situations. A symphony orchestra could not exist if it were not a permanently funded organization. Musicians could not establish continuity and excellence without the outlet of a stable organization such as a symphony orchestra. Other musical groups tend to draw strength from the establishment of an organization that employs selected talent, high standards, financial support, and good leadership. Dancers need the same things. A strong dance performing unit will attract important artists and will support the growth of other local groups.

In 1937 there was a strong move to found a permanent ballet company in connection with the Hollywood Bowl summer seasons and the winter concerts of the Los Angeles Philharmonic. The September 1938 edition of the *Dancers' Bulletin* carried a report on this matter.

> Our initial attempts to convince the Southern California Symphony Association of the need for a permanent Hollywood Bowl Ballet on a seasonal basis has had two by-products. First is the economic gain made this season in the matter of wages and rehearsal hours. Second is the amplification of the permanent ballet company into a Los Angeles Ballet company, employed nine months of the year, in the Bowl in the summer, the symphony's winter series and in a series of concerts on tour.[11]

By the fall of 1939 the discussions about a permanent Los Angeles Ballet company had reached a somewhat more definitive stage. The Dancers' Federation announced the formation of a support organization, the Southern California Dance Association. The idea was that this group would parallel the Southern California Symphony Association, which provided support for the Los Angeles Philharmonic. An organization was formed called the Permanent Ballet for Southern California, and David Thimar was elected as the first president. Lincoln Kirstein's Ballet Caravan was to appear in December 1939 at the Philharmonic Auditorium, and the performance of 1 December was announced as a benefit performance for the newly formed Los Angeles Ballet company.

There was no doubt in anyone's mind that the company would be formed. The October 1939 headline of the *Dancers' Bulletin* contained the following article in bold, dark print: "Permanent Ballet Formed!" In that same issue of the *Bulletin* there were four statements of congratulations to the permanent ballet company that was supposedly being formed in Los Angeles. Leopold Stokowski, L. E. Behymer, Merle Armitage, and Mrs. Leiland Atherton Irish all wrote strong statements of support and noted that such an organization was long overdue and essential to dance in Los Angeles. The dancers themselves voiced their needs and hopes.

> We as dancers have realized the need for such a company, and it has become quite clear at last, that until such a group is established, Southern California dancers cannot have the recognition and security their talent deserves. Los Angeles is large and it is maturing artistically. There is every reason to look forward to its becoming one of the foremost cultural centers in the country—with the look of things on the

other side of the water, we might say, in the world. Audiences are increasing. There are unique opportunities here to support a permanent company. The symphony season and the opera companies are sufficient background in themselves. . . . The Dancers' Federation in line with its program for advancement of dancers sees the establishment of a permanent Ballet Company as another step towards securing economic stability for the dance profession.[12]

The Los Angeles Ballet company never became a reality, although the idea of having a permanent ballet company in Los Angeles made a lot of sense. There were many trained dancers in the city by the late 1930s. They had come from all over for a variety of reasons—the climate, the scenery, Hitler, changes on Broadway, and the depression. With the advent of the "immigrant" dancers came new schools and more and better training, which also meant there were numerous local dancers with higher standards of professionalism than before.

There is no question that many of the dancers and choreographers had been lured to Los Angeles by the economic potential of the movies. Helen Caldwell remembered that in 1929 Michio Ito made $100,000 working in films when he first came to Los Angeles. Ernest Belcher earned a handsome living from his work in the movies. Theodore Kosloff made money very early with this new medium, and Lester Horton worked in films periodically to supplement his meager concert income. When the depression hit the United States the movie industry remained solvent, and work was available on the film lots of Hollywood—work that by the standards of those days was extremely lucrative. Lois Lacy, who came from Missouri with her family to be in the movies, was a Busby Berkeley dancer in the 1930s. In 1933 her salary of $50 helped support seven people in her family.[13]

In addition to the work and good salaries available in the movies, housing was cheap. Land was incredibly inexpensive. In those days it was even possible to pick oranges, lemons, tangerines, and other fruit from the trees in one's backyard. The climate in southern California seemed a miracle to those accustomed to difficult snowy winters. The physical landscape exerted a strong pull on the imagination. The ocean was close at hand but so were the mountains and the desert.

For many of the dancers the opportunity to come to Los Angeles, work in the movies, and live in what seemed like paradise was a dream come true. They saw themselves making money while associating with other intellectuals and artists. The optimism expressed by Adolph Bolm in an article in *The American Dancer* in 1931 was probably shared by many. The writer W. E. Kirby voiced Bolm's thoughts as follows:

Now that the films have practically dropped the Broadway type production he feels that interpretive and classic dances will be received with a hearty welcome by the intelligent theatre goer. Mr. Bolm has found Hollywood to be a gathering place for leaders in the arts. He is amazed at the number of people to be found in the film colony that he has met previously in his travels. Artists, writers, dancers and singers, many of the people he has worked with in various cities of the world are to be found rubbing elbows with one another speaking their native languages and working for a common end. If Hollywood is not productive of a cultural expression of this period it is not because we do not have the brains and the genius in our midst.[14]

In 1937, when the idea emerged for a Los Angeles Ballet company, there was no longer the optimism among the choreographers about the creative potential of dance in the movies. They were most anxious to have a stable creative outlet in the form of an organization that would have artistic opportunities for them. The movies had not been very open to the work of the concert choreographers. Most of the dances that Adolph Bolm created for the movie *The Mad Genius* were left on the cutting room floor. One of the women who worked with Benjamin Zemach on the movie *She* remembered that anything good or interesting that Zemach did in the film was eliminated; the directors kept asking for shots that were more sensational than artistic.[15]

The artists who saw the possibilities of dance in the movies were inevitably disappointed by the attitude of Hollywood toward both art and dance. Agnes de Mille was offered the chance to do the dances for Irving Thalberg's version of *Romeo and Juliet* starring Norma Shearer.

> I was getting five hundred dollars a week . . . the job was to last for six months. The dances were finished in three weeks. . . . What to do? I had to keep the company of thirty-two busy for six hours a day. We gave classes in everything . . . the dances were lovely. The madrigals by Byrd, Morley, and Dowling were the finest counterpoint I had ever done. And the pavane, which was to be Juliet's introduction to Romeo, was really strong. . . . When it came time for filming Romeo the set was large and magnificent, the costumes exquisite, the music enchanting, and the time for shooting eight days, more than adequate. . . . But although Cukor had seen the dances, he had no plans for photographing them. Thalberg was not interested at all, and the cameras were simply halted. The dances were either not filmed at all or in bits, the directors and producers feeling stubbornly that the story must be maintained even at the cost of the choreography.[16]

Perhaps if there had been just one bold visionary who championed dance in Los Angeles, all the talent that was quartered in the city would have been marshalled into a brilliant permanent southern California company. Lincoln Kirstein in New York was able to mold a company of power and beauty when he offered George Balanchine total support in a new ballet venture in 1933. Balanchine's genius and Kirstein's money and vision created the New York Ballet, one of the major companies of the world. Had there been a Lincoln Kirstein and a George Balanchine in Los Angeles in 1939, who would have salvaged the concept of a ballet company, would the city and the community have supported such a company? Would the dancers have supported such a company, or would the lure of financial gain from the movies always exercise too much power and mitigate against the more stringent demands of the art form?

In 1987 there seemed to be a resolution of many of the problems that have faced dance in Los Angeles. The Joffrey Ballet is now a resident company at the Los Angeles Music Center. Bella Lewitzky has been working steadily toward her vision of a Dance Gallery that will promote local, national, and international dance; groundbreaking took place in September 1986. Although the entertainment industries are still strong in Los Angeles, art is attracting more sponsorship and professional concert dance is becoming stronger.

Dance is a fragile, ephemeral art form, and this has been the story of an era and a place where some of its pioneers found a home that would nurture them and their work. In the environment of Los Angeles they choreographed and taught, and they helped make American dance the exciting and multifaceted art form it is today.

Notes

Chapter 1

1. Most of the information on Norma Gould comes from her scrapbooks, manuscripts, programs, school brochures, costumes, and class notes. These were retrieved from the garbage in 1968 by Karoun Toutikian, who happened to visit Gould just after she had been moved to the Arizona Convalescent Home in Santa Monica. I first interviewed Toutikian in February 1980 after finding her name on the cast lists for the Hollywood Bowl. She is a woman deeply involved in dance and the dance history of Los Angeles: as colleague and teacher for Ruth St. Denis, as performer with Lester Horton and Benjamin Zemach, and currently as an artist recording on video the St. Denis heritage. Toutikian knew and studied with Norma Gould. She gave me all the material when I began my research and writing.

2. The school was built in downtown Los Angeles. It is now called Francis Polytechnic High School and is located in the Van Nuys area of Los Angeles. The yearbook and information on the school are available in their archives.

3. Ted Shawn, with Gray Poole, *One Thousand and One Night Stands* (1960; Reprint, New York: Da Capo Press, 1979), p. 14.

4. Ibid., pp. 14–15.

5. Ibid., p. 15 (for all comments on the early film).

6. Ibid., p. 16.

7. Ibid.

8. These excerpts are in a small pamphlet, *Address at Moonshine* (New York: privately printed, 1911). This was among the memorabilia salvaged by Los Angeles dancer Karoun Toutikian after Gould's death. The copyright was granted Bliss Carman in 1911. The title page on the inside of the pamphlet reads as follows: "Address to the graduating class MCMXI of the Unitrinian School of Personal Harmonizing." The autograph of King is dated February 1914.

9. Shawn, p. 23.

10. Advertisement for forthcoming events found in 1921 Los Angeles Philharmonic Programs.

11. The normal school became the University of California, Southern Branch, in 1919–20. In 1927 it became the University of California at Los Angeles. In 1958 the "at" became a comma, and UCLA became a common abbreviation.

12. The UCLA Archives, in Powell Library, have all the old bulletins and catalogues for the normal school and the University of California, Southern Branch, as well as the early Berkeley catalogues. Norma Gould is on the faculty listings from 1919 through 1923 as Assistant in Gymnasium.

13. For further discussion and bibliography see: Naima Prevots, "American Pageantry and American Modern Dance," *Dance History Scholars Proceedings, Sixth Annual Conference,* Ohio State University, February 1983, pp. 59–70.

14. Norma Gould typed the lectures. There are 20 for the regular semester course and 12 for the summer. She included a complete bibliography, homework assignments, and suggestions for production. Lecture topics included: origin and history of pageantry; principles of pageantry; pageant for schools, colleges, universities; pageant composition, production, organization.

15. All these articles are in Gould's scrapbooks. For the most part there is no information about author or newspaper. In 1924 at USC summer session Gould taught an undergraduate course, "Technique of Dance Rhythm," and a graduate course, "Classic Dance Interpretation."

16. Ibid.

17. The Dance Collection, New York Public Library, has a Marion Morgan clipping file. Morgan's picture is on the front of the Beegle and Crawford book on pageants (see bibliography). A scrapbook given to me by Lance Bowling in March 1987 lists dancers from the Marion Morgan School as participants in a Thanksgiving Day Pageant, 27 November 1920, Hollywood Bowl site. Genevieve Kelso, on the faculty listing in the bulletin as "formerly manager of the Marion Morgan Dancers," taught at University of California, Southern Branch, summer session 1922.

18. Personal interview with Karoun Toutikian, February 1980.

19. Telephone interview with Bella Lewitzky, February 1980.

20. This is from a 1938 Dance Theatre announcement. One entire scrapbook in my possession is devoted to Dance Theatre and contains programs from 1932 through 1942.

Chapter 2

1. Unpublished autobiographical notes written by Ernest Belcher. Hereafter cited as "Belcher autobiographical notes." Belcher Collection, Special Collections, UCLA.

2. Mary Clarke, *The Sadler's Wells Ballet* (London: Adam and Charles Black, 1955), p. 31.

3. G. B. L. Wilson, *A Dictionary of Ballet* (London: Penguin, 1957), p. 282. Zanfretta was born in 1862 and died in 1952.

4. Belcher autobiographical notes.

5. Quoted in *London Dancing Times,* December 1913, p. 132.

6. Belcher autobiographical notes.

7. Interview with Belcher, "Early Career in Europe," KFAC Radio, Los Angeles, 16 March 1935, by Alma Gowdy and James Vandivere. The transcript is in the Belcher Collection, UCLA.

8. Faith Service, "Ernest Belcher: The Teacher of 'It,'" *The Dance Magazine,* August 1928, p. 18.

9. Personal interview with Marge Champion, 24 June 1986.

10. Belcher autobiographical notes.

11. B. Griffith, "Where Many in Movieland Get Dancing Inspiration," *The Dancing Master,* April 1929, p. 108.

12. Leland Windreich, "June Roper," *Dance Chronicle* 10, no. 1 (1987): 109.

13. Interview with Maria Tallchief, 1964, by Marion Horosko. Dance Collection, New York Public Library, New York.

14. Windreich, p. 109.

15. Belcher Collection, UCLA. The collection has a large number of school catalogues covering the 1920s through the 1940s. All the catalogues are large, with extensive information about classes, teachers, Belcher himself, and various students who became famous and were involved in movies or show business.

16. Letter received from Lina Basquette, 29 May 1986.

17. Ibid.

18. Letter from Alice Perissi to Marge Champion, 1 March 1973.

19. Letter from Gower Champion to Marge Champion, n.d.

20. Ann Barzel, "European Dance Teachers in the U.S.," *Dance Index,* April–June 1944, p. 92.

21. Windreich, p. 109.

22. Letter received from Lina Basquette, 29 May 1986.

23. Personal interview with Marge Champion, 24 June 1986.

24. Letter received from Lina Basquette, 29 May 1986.

25. Telephone interview with Lina Basquette, 20 May 1986.

26. Ruth Eleanor Howard, "Dancing Has Brought a New Angle to Talkies," *The American Dancer,* November 1929, pp. 14–15.

27. Lina Basquette first left Los Angeles with her mother for New York in 1922, returned briefly to Los Angeles, and then worked on Broadway between 1923 and 1925. She married Sam Warner in 1925, returning once again to Los Angeles. He died after they had been married one year, leaving her with a child.

28. Barzel, "European Dance Teachers in the U.S.," p. 92.

29. Renee Dunia Hawley, "Ernest Belcher: The Father of Dance in Southern California," p. 24. Belcher Collection, UCLA.

30. Unpublished typewritten notes, loose in the Belcher Collection, UCLA.

31. Service, p. 18.

32. Belcher Collection, UCLA.

33. Ibid.

34. Interview with Belcher, KFAC radio.

35. It is not clear what Belcher wrote this for and how it was used, even if it was ever published or printed. Belcher Collection, UCLA.

36. Undated article, Belcher Collection, UCLA.

37. A copy of the book is in the Belcher Collection, UCLA.

38. Personal interview with Marge Champion, 24 June 1986.

Chapter 3

1. David Leddick, "Baldina," *Dance Magazine*, November 1965, p. 22.

2. Leddick, p. 21.

3. Nesta Macdonald, *Diaghilev Observed by Critics in England and the United States, 1911–1929* (New York: Dance Horizons; London: Dance Books, 1975), p. 18.

4. Ibid.

5. Ibid., p. 19.

6. Ibid., p. 18. She quotes a review of 1 July 1909 that appeared in *The Stage*. "They were originally billed to appear in an Egyptian love-ballet, but this arrangement was cancelled, and very wisely too, for they are seen to better advantage in the short selection of dances which they now present."

7. Barbara Naomi Cohen, "The Borrowed Art of Gertrude Hoffman," *Dance Data*, no. 2 (New York: Dance Horizons, 1977), p. 3. In the 1912 program of the Hoffman venture *Cleopatre* had no accents and *Schéhérazade* was spelled *Sheherazade*.

8. Ibid., p. 2.

9. Ibid.

10. Ibid., p. 13.

11. Oliver M. Sayler and Marjorie Barkentin, "On Your Toes—America! The Story of the First Ballet Russe," in Cohen, p. 20. Barkentin and Sayler started to work on an authorized biography of Morris Gest in 1935 titled "If This Be Madness." The manuscript was never published and is now lost, but the chapter on the Ballet Russe was not lost, as noted in Cohen.

12. Sayler and Barkentin, pp. 22–23, as noted in Cohen.

13. Archives for Performing Arts, San Francisco.

14. Program note, Archives for Performing Arts, San Francisco.

15. The 1917 picture was not successful; instead of the agreed $10,000 remuneration, Kosloff was offered stock in a recently organized film company—Paramount. As a result he became a wealthy man, later investing in real estate in Los Angeles.

16. John Sanders, "Los Angeles Grand Opera Association: The Formative Years, 1924–1926," *Southern California Quarterly* 4, no. 4 (Fall 1973): 276.

17. Sanders discusses the rivalry in opera companies in Los Angeles from 1924 to 1926. The Los Angeles Grand Opera Association was organized in 1924 by Gaetano

Merola as a logical joint venture with the San Francisco Grand Opera Association. Merle Armitage was general business manager, and George Leslie Smith, who had brought the San Carlo Opera in February, was the local manager. In 1925 the ties between the San Francisco and Los Angeles Operas were broken. Merola then decided to bring the San Francisco company to Los Angeles as the California Opera Company. L. E. Behymer acted as manager with Rena MacDonald. In 1925 both the Los Angeles Opera and the California Opera gave seasons. In 1926 both groups in Los Angeles merged to create one Los Angeles Opera Company.

18. Bertha Wardell, "Scheherazade in Hollywood," *The Dance* (January 1927): 31, 64. On p. 64 Kosloff talks about the Kosloff prologues at the Circle Theatre: " 'Have you seen the dancers in the Russian prolog of 'The Volga Boatman' at the Circle Theatre?' Mr. Kosloff asked. 'Those girls are my best dancers. They drew their designs, sewed, and painted their own costumes.' "

19. The souvenir program for the 1926 Kosloff ballet is in the Kosloff file in the Archives for Performing Arts, San Francisco.

20. Wardell, p. 31. The entire article is devoted to a discussion of the ballet at the Philharmonic in the 1927 season.

21. Cohen, p. 8.

22. The 1909 *Les Sylphides* used the following music as listed in Richard Buckle, *Diaghilev* (New York: Atheneum, 1979), p. 140: *Overture Prelude,* op. 28, no. 7; *Nocturne,* op. 32, no. 2; *Valse,* op. 70, no. 1; *Mazurka,* op. 33, no. 2; *Mazurka,* op. 67, no. 3; *Overture,* op. 28, no. 7; *Valse,* op. 64, no. 2; *Valse Brilliante,* op. 18, no. 1. In *Fokine, Memoirs of a Ballet Master* translated by Vitale Fokine (Boston: Little, Brown and Co., 1961), p. 103, there is a description of the original *Chopiniana.* The order of the dances was: polonaise, mazurka, nocturne, mazurka, waltz, and tarantella.

23. Program for the evening of Kosloff ballets in 1938. In Archives for Performing Arts, San Francisco.

24. After Diaghilev's death in 1929, René Blum took over the contracts for the Ballets Russes. In 1932 he was joined by Colonel de Basil, and they put on a successful Monte Carlo season. From 1933 to 1936 de Basil reorganized the company and changed the name twice: Ballets Russes de Monte Carlo (1932), and Monte Carlo Ballet Russe (1933 to 1936). In 1936 Blum and de Basil broke their association. Blum organized a new Ballet Russe de Monte Carlo with Fokine as choreographer. De Basil in 1937 hired Massine and called his company Colonel W. de Basil's Ballet Russe. In 1938 de Basil hired Fokine and called his company Covent Garden Ballet Russe, while Massine formed a separate company soon to function as the Ballet Russe de Monte Carlo. De Basil reformed his company as Educational Ballet Russe (1939) and Original Ballet Russe (1940).

25. *The Dancing Times,* January 1957, carried an obituary of Kosloff by Winifred Edwards (Vera Fredowa). She wrote that between "1924 and 1934 Kosloff opened schools in San Francisco," p. 191.

26. *Dance News,* January 1957, p. 13.

27. George Amberg, *Ballet, The Emergence of an American Art* (New York: Mentor Books, 1949), p. 34.

Chapter 4

1. Slightly different dates have been given for his birth. The date given in chapter title is taken from a membership card for insurance with Mutual of Omaha found in the Archives for Performing Arts, San Francisco. The "O" in his name stands for "Orlay."

2. Serge Oukrainsky, *My Two Years with Pavlowa* (Los Angeles, San Francisco, New York: Suttonhouse Publishers, 1940), p. 13.

3. Ibid., pp. 25–26.

4. Ibid., p. 129.

5. Ibid., p. 39.

6. Ibid.

7. Ibid., p. 56.

8. An unpublished manuscript by Oukrainsky is in the Archives for Performing Arts, San Francisco. The title is "My Life in Ballet." It was written in collaboration with Antoinette Simanovich and is undated. The information on Pavley is in the back of the manuscript, p. 2.

9. Selma Jeanne Cohen, *Doris Humphrey, An Artist First* (Connecticut: Wesleyan University Press, 1972), p. 15.

10. Ibid., p. 16.

11. Barzel, "European Dance Teachers in the United States," p. 87.

12. Programs in Archives for Performing Arts, San Francisco.

13. Copyright No. 287096, as listed in Archives for Performing Arts, San Francisco.

14. Unpaginated section of Oukrainsky manuscript, "My Life in Ballet."

15. Program in collection of Archives for Performing Arts, San Francisco.

16. Oukrainsky, *Anna Pavlowa*, p. 89.

17. Serge Oukrainsky, "The Dance, What It Is, Was and Should Be," *The American Dancer*, June 1927, p. 16.

18. Oukrainsky, *Anna Pavlowa*, pp. x, xi.

19. Ibid., p. xi.

20. Ibid.

21. Oukrainsky, "My Life in Ballet," p. 103.

22. Ibid., p. 152.

23. Ann Barzel, "Chicago's 'Two Russians': Andreas Pavley and Serge Oukrainsky," *Dance Magazine*, June 1979, p. 63.

24. Ibid., p. 67.

25. Ibid., p. 64.

26. Eleanore Flaige also spelled her name Eleanora Flaig and is listed both ways in sources in the Dance Collection, New York Public Library.

Chapter 5

1. During his first years in America he spelled his name Adolf.

2. Merle Armitage, *Dance Memoranda* (New York: Books for Libraries Press, 1969), p. 46.

3. Hamilton Easter Field, "Adolph Bolm and *The Birthday of the Infanta*," *Arts and Decoration* 12 (1920).

4. R. C. Brownell, 29 November 1915, from Geneva, Switzerland. Bolm Clipping File, Dance Collection, New York Public Library.

5. Bolm Clipping File.

6. Frederick H. Martens, "*Sadko* and Its Author: 'A New Russian Ballet'," *Musical America*, 7 October 1916. Bolm Clipping File.

7. Bolm Clipping File.

8. Martens.

9. Bolm Clipping File.

10. Harry Birnbaum, "Adolf Bolm Describes 'Danse Macabre,' His New Ballet," *Musical America*, 4 August 1917, p. 5.

11. Undated, unsigned review. Bolm Clipping File.

12. Birnbaum.

13. Undated, unsigned review. Bolm Clipping File.

14. John Martin, *Ruth Page: An Intimate Biography* (New York and Basel: Marcel Dekker, 1977), p. 4.

15. Ibid., p. 29.

16. Olin Downes, *New York Times*, 27 March 1921. Bolm Clipping File.

17. *Theatre Arts Monthly*, May 1931, p. 359.

18. The three references are as follows: Anatole Chujoy and P. W. Manchester, *The Dance Encyclopedia*, 3d. rev. ed. (New York: Simon and Schuster, 1967), p. 145; Armitage, *Dance Memoranda*, p. 47; and John Dougherty, "Perspective on Adolph Bolm," Parts 1–3, *Dance Magazine*, January–March 1963.

19. 1931 Hollywood Bowl scrapbook, Hollywood Bowl Museum Archives, Hollywood.

20. Cyril W. Beaumont, *Complete Book of Ballets* (New York: Garden City Publishing, 1941), pp. 646–47.

21. John Dougherty, "Perspective on Adolph Bolm," Part 2, February 1963, p. 54.

22. Dougherty, "Perspective on Adolph Bolm," Part 3, March 1963, p. 50.

23. Irving Deakin, "America Nurtures the Seed" in *Ballet Profile* (New York: Dodge Publishing, 1936), pp. 97–132.

24. Dougherty, "Perspective on Adolph Bolm," Part 3, p. 52.

Chapter 6

1. Ito's birthdate is often given as 1893, but Helen Caldwell, in *Michio Ito, The Dancer and His Dances* (Berkeley: University of California Press, 1977), noted it is more likely 1892 and discusses this on p. 158, note 5 to chapter 2.

2. Oscar G. Brockett and Robert R. Findlay, *Century of Innovation: A History of European and American Theatre and Drama Since 1870* (Englewood Cliffs, N.J.: Prentice-Hall, 1973), p. 203.

3. John Martin, *America Dancing* (1936; Reprint, New York: Dance Horizons, 1968), p. 170.

4. Caldwell, p. 85.

5. Ezra Pound and Ernest Fenellosa, *The Classic Noh Theatre of Japan* (New York: New Directions Paperback, 1959), p. 69.

6. Caldwell, p. 98.

7. Ibid., p. 3.

8. Ibid., p. 34.

Chapter 7

1. Brockett and Findlay, p. 263.

2. Ibid., pp. 258, 259.

3. Personal interview with Benjamin Zemach, 2 August 1980, in Berkeley, California, at the home of his daughter, Margot Zemach.

4. Ibid.

5. Letter received from Benjamin Zemach, January 1983. The spellings of names are Zemach's.

6. Ibid.

7. Ibid.

8. Elizabeth Selden, *The Dancer's Quest: Essays on the Aesthetics of Contemporary Dance* (Berkeley: University of California Press, 1935), pp. 80–81.

9. Ibid., p. 82.

10. Telephone conversation with Frieda Flier Maddow, 20 August 1986.

11. Isabel Morse Jones, *Hollywood Bowl* (New York and Los Angeles: G. Schirmer, 1936), p. 173.

12. Personal interview with Amielle Zemach, New York, 28 October 1982.

13. Personal interview with Benjamin Zemach, 2 August 1980.

14. Personal interview with Amielle Zemach, October 1982.

15. Personal interview with Benjamin Zemach, 2 August 1980.

Chapter 8

1. Larry Warren, *Lester Horton: Modern Dance Pioneer* (New York and Basel: Marcel Dekker, 1977), pp. 6–7.

2. Christina L. Schlundt, *The Professional Appearances of Ruth St. Denis and Ted Shawn: A Chronology and an Index of Dances,* 1906–1932 (New York: New York Public Library, 1962). The information on the 1922–23 Denishawn tours is on pp. 41–47.

3. Personal interview with Karoun Toutikian, 8 June 1986.

4. Indianapolis newspaper, dated July 1927, from the collection of Karoun Toutikian.

5. Ibid.

6. Information from 1929 *Hiawatha* program, saved and given to me by Karoun Toutikian.

7. Newspaper article dated only 1929 from Toutikian's collection.

8. Personal interview with Elizabeth Talbot-Martin, 15 November 1983.

9. Telephone interview with William Bowne, 13 November 1983.

10. Macdonald, pp. 87–88.

11. Ibid., p. 88.

12. Serge Lifar, *Diaghilev* (New York: Putnam, 1976), p. 200.

13. Richard Buckle, *Diaghilev* (New York: Atheneum, 1979), p. 368.

14. Ibid., p. 252.

15. Review by W. E. Oliver from the collection of Frank Eng. No newspaper credit or date given.

16. Personal interview with Frank Eng, 10 May 1980.

17. Both these reviews are from the collection of Frank Eng. They are undated with no newspaper credit or dates.

18. Telephone interview with Bella Lewitzky, 10 March 1980.

19. Telephone interview with William Bowne, 11 March 1980.

20. Review by W. E. Oliver from the collection of Frank Eng. Newspaper and date unknown.

21. Telephone interview with Bella Lewitzky, 9 March 1980.

22. Lester Horton, "An Outline Approach to Choreography," *Educational Dance* 3, no. 3 (August–September 1940): 4.

Epilogue

1. *Dancers' Bulletin* 1, no. 1 (September 1938): 1.

2. Ibid.

3. Personal interview with Benjamin Zemach, 2 August 1980.

4. Personal interview with Karoun Toutikian, March 1980.

5. Personal correspondence with Benjamin Zemach, January 1983.

6. Florence Gordon, "Federation Aids Union Victory," *Dancers' Bulletin* 1, no. 1 (September 1938): 2.

7. "AGMA Dancers Hold Meeting," *Dancers' Bulletin* 1, no. 1 (September 1938): 2.

8. "Unity Keynotes Federation Growth," *Dancers' Bulletin* 1, no. 1 (September 1938): 1.

9. Grace Koopal, *Miracle of Music* (Los Angeles: Anderson, Ritchie, Simon, 1972), p. 160.

10. Koopal, p. 174.

11. "Unity Keynotes Federation Growth," p. 1.

12. "Permanent Ballet Formed," *Dancers' Bulletin* 1, no. 3 (October 1939): 1.

13. Personal interview with Lois Lacy, June 1980.

14. W. E. Kirby, "Bowl Engagement Announced by Adolph Bolm," *The American Dancer*, May 1931, p. 9.

15. Personal interview with Frieda Flier Maddow, June 1980.

16. Agnes de Mille, *Speak to Me, Dance with Me* (Boston and Toronto: Atlantic, Little, Brown, 1973), pp. 348–54.

Bibliography

Books

Amberg, George. *Ballet, The Emergence of an American Art*. New York: Mentor Books, 1949.

Armitage, Merle. *Accent on America*. New York: E. Weyhe, 1944.

———. *Accent on Life*. Ames: Iowa State University Press, 1965.

———. *Dance Memoranda*. New York: Books for Libraries Press, 1969.

Arvey, Verna. *Choreographic Music: Music for the Dance*. New York: E.P. Dutton and Co., 1941.

Balanchine, George, and Mason, Frances. *Balanchine's Complete Stories of the Great Ballets*. New York: Doubleday and Co. 1977.

Banham, Reyner. *Los Angeles, The Architecture of Four Ecologies*. New York: Pelican Books, 1982.

Bates, Esther Willard. *Pageants and Pageantry*. Boston: Gin and Co., 1912.

Baxter, John. *Hollywood in the Thirties*. San Diego: A.S. Barnes and Co., 1968.

Beaumont, Cyril W. *Complete Book of Ballets*. New York: Garden City Publishing, 1941.

———. *Michel Fokine and His Ballets*. New York: Dance Horizons, 1981.

Beegle, Mary Porter, and Crawford, John Randall. *Community Drama and Pageantry*. New Haven: Yale University Press, 1916.

Berg, Shelley. *Le Sacre du Printemps*. Ann Arbor, Mich.: UMI Research Press, 1988.

Brockett, Oscar G., and Findlay, Robert R. *Century of Innovation: A History of European and American Theatre and Drama Since 1870*. Englewood Cliffs, N.J.: Prentice-Hall, 1973.

Brownlow, Kevin, and Kobal, John. *Hollywood: The Pioneers*. New York: Alfred A. Knopf, 1979.

Buckle, Richard. *Diaghilev*. New York: Atheneum, 1979.

Burleigh, Louise. *The Community Theatre*. Boston: Little, Brown and Co., 1979.

Caldwell, Helen. *Michio Ito, The Dancer and His Dances*. Berkeley: University of California Press, 1977.

Cary, Diana Serra. *Hollywood's Children: An Inside Account of the Child Star Era*. Boston: Houghton Mifflin, 1979.

Caughey, John. *Los Angeles: Biography of a City*. Berkeley: University of California Press, 1976.

Chasins, Abram. *Leopold Stokowski: A Profile*. New York: Hawthorn Books, 1979.

Cheney, Sheldon. *The Art Theatre: A Discussion of Its Ideals, Its Organization and Its Promise as a Corrective for Present Evils in the Commercial Theatre*. New York: Alfred A. Knopf, 1917.

———. *The New Movement in the Theatre*. New York: Mitchell Kennerley, 1914.

————. *The Open Air Theatre.* New York: Mitchell Kennerley, 1914.

Chujoy, Anatole, and Manchester, P. W., eds. *The Dance Encyclopedia.* 3d. rev. ed. New York: Simon and Schuster, 1967.

Cina, Zelda, and Crane, Bob. *Hollywood: Land and Legend.* Westport, Conn. Arlington House, 1980.

Clarke, Mary. *The Sadler's Wells Ballet.* London: Adam and Charles Black, 1955.

Cohen, Selma Jean. *Doris Humphrey: An Artist First.* Middletown, Conn.: Wesleyan University Press, 1972.

Craig, Gordon. *On the Art of the Theatre.* 1911. Reprint. London: Butler and Tanner, 1957.

Dalcroze, Jaques [Emile Jaques-Dalcroze]. *The Eurhythmics of Jaques-Dalcroze.* 2d. rev. ed. London: Constable, 1917.

Davol, Ralph. *A Handbook of American Pageantry.* Taunton, Mass.: Davol Publishing, 1914.

Deakin, Irving. *Ballet Profile.* New York: Dodge Publishing, 1936.

de Mille, Agnes. *Dance to the Piper.* Boston: Little, Brown and Co., 1952.

————. *Speak to Me, Dance with Me.* Boston and Toronto: Atlantic, Little, Brown, 1973.

Dickinson, Thomas H. *The Case of American Drama.* Boston and New York: Houghton Mifflin, 1915.

Dunning, Jennifer. *"But First a School."* New York: Elizabeth Sifton Books, Viking Penguin, 1985.

Eliot, T. S. [Thomas Stearns]. *On Poetry and Poets.* London: Faber and Faber, 1957.

Fokine, Michel. *Fokine, Memoirs of a Ballet Master.* Trans. by Vitale Fokine. Boston: Little, Brown and Co., 1961.

Fonteyn, Margot. *Pavlova: Portrait of a Dancer.* New York: Viking Penguin, 1984.

Gebhard, David, and Von Breton, Harriette. *Los Angeles in the '30s, 1931–1941.* Salt Lake City: Peregrine Smith, 1975.

Grigoriev, S. L. *The Diaghilev Ballet, 1909–1929.* Trans. and ed. by Vera Bowen. Harmondsworth, Middlesex: Penguin Books, 1960.

Haskell, Arnold, and Nouvel, Walter. *Diaghileff: His Artistic and Private Life.* New York: Da Capo Press, 1978.

Heilbut, Anthony. *Exiled in Paradise.* New York: Viking Press, 1983.

Hill, Lawrence L. *Can Anything Good Come Out of Hollywood.* Los Angeles: Los Angeles Times Press, 1923.

Horwitz, Dawn Lille. *Michel Fokine.* Boston: Twayne Publishers, 1985.

Jackman, Jarrell C., and Borden, Carla M. *The Muses Flee Hitler.* Washington, D.C.: Smithsonian Institution, 1983.

Jones, Isabel Morse. *Hollywood Bowl.* New York and Los Angeles: G. Schirmer, 1936.

Koopal, Grace. *Miracle of Music.* Los Angeles: Anderson, Ritchie, Simon, 1972.

Lasky, Betty. *RKO: The Biggest Little Major of Them All.* New York: Prentice-Hall, 1984.

Lederman, Minna. *Stravinsky in the Theatre.* New York: Da Capo Press, 1975.

Lieven, Peter. *The Birth of the Ballets-Russes.* 1936. Reprint. New York: Dover Publications, 1973.

Lifar, Serge. *Diaghilev.* New York: Putnam, 1976.

Los Angeles: A Guide to the City and Its Environs Compiled by Writers' Program of the Work Projects Administration in Southern California. American Guide Series, Sponsored by the Los Angeles Court Board of Supervisors. New York: Hastings House Publishers, 1984.

Macdonald, Nesta. *Diaghilev Observed by Critics in England and the United States, 1911–1929.* New York: Dance Horizons; London: Dance Books, 1975.

Mackaye, Percy. *The Civic Theatre in Relation to the Redemption of Leisure: A Book of Suggestions.* New York and London: Mitchell Kennerley, 1912.

————. *The Playhouse and the Play and Other Addresses Concerning the Theatre and Democracy in America.* New York: Macmillan, 1909.

————. *A Substitute for War*. New York: Macmillan, 1915.

Martin, Frank, et al. *Emile Jaques-Dalcroze: L'Homme, Le Compositeur, Le Créateur de la Rythmique*. Neuchâtel, Suisse: Editions de la Bacannière, 1965.

Martin, John. *America Dancing*. 1936. Reprint. New York: Dance Horizons, 1968.

————. *Introduction to the Dance*. 1939. Reprint. New York: Dance Horizons, 1965.

————. *Ruth Page: An Intimate Biography*. New York and Basel: Marcel Dekker, 1977.

Maynard, Olga. *The American Ballet*. Philadelphia: Macrae Smith, 1959.

McDonagh, Don. *The Complete Guide to Modern Dance*. New York: Doubleday, 1976.

McWilliams, Carey. *Southern California: An Island on the Land*. Salt Lake City: Peregrine Smith, 1983.

Moore, Colleen. *Silent Star*. New York: Doubleday, 1968.

Mosley, Leonard. *Zanuck: The Rise and Fall of Hollywood's Last Tycoon*. Boston and Toronto: Atlantic, Little, Brown, 1984.

Newmark, Harris. *Sixty Years in Southern California: 1853–1913*. Los Angeles: Zeitlin and Ver Grugge, 1970.

Nijinska, Bronislava. *Bronislava Nijinska: Early Memoirs*. Trans. and ed. by Irina Nijinska and Jean Rawlinson. New York: Holt, Rinehart, and Winston, 1981.

Northcutt, John Orlando. *Magic Valley: The Story of the Hollywood Bowl*. Los Angeles: Oshenko, 1967.

Oukrainsky, Serge. *My Two Years with Anna Pavlowa*. Los Angeles, San Francisco, New York: Suttonhouse Publishers, 1940.

Page, Ruth. *Page by Page*. New York: Dance Horizons, 1978.

Parker, David L., and Siegel, Esther. *Guide to Dance in Film: A Catalog of United States Productions Including Dance Sequences, With Names of Dancers, Choreographers, Directors, and Other Details*. Performing Arts Information Guide Series, Vol. 3. Detroit: Gale Research, 1978.

Pound, Ezra, and Fenellosa, Ernest. *The Classic Noh Theatre of Japan*. New York: New Directions Paperback, 1959.

Reinhardt, Gottfried. *The Genius: A Memoir of Max Reinhardt*. New York: Alfred A. Knopf, 1979.

Rodrigues, Jose, ed. *Music and Dance in California*. Hollywood: Bureau of Musical Research, 1940.

Rolland, Romain. *The People's Theatre*. Trans. by Barrett H. Clark. New York: Henry Holt, 1918.

Rood, Arnold. *Gordon Craig on Movement and Dance*. New York: Dance Horizons, 1977.

Saunders, Richard Drake, ed. *Music and Dance in California and the West*. Hollywood: Drake-William, 1948.

Sayler, Oliver M., ed. *Max Reinhardt and His Theatre*. Trans. by Barrett H. Clark. New York: Henry Holt, 1918.

Schlundt, Christina L. *The Professional Appearances of Ruth St. Denis and Ted Shawn: A Chronology and an Index of Dances, 1906–1932*. New York: New York Public Library, 1962.

Selden, Elizabeth. *The Dancer's Quest: Essays on the Aesthetic of Contemporary Dance*. Berkeley: University of California Press, 1935.

————. *Elements of the Free Dance*. New York: A.S. Barnes, 1930.

Shawn, Ted. *Every Little Movement: A Book About François Delsarte*. New York: Dance Horizons, 1963.

————. *One Thousand and One Night Stands*. 1960. Reprint. New York: Da Capo Press, 1979.

Shelton, Suzanne. *Divine Dancer: A Biography of Ruth St. Denis*. New York: Doubleday, 1981.

Sound Waves. Catalogue of Exhibit. Los Angeles: Hollywood Bowl Museum, 1986.

Stanislavsky, Constantin. *My Life in Art.* New York: Theatre Books, 1952.

Starr, Kevin. *Inventing the Dream: California Through the Progressive Era.* New York and Oxford University Press, 1985.

Stewart, Virginia, and Armitage, Merle. *The Modern Dance.* 1935. Reprint. New York: Dance Horizons, 1970.

Stravinsky, Igor, and Craft, Robert. *Dialogues.* Berkeley and Los Angeles: University of California Press, 1982.

———. *Expositions and Developments.* Berkeley and Los Angeles: University of California Press, 1981.

———. *Themes and Conclusions.* Berkeley and Los Angeles: University of California Press, 1982.

Taper, Bernard. *Balanchine: A Bibliography.* New York: Times Books, 1984.

Torrence, Bruce. *Hollywood: The First Hundred Years.* Hollywood: Hollywood Chamber of Commerce and Fiske Enterprises, 1979.

Ussher, Bruno David. *Who's Who in Music and Dance in Southern California.* Los Angeles: Bureau of Musical Research, William J. Perlman, 1933.

A Vision for Music. Hollywood Bowl Museum Catalogue of Opening Exhibit. Hollywood: Hollywood Bowl Museum, 1985.

Warren, Larry. *Lester Horton: Modern Dance Pioneer.* New York and Basel: Marcel Dekker, 1977.

Weaver, John D. *El Pueblo Grande: A Non-Fiction Book about Los Angeles.* Los Angeles: Anderson, Ritchie, Simon, 1973.

White, Eric Walter. *Stravinsky: The Composer and His Work.* Berkeley and Los Angeles: University of California Press, 1966.

Wilson, G. B. L. *A Dictionary of Ballet.* London: Penguin, 1957.

Yeats, William Butler. *Four Plays for Dancers.* New York: Macmillan, 1921.

Articles, Journals, Pamphlets and Periodicals

"Address to the Graduating Class MCMXI of the Unitrinian School of Personal Harmonizing." *Address at Moonshine.* New York: privately printed by Bliss Carmen, 1911.

"AGMA Dancers Hold Meeting." *Dancers' Bulletin* 1, no. 1 (September 1928).

"Album Souvenir de 'La Saison Russe.'" Reprint. *Dance Data,* no. 2. New York: Dance Horizons, 1977.

Barzel, Ann. "Chicago's 'Two Russians': Andreas Pavley and Serge Oukrainsky." *Dance Magazine,* June 1979.

———. "European Dance Teachers in the United States." *Dance Index,* April–June 1944.

Birnbaum, Harry. "Adolf Bolm Describes 'Danse Macabre' His New Ballet." *Musical America,* 4 September 1917.

Bolm, Adolph. "Impressions of a Partner; Before and After the World Spotlight Found Pavlova." *Dance Magazine,* August 1931.

[Article on Bolm]. *Musical America,* 13 November 1916. Bolm Clipping File, Dance Collection, New York Public Library.

Brownell, R. C. [Article on Bolm]. *Musical America,* 29 November 1915. Bolm Clipping File, Dance Collection, New York Public Library.

Cohen, Barbara Naomi. "The Borrowed Art of Gertrude Hoffman." *Dance Data,* no. 2. New York: Dance Horizons, 1977.

Dancers' Bulletin 1, no. 1 (September 1938).

Dancers' Bulletin 1, no. 3 (October 1939).

"Dancing and Art: Miss Norma Gould, Los Angeles' Talented Young Artist to Establish Temple of Dancing." *Pipes o' Pan* 2, no. 1 (ca. 1920).

Dougherty, John. "Perspective on Adolph Bolm," Parts 1–3, *Dance Magazine*, January–March 1963.

Edwards, Winifred. Kosloff obituary. *Dance News*, January 1957.

Eliot, T. S. [Thomas Sterns]. "Ezra Pound." *Poetry*, September 1946.

Field, Hamilton Easter. "Adolph Bolm and *The Birthday of the Infanta.*" *Arts and Decoration* 12 (1920).

Gleason, Dorothy. "Norma Gould, Dancer." *El Noticiero* 5, no. 12 (December 1965).

Gordon, Florence. "Federation Aids Union Victory." *Dancers' Bulletin*, September 1938.

Gould, Norma. "At What Age Should Children Study Dancing." *Artland Magazine*, January 1927.

———. "Dancing: The Fountain of Youth." *The American Dancer*, July 1928.

Griffith, B. "Where Many in Movieland Get Dancing Inspiration." *The Dancing Master*, April 1929.

Horton, Lester. "An Outline Approach to Choreography." *Educational Dance* 3, no. 3 (August–September 1940).

Howard, Ruth Eleanor. "Dancing Has Brought a New Angle to Talkies." *The American Dancer*, November 1929.

———. "Dancing in Southern California." In *Who's Who in Music and Dance in Southern California*, pp. 52–53. Los Angeles: Bureau of Musical Research, 1933.

Jordan, Stephanie. "Ted Shawn's Music Visualizations." *Dance Chronicle* 7, no. 1 (1984).

Karsavina, Tamara. Bolm obituary. *Dancing Times*, July 1951.

Kirby, W. E. "Bowl Engagement Announced by Adolph Bolm." *The American Dancer*, May 1931.

Leddick, David. "Baldina." *Dance Magazine*, November 1965.

Mad Genius. Review of film. *Theatre Arts Monthly*, May 1931.

Maracci, Carmelita. "Face the Music before You Dance." In *Music and Dance in California*. Los Angeles: Bureau of Musical Research, 1940.

Martens, Frederick H. "*Sadko* and Its Author: 'A New Russian Ballet.'" *Musical America*, 7 October 1916. Bolm Clipping File, Dance Collection, New York Public Library.

Oukrainsky, Serge. "The Dance, What It Is, Was and Should Be." *The American Dancer*, June 1927.

Padlocked. Review of film. *Variety*, 8 August 1926.

"Permanent Ballet Formed." *Dancers' Bulletin* 1, no. 3 (October 1939).

Pierre, Dorathi Bock. Review of *Le Sacre du Printemps*. Choreography by L. Horton, 5 August 1937. *The American Dancer*, October 1937.

Prevots, Naima. "American Pageantry and American Modern Dance." *Dance History Scholars Proceedings, Sixth Annual Conference*. Ohio State University. 11–13 February 1983.

———. "Carrying the Torch from the '32 Games." *Los Angeles Times*, 29 July 1984.

Rosen, Lillie F. "A Conversation with Bella Lewitzky." *Ballet Review* 10, no. 3 (n.d.).

Sanders, John. "Los Angeles Grand Opera Association: The Formative Years, 1924–1926." *Southern California Quarterly* 4, no. 4 (Fall 1973).

Service, Faith. "Ernest Belcher: The Teacher of 'It.'" *Dance Magazine*, August 1928.

St. Denis, Ruth. "The Southland's Dance Inheritance." In *Who's Who in Music and Dance in Southern California*, pp. 49–51. Los Angeles: Bureau of Musical Research, 1933.

"Unity Keynotes Federation Growth." *Dancers' Bulletin*, September 1938.

Wardell, Bertha. "Scheherazade in Hollywood." *The Dance* 31, no. 64 (January 1927).

Windreich, Leland. "June Roper." *Dance Chronicle* 10, no. 1 (1987).

Newspapers

At the Hawk's Well. Review. Choroegraphy by M. Ito. *Los Angeles Times,* 29 August 1929.
"Belcher Tells Dream of Organizing Truly American Ballet." *Hollywood Citizen News,* 12 May 1931.
[Review of Belcher program]. *Hollywood Citizen News,* 19 August 1931.
[Article on Belcher]. *London Dancing Times,* December 1913.
[Article on Bolm program]. *New York Telegraph,* 13 February 1921.
[Review of Bolm program]. *Minneapolis Journal,* 2 March 1916.
Brown, Gilbert. "Kosloff Ballet Is Triumph." *Los Angeles Record,* 13 October 1925.
Carmen. Review. Choreography by E. Belcher, 8 July 1922. *Los Angeles Times,* 9 July 1922.
Cowdy, Alma. Review of *A Victory Ball.* Choreography by B. Zemach, 1 August 1935. *Los Angeles Herald Express,* 2 August 1935.
Daggett, Charles. Review of *Prince Igor.* Choreography by M. Ito. *Los Angeles Record,* 16 August 1930.
"Dancers Appear in Original Roles—Artistic Program Enjoyed by Ebell Members and Their Guests." Unidentified newspaper, 27 March 1920. Gould Scrapbooks, Author's Collection.
Danse Macabre. Review. Choreography by A. Bolm, n.d. Bolm Clipping File, Dance Collection, New York Public Library.
[Article on *Dionysia*]. Choreography by N. Gould. *Pasadena Star News,* 1 May 1920.
[Article on *Dionysia*]. Choreography by N. Gould. *Los Angeles Evening Express,* 6 May 1920.
Downes, Olin. [Article on Bolm]. *New York Times,* 27 March 1921. Bolm Clipping File, Dancing Collection, New York Public Library.
Elysia (A Grecian Divertissement). Review. Choreography by E. Belcher, 8 August 1932. *Los Angeles Times,* 6 August 1932.
Fragments of Israel. Review. Choreography by B. Zemach. *Los Angeles Times,* 30 July 1933.
[Article on Gould program]. *Los Angeles Evening Express,* 1 June 1916.
[Article on Gould program]. *Los Angeles Tribune,* 27 April 1915.
Greene, Patterson. Review of *Prince Igor.* Choreography by M. Ito. *Los Angeles Examiner,* 16 August 1930.
Jones, Isabel Morse. Review of Divertissements by Pavley, Oukrainsky, and company, 30 August 1928. *Los Angeles Times,* 31 August 1928.
———. Review of *Etenraku.* Choreography by M. Ito, 19 August 1937. *Los Angeles Times,* 20 August 1937.
———. "New Dance Explained as Evolution." *Los Angeles Times,* 14 October 1937.
Knisely, Bertha McCord. Review of Gould program, 30 August 1929. *Los Angeles Saturday Night,* 7 September 1929.
———. Review of *Spirit of the Factory.* Choreographed by A. Bolm, 28 July 1931. *Los Angeles Saturday Night,* 31 July 1931.
[Article on Kosloff]. *Los Angeles Times,* March 1929. Annual Scrapbooks, Music Collection, Los Angeles Public Library, Main Branch.
[Article on Kosloff]. *Los Angeles Times,* February 1929. Annual Scrapbooks, Music Collection, Los Angeles Public Library, Main Branch.
"LA Takes Lead as Dance Center." *Los Angeles Times,* 1929.
Martin, John. Review of *Spirit of the Factory.* Choreography by A. Bolm. *New York Times,* 6 September 1931.
Mayer, Mary. "Kosloff Declares New Repetition of Old." *Los Angeles Times,* 12 June 1932.
Murrill, Jan. Review of *Spirit of the Factory.* Choreography by A. Bolm, 28 July 1931. *Los Angeles California Record,* 29 July 1931.

Oliver, W. E. Review of *Le Sacre du Printemps*. Choreography by L. Horton. Unidentified newspaper, n.d. Frank Eng Collection.

[Article on Oukrainsky and Pavley]. *Los Angeles Times,* 1 May 1927.

[Article on Oukrainsky and Pavley]. *Los Angeles Times,* 29 May 1927.

"Russian Ballet Seen in 'Sadko': New Submarine Dance-Story Is a Rare Delight to the Eye." *Philadelphia Public Ledger,* 25 November 1916.

Saunders, Richard Drake. Review of *Spirit of the Factory*. Choreography by A. Bolm. *Hollywood Citizen News,* 29 July 1931.

———. Review of *Prince Igor*. Choreography by M. Ito. *Hollywood Citizen News,* 16 Aug 1930.

The Song of Hiawatha. Review. Choreography by L. Horton, 4 July 1927. Indianapolis newspaper, July 1927. Karoun Toutikian Collection.

Spanish Choreographic Episode. Review. Choreography by A. Bolm. Unidentified newspaper, n.d. Bolm Clipping File, Dance Collection, New York Public Library.

Spirit of the Factory. Article on choreography by A. Bolm, 28 July 1931. *Los Angeles Times,* 26 July 1931.

Spirit of the Factory. Review. Choreography by A. Bolm, 28 July 1931. *B'nai B'rith Messenger,* 29 July 1931.

Swisher, Viola Hegyi. Review of *A Victory Ball*. Choreography by B. Zemach, 1 August 1935. *Hollywood Citizen News,* 2 August 1935.

Ussher, Bruno David. Review of *Spirit of the Factory*. Choreography by A. Bolm, *Los Angeles Evening Express,* 29 July 1931.

"Victory Ball Symphony Due at Bowl Written as Protest on Indifference to War Cost." *Hollywood Citizen News,* 1 August 1935.

Willis, Dorothy. Article on *Jeanne d'Arc*. Choreography by N. Gould. *Los Angeles Evening Express,* 1 June 1916.

———. Review of *Naia*. Choreography by N. Gould. *Los Angeles Evening Express,* 13 June 1917.

"Zemach Ballet Distinctive . . . Unusual Offering . . . Hebrew Folk Dance Basis." *Hollywood Citizen News,* 4 August 1933.

Letters and Interviews

Basquette, Lina. Telephone interview, 10 May 1986.

———. Letter to author, 25 May 1986.

Belcher, Ernest. "Early Career in Europe." Interview by Alma Gowdy and James Vandivere, 16 March 1935. KFAC Radio, Los Angeles. Transcript in the Belcher Collection, Special Collections, University of California, Los Angeles.

Bowne, William. Telephone interview, 11 March 1980.

———. Telephone interview, 13 November 1983.

Caldwell, Helen. Personal interview, March 1980.

Champion, Gower. Letter to Marge Champion, n.d.

Champion, Marge. Personal interview, 24 June 1986.

Eng, Frank. Personal interview, 10 May 1980.

Lacy, Lois. Personal interview, June 1980.

Lewitzky, Bella. Telephone interview, 10 March 1980.

———. Telephone interview, February 1980.

Maddow, Frieda Flier. Personal interview, June 1980.

———. Telephone interview, 20 August 1986.

Perissi, Alice. Letter to Marge Champion, 1 March 1973.

Pierre, Dorathi Bock. Telephone interview, February 1980.

Reinhold, Gottfried. Personal interview, March 1984.

Talbot-Martin, Elizabeth. Personal interview, November 1985.

Tallchief, Maria. Interview by Marion Horosko, 1964. Dance Collection, New York Public Library.

Toutikian, Karoun. Personal interview, February 1980.

———. Personal interview, March 1980.

———. Personal interview, 8 June 1986.

Zemach, Amielle. Personal interview, 28 October 1982.

Zemach, Benjamin. Personal interview, 2 August 1980.

———. Letters to author, January, May, November 1983.

Zemach, Margot. Letter to author, 2 January 1982.

Unpublished Sources

Belcher, Ernest. Unpublished autobiographical notes. Belcher Collection, University Research Library, Special Collections, University of California, Los Angeles.

Gould, Norma. "The Art of Pageantry." Essay, ca. 1920s. Gould Scrapbooks, Author's Personal Collection.

———. Dance Theatre announcement, 1938. Gould Scrapbooks, Author's Personal Collection.

———. "Dancing in Its Relation to Other Arts." Essay, October 1926. Gould Scrapbooks, Author's Personal Collection.

———. "Dianidra: A Miniature Dance Drama in Three Acts." Script, ca 1920s. Gould Scrapbooks, Author's Personal Collection.

———. "Dramatic Dancing and Opera Ballet." Essay, November 1926. Gould Scrapbooks, Author's Personal Collection.

———. Lectures given at UCLA and USC. Gould Scrapbooks, Author's Personal Collection.

Hawley, Renee Dunia. "Ernest Belcher: The Father of Dance in Southern California." Belcher Collection, University Research Library, Special Collections, University of California, Los Angeles.

Los Angeles Polytechnical High School Yearbook, 1908. Francis Polytechnic High School Archives.

Nordskog, Arne Andrae. "Earliest Musical History of the Hollywood Bowl." Art, Music and Recreation Department, Los Angeles Public Library, Main Branch.

Oukrainsky, Serge. "My Life in Ballet." Ed. Antoinette Simanovich. No. 287096. Dance Collection, Archives for Performing Arts, San Francisco.

Rochlin, Miriam, producer. *The Art of Benjamin Zemach.* Film. Dance Collection, New York Public Library.

Archives and Collections

Archives for Performing Arts, San Francisco (now in opera house).

Belcher Collection. University Research Library, Special Collections, University of California, Los Angeles.

Belcher Collection. Author's Personal Collection, Los Angeles.

Bolm Clipping File. Dance Collection, New York Public Library, New York.

Adolf Bolm Papers. George Arents Research Library for Special Collections. Syracuse University, New York.

Bowling, Lance. Private Collection, Los Angeles.

Eng, Frank. Private Collection (Horton material), Nevada.

Gould Scrapbooks. Author's Personal Collection, Los Angeles.

Hollywood Bowl Museum Archives, Hollywood.

Horton Collection. Author's Personal Collection, Los Angeles.

Los Angeles Philharmonic Archives, Los Angeles.

Los Angeles Public Library, Main Branch. Music Collection, Yearly Scrapbooks. Los Angeles.

New York Public Library, Dance Collection, New York.

Toutikian, Karoun. Private Collection, Los Angeles.

University Catalogues. University Archives, Doheny Library, University of Southern California, Los Angeles.

University Catalogues. University Archives, Powell Library, University of California, Los Angeles.

Zemach, Amielle. Private Collection (Zemach material), Los Angeles.

Zemach Collection. Author's Personal Collection, Los Angeles.

Index